SHADOW LIFE

SHADOW LIFE

A Portrait of Anne Frank and Her Family

BARRY DENENBERG

SCHOLASTIC INC.
NEW YORK TORONTO LONDON AUCKLAND SYDNEY
MEXICO CITY NEW DELHI HONG KONG BUENOS AIRES

ACKNOWLEDGMENTS

My deepest thanks to David Caplan, Amy Griffin, Sheila Keenan,
John Marchesella, Terra McVoy, Arlene Robillard,
Mark Seidenfeld, Liz Szabla, and everyone at
Scholastic who worked so hard on *Shadow Life*.

PHOTO CREDITS

Cover, Page 197: © Anne Frank Fonds, Basel/Anne Frank House,
Amsterdam/Getty Images

ISBN 0-439-87438-6

12 11 10 9 8 7 6 5 4 3 2 1   6 7 8 9 10 11/0

Printed in the U.S.A.   40

First Scholastic paperback printing, March 2006

Designed by David Caplan

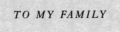

TO MY FAMILY

CONTENTS

INTRODUCTION

I FIRST READ *Anne Frank: The Diary of a Young Girl* (I was ashamed to realize) in 1994, while preparing to write one of the first books in Scholastic's Dear America series. I read numerous diaries, but it was Anne Frank's diary that had the biggest impact on me and eventually on the book I was writing.

At first Anne's diary annoyed me: It was fragmented, unstructured, unedited, and unrelentingly precocious and self-absorbed. But it was also unashamedly introspective and unself-consciously intimate. Fortunately it dawned on me that this was exactly what the diary would sound like of an intelligent thirteen-year-old girl with the talent and inclination to record her thoughts and experiences. I kept Anne's diary close at hand throughout the writing process of that book and referred to it frequently.

Three years later, in 1997, I read a provocative and what turned out to be inspirational article in the *New Yorker*: Cynthia Ozick's "Who Owns Anne Frank?" It caused me to question my understanding of the diary and subsequently the way the Holocaust is presented to young readers.

Although I am Jewish and throughout my life had read about World War II and the Holocaust, Ozick's article showed me how truly ignorant I was on the subject. I read all the books mentioned in it and watched Jon Blair's Academy Award–winning documentary *Anne Frank Remembered* — a further inspiration.

I decided that my next project would be a compelling and complete portrait of Anne Frank, her family, and the times they lived in. Five years later, when my research, note-taking, and organization of materials was complete, I began to contemplate the structure of *Shadow Life*.

I wanted to make the first part of Anne Frank's life, in prewar Frankfurt and Amsterdam, as rich, detailed, and alive as possible. That section, I thought, would be best told in a conventional, narrative fashion.

But the second part, the family's two years in hiding, could not. I didn't want to simply recapitulate what Anne had written, but illuminate it. I was unsure of the right way to approach it and reread Anne's diary, hoping for a sign.

It was there.

On Friday, October 16, 1942, Anne wrote:

"Margot and I got into the same bed together last evening; it was a frightful squash, but that was just the fun of it. She asked if she could read my diary. I said, 'Yes — at least bits of it'; and then I asked her if I could read hers."

Margot, Anne's introspective, self-effacing older sister, must have also kept a diary during their time in hiding (and possibly before). As if to accentuate the miracle of Anne's diary surviving, Margot's — like so many others — must have disappeared in the chaos and destruction of the war.

Imagining and re-creating Margot Frank's diary was an undertaking that could not be passed up, because it allowed me to accomplish so many important things:

≡ The everyday matters of the family's years in hiding could be described without being redundant for those who had already read the diary or wished to after reading *Shadow Life*.

≡ The reader could get a different perspective on Anne — what better source than her older sister? — and her intense relationship with her family.

⹀ The personalities and dynamics of the other people in hiding could be seen through a lens different from Anne's.

⹀ Readers could learn something of Margot, like Anne, a teenager forced to witness the world she loved disintegrate.

⹀ Margot's highly regarded intelligence and political interests could be a valid vehicle for conveying what was happening historically in both the Netherlands and the world.

⹀ Writing as Margot would allow me to confront one of, if not *the,* critical issue raised by Cynthia Ozick: Anne and her family's Jewishness. Unlike her irreligious father and free-spirited sister, Margot was, like her mother, a practicing Jew as well as an earnest young Zionist who dreamed of someday immigrating to what is today Israel and becoming a midwife.

Biographers of Anne Frank understandably use Margot only to more fully realize their picture of Anne. As in life, Margot is not the focus of attention, Anne is. But fortunately there is some historical information available and several revealing letters written by Margot to a pen pal in Iowa, which Anne had preserved in her diary. These letters reveal that Margot was pragmatic, affectless, and wise beyond her years. It is almost as if childhood and her teenage years were something Margot couldn't be bothered with. These letters gave me valuable additional insight into her personality and provided the parameters of how she would speak and write. I developed an intricate profile of Margot, which I kept beside me along with her letters while imagining her diary.

But my problems weren't over. The third part of *Shadow Life* presented yet another challenge.

Early in my research, I came to have a much better understanding of why Ozick — and so many others writing about the Holocaust — believed "... the diary itself, richly crammed though it is with incident and passion, cannot count as Anne Frank's story. A story may not be said to be a story if the end is missing."

How was I to present the "end" — the last seven months of Anne Frank's life — in a way that was historically accurate and would truly speak to my audience?

I found my answer in *Voices from Vietnam,* which I had written ten years earlier. The book originally combined my historical narrative with first-person accounts of the men and women who had served in the Vietnam War. After three years of research and writing, however, something was not right. Getting it right had become a frustrating, daily struggle. Early one morning, I decided to remove nearly 80 percent of my writing (leaving just enough narrative to provide the necessary chronology and historical background) so that the "voices" could come through loud and clear.

By relying on first-person narratives for Part Three of *Shadow Life,* I hoped the voices of the survivors of Westerbork, Auschwitz, and Bergen-Belsen would also come through. Part Three is constructed as an oral history by the people who were in those same concentration camps, many at the same time as and alongside Anne and her family — some up until the end.

Ozick rightly takes issue with a line taken out of context from Anne's diary, the one that concludes the 1955 play and the 1959 movie: ". . . in spite of everything I still believe that people are really good at heart."

Of course, no one familiar with Anne Frank's last days would think she continued to feel this way. But tragically this same misleading line, erroneously implying that there is something uplifting in Anne's brief life and unspeakably horrific death, is still being used today as part of the Holocaust curriculum for many middle- and upper-school students.

Recent historical scholarship meant for adult readers has been providing newly conceived and researched analysis as well as valuable accounts of the Holocaust that are important additions to the already vast literature. This same evolution in thought and writing on the subject should be made available to young readers. It is time to reintroduce the story of Anne Frank to a new generation.

As I write this, we are approaching what would be Anne Frank's seventy-fifth birthday. February–March 2005 will mark the sixtieth anniversary of her death.

We live at a time when insensitivity to the value of human life is on the rise; reading about Anne Frank is, it seems to me, especially urgent and meaningful now.

If there is any hope it lies within us.

Perhaps we will finally understand that the object of hate, violence, and evil may be a child just like ourselves. Perhaps even a young girl living in Amsterdam who has just celebrated her thirteenth birthday and has joyously received the only gift she cared about — a diary. Someone with her whole life before her . . .

Maybe if we realize that each life is precious, then the diary that Anne was given can be a gift to us, too.

BARRY DENENBERG

MAY 2004

PART ONE

LIVING

Frankfurt, Germany

1933

In 1932, the National Socialist German Workers' Party, its members known as Nazis (*NA*tionalso*ZI*alistische), was democratically elected (polling fourteen million votes) to preside over the government. The head of the party, forty-three-year-old Austrian-born Adolf Hitler, was appointed chancellor in January 1933.

The election took place three years after the New York Stock Exchange crashed, triggering a worldwide economic depression. In Germany, unemployment was at an all-time high — directly and tragically affecting thirteen million people, if spouses and children were considered. Men walked the streets wearing signs asking for jobs, any jobs. It was estimated that nearly half a million people were homeless. The result of all this was deplorable living conditions for many German citizens.

Added to this were the financial payments Germany had to make to the countries that were victorious in the First World War, a provision of the Treaty of Versailles, which had ended that war. The overwhelming majority of the German population considered these payments harsh and humiliating, and even more punitive and unfair when combined with the current, severe economic crisis.

There was widespread unrest and an atmosphere of desperation. Germans rightly feared for their future and sought reasons for their plight and an end to their misery.

Adolf Hitler offered both.

According to Hitler there were two reasons for Germany's problems: the punishing stipulations of the Treaty of Versailles and the Jews. Although the Jewish people constituted less than 1 percent of the population, Hitler and an increasing number of German citizens claimed they accounted for 100 percent of the country's problems.

Adolf Hitler proclaimed and preached the racial superiority of the German people. Germans were stronger, smarter, and better than other races. Their destiny was to dominate the earth. Maintaining the racial purity of the German people was essential, he said. He promised to make Germany Europe's most powerful country once again. He promised to take over adjoining land that rightfully belonged to

Germany, providing the "living space" they needed to prosper and thrive.

He was addressing an audience that was becoming increasingly militaristic, racist, and anti-Jewish.

To celebrate their victory at the polls, an estimated two million Nazi followers unleashed a nationwide campaign of intimidation and terror aimed at their opponents and all Jews.

Jewish writers, film directors, conductors and composers, philosophers, psychiatrists, and scientists (eventually including Albert Einstein) were forced to leave Germany.

In towns and cities across Germany, students who embraced the new Fascist philosophy took books that were written by Jews or were otherwise unacceptable from the libraries and burned them. These book burnings appeared spontaneous but were directed by Nazi Party officials who provided the lists of which books were to be destroyed.

The Nazi Party declared a boycott of Jewish-owned businesses: Anti-Jewish slogans were painted on shop windows and signs were put up warning people not to shop there. Guards were posted outside to ensure that anyone who would have chosen to ignore the boycott was not allowed to.

Hundreds of thousands of people were arrested, supposedly

for political crimes, and hundreds and hundreds of others were kidnapped, beaten, tortured, and killed, all while the police stood by and did nothing. Gangs of "Brownshirts" (as Nazi followers were called because of the color of their uniforms) roamed the streets of German cities looking for victims and shouting "Down with the Jews."

Otto and Edith Frank and their two daughters, Margot Betti (born February 16, 1926) and Annelies Marie (born June 12, 1929), were German Jews living in Frankfurt.

In 1925, thirty-six-year-old Otto, who had grown up in Frankfurt, married twenty-five-year-old Edith Holländer. Otto was charming, cultured, intelligent, and shrewd. He had gone to the university for a year and then traveled. At one point he lived in New York City, working in Macy's Department Store, which was owned by his classmate's relatives. He had the makings of the salesman and business-man he was to become. In the First World War he served as a German officer.

Edith came from a wealthy family and her large dowry was a factor for practical Otto, whose family fortunes had ebbed. Despite her youth she was somewhat old-fashioned, spoke only when she had something to say, and was courte-ous and thoughtful.

Neither was particularly religious, although Edith, unlike Otto, went to the synagogue. They observed some of the traditions of their religion, but not often and never strictly.

Like many Germans who were Jewish, they considered themselves Germans first: assimilated members of the population at large. Otto especially was a modern, liberal, progressive thinker, unbound by religious dogma. Reading, not religion, was sacred in the Frank household. Both Edith and Otto viewed the country of their birth as the most cultured and civilized place on earth.

That was about to change.

When they were first married they lived with Otto's mother and then, as economic and "other factors" dictated, they moved. Once they had to move because their landlord turned out to be a supporter of the Nazi Party's anti-Jewish views. No matter where they lived or how small or large their home, their main concern was that the children be happy and safe.

In the warmer months they played outside: Margot in the street with her many friends and Anne in the sandbox or large metal outdoor bath. When it snowed Margot towed her baby sister around on a sleigh.

Kathi, their trusted housekeeper, helped care for the

children, returning to help out even after she was married. Gertrude, a loving neighbor, also was like a member of the family.

Otto and Edith were glad their two daughters were growing up in a religiously diverse environment: Their friends were Catholics, Protestants, and Jews.

Otto was a particularly attentive and loving father. Most fathers of his time and place were solely concerned with obedience and proper behavior (if they were concerned at all). "Pim," as he was called by his children (although no one knows why), would come home for lunch in the afternoons and play with and bathe his girls at night.

Margot was easy to care for. She slept through the night from the time she was born and never cried. She was a happy, contented child. Anne's difficult delivery was a harbinger of things to come. She had trouble breathing and let everyone know about it. She didn't sleep at night and cried out for days on end. Edith kept a baby book for both girls. Margot's went on at length, but Anne's was brief, to the point, and mostly medical.

Proper Edith took great pains with both girls' appearances. Their dresses were always freshly starched and ironed, their hair washed and combed. No matter how long or

1. Autobiographical Investigations

SO, THE ONE AGREEABLE bonus of all this is that I finally found a way of gaining admittance to Oxford University. Here I am in Somerville College on the Woodstock Road experiencing a simulacrum of the varsity life. While I have a room off a staircase in a quadrangle in a women's college there are no women (apart from nurses and domestic staff) – the undergraduettes having been decanted to Oriel College for the duration of the war. We are all men here, wounded officers from France and other battlefields with our various incapacities – some shocking (the multiple amputees, the burned) and some invisible: the catatonic victims of mental dementia caused by the concussion of huge guns and images of unconscionable brutality and awfulness. Somerville, now part of the 3rd Southern General Hospital, as the Radcliffe Infirmary, a few yards further up the Woodstock Road, has been renamed.

Florence Duchesne shot me three times and caused four wounds. Let's begin with the last. Her third and final squeeze of the trigger sent a bullet through my chest, high on the right side, entering two inches below my collar-bone and exiting by my shoulder blade. Her second shot blasted through my left hand – that I'd raised in futile protection – and sped on, under through it and through the muscle of my left shoulder. I recall seeing – in a split second – the flower of blood bloom on the palm of my hand as the bullet passed through. The scar has healed but I have enduring stigmata – one in the middle of my palm, one on the back of my hand – puckered brown and round, the size of a sixpence. Her first shot was a miss, of sorts.

certainly: she hadn't raised the gun sufficiently when she fired and I was hit in the top of my left thigh where the bullet smashed into a small bundle of change in my pocket, driving some of the coins deep into the rectus femoris muscle. The surgeon later told me he'd extracted four francs and sixty-seven centimes – he gave them to me in a small envelope.

The shot in the chest caused my lung to collapse and I think produced the copious flow of blood that I saw before I passed out. My good fortune – if such a concept is valid in a case of multiple gunshot wounds – is that six of my seven wounds were entry and exit. Only the pocketful of coins denied egress and – now I'm feeling much better – only my thigh still causes me discomfort and makes me walk with a limp and, for the moment, compels the use of a cane.

I'm also lucky in that, after Florence Duchesne shot me and disappeared, some mechanic or stoker emerged from the engine room and found me lying there in the widening pool of my own blood. I was swiftly taken to a small nursing home in Evian and then Massinger, who eventually tracked me down, had me transferred immediately across country by private motor ambulance to the British base hospital at Rouen.

I convalesced there for four weeks as my injured lung kept filling with blood and had to be aspirated regularly. My left hand was in a cast as some small bones had been broken by the bullet on its way through but the persistent problem was my left thigh. The bullet and the small change were extracted in Rouen but the wound seemed continually to re-infect itself and had to be drained and cleaned and re-dressed. I was obliged to walk around on crutches for most of my stay there.

I was shipped back to England and Oxford towards the end of August. My mother came to visit me almost as soon as I was installed in Somerville. She rushed into my room wearing black and for a fraught, shocked moment I thought Florence Duchesne had returned to finish me off. Crickmay Faulkner had died a

PART FOUR

LONDON, 1915

month before – while I was in Geneva, in fact – and my mother was still in mourning.

She told me that the worst night of her life had occurred when she received the telegram that I was 'missing in action'. Crickmay was close to death and she thought her son had been snatched away, also. The next morning, however, she had a visit from a 'naval officer' – bearded, with a most curious, eerie smile, she said – who had come all the way to Claverleigh to tell her that I was believed to have been captured, unharmed. She found it very hard to understand how it came about that I was now in hospital in England, 'riddled with bullets'. I told her that the naval officer (it could only have been Fyfe-Miller) had been well intentioned but not in possession of all the facts.

Despite her new status of widow she seemed in excellent spirits, I had to admit, and she'd made the most of her mourning subfusc with a lot of black lace and ostrich feathers on display. Crickmay's passing was a blessing, she said, much as she loved him, sweet old man, and Hugh was preparing a perfectly adorable cottage on the estate to serve as a kind of dower house for her. The charity fund was growing incrementally and she was to be presented at court to Queen Mary. After we had walked through the quadrangle and I had seen her into her taxi, one of my fellow wounded – who knew about my former life – wondered if she were an actress. When I told him no, he asked, 'Is she your girl?' War affects people in all manner of different ways, I suppose – in my mother's case she was flourishing, visibly rejuvenated.

I received a telegram from Munro today, commiserating and congratulating simultaneously, and saying that we needed to assess the intelligence from the Glockner letters. And when that moment came he had a proposition to put to me. I reasoned that with Glockner dead the pressure to find the War Office source might have reduced somewhat – whoever our traitor was would have to seek out someone new to communicate with and that would obviously take some time.

★ ★ ★

Hamo has just left. He was very affected to see me – I was in bed, having just had my lung aspirated again – a concern that took the form of very specific questions about my wounds: what exactly were the physical sensations I felt at the moment of impact? Was the pain instant or did it arrive later? Did I find that the shock anaesthetized me in any way? Did the numbness endure for the length of time I lay out on the battlefield – and so on. I answered him as honestly as I could but kept deliberately vague about the reality of who had shot me and where. 'I had the strangest feelings when I was wounded, that's why I ask,' Hamo said. 'I've seen men screaming in agony from a broken finger, yet there I was, blood everywhere, and all I felt was a kind of fizzing, like pins and needles.' When he left he took my hand and squeezed it hard. 'Glad to have you back, dear boy. Dear brave lad.'

I walked up St Giles this evening all the way to the Martyrs' Memorial and back – as far as I've walked anywhere since Geneva. I stopped in a pub on the return journey and had half a pint of cider. People looked at me oddly – my pallor and my stick signalling the 'price' I've paid, I suppose. I keep forgetting I'm an officer in uniform (Munro has arranged for me to be resupplied). Lt. Lysander Rief, East Sussex Light Infantry, recovering from wounds. It was a warm late summer evening and St Giles with its ancient, soot-black college to one side and the Ashmolean Museum on the other looked timeless and alluring – motor cars and tradesmen's lorries excepting, of course – and I rather envied people who had had the chance to study and live here. Too late for me now, alas.

I was sitting on a bench in the front quad this afternoon, around the corner from the porter's lodge, reading a newspaper in the sun, when one of the nurses appeared. 'Ah, there you are, Mr Rief. You've just had a visitor in your room. We didn't know where you were.' And stepping diffidently into view came Massinger, in civilian clothes.

He sat beside me on the bench, very tense and awkward, and seemingly unwilling to look me in the eye.

'I never thanked you properly,' I said, wanting to ease the mood. 'Whisking me off to Rouen. Private ambulance and all that. The best of care, really.'

'I owe you an apology, Rief,' he said, looking down at his hands in his lap, fingers laced as if he were at prayer. 'I can't tell you how glad I was to see you alive in Evian. How glad I am today.'

'Thank you,' I said. Then, curious, asked, 'Why so? Particularly.'

'Because I think – I have this horrible feeling that I ordered you killed. Terrible error, I admit. I got it all wrong.'

He explained. There had been a rapid exchange of telegrams between him and Madame Duchesne on the Monday morning after Glockner's death had been discovered and reported. Madame Duchesne had been very suspicious, convinced that it had something to do with me and my meeting with him. They had even spoken by telephone about an hour before my steamer was due to depart. Massinger had received my telegram by then and knew from the steamer timetable when I would be leaving. At this point he had ordered Madame Duchesne to accompany me on the boat, interrogate me and, if she had any reason to believe I was a traitor, she was to take the necessary steps to bring me to justice.

I listened to this in some shock.

'Then when I saw her at Evian she told me she'd shot you,' Massinger said. 'You can imagine how I felt.'

'Saw her?'

'We met on the quayside. She said you had lied about the cipher-key – the source text. She said you were hiding something. She was convinced that you had murdered Glockner. She was incredibly suspicious of you. I think your disguise was enough proof for her.'

'Yes, how did you know that I'd disguise myself?'

Massinger looked a little taken aback at this, confused.

'Munro told me. Or was it Fyfe-Miller? About what happened in Vienna when I saw them there.'

'You were in Vienna?'

'Off and on. Mainly last year before the war began – while I was setting up the network in Switzerland. Everybody spoke about your escape.'

'I see . . .' I was puzzled to learn about my notoriety. I put it to the back of my mind. 'Anyway, I didn't think I was obliged to tell Madame Duchesne everything. Why should I? I was about to meet you and report in full, for Christ's sake – on French soil. And all the while you'd ordered me killed.'

Massinger looked a bit sick and grimaced.

'Actually, I didn't in so many words. Madame Duchesne was going on and on, raising her suspicions about you. So I said –' he paused. 'My French is a bit rusty, you see. I don't know if I made myself totally clear to her. I tried to reassure her and I said words to the effect that we cannot assume he – you – is not a traitor. It's unlikely, but, in the event it was confirmed, you would be treated without compunction.'

'Pretty difficult to say that in French even if you were fluent,' I said.

'I was a bit out of my depth, you're right. I got confused with "*traître*" and "*traiter*", I think.' He looked at me sorrowfully. 'I have this ghastly feeling I said you were a "*traître sans pitié*" . . .'

'That's fairly unequivocal. A "merciless traitor".'

'Whereas I was trying to say –'

'I can see where the confusion arose.'

'I've lain awake for nights going through what I might actually have said to her. We were all rather thrown by Glockner's death. Panic stations, you know.'

'That's all very well. The woman shot me three times. Point-blank range. All because of your schoolboy French.'

'How did Glockner die?' he asked, clearly very keen to change the subject.

'A heart attack – so Madame Duchesne told me.'

'And he was fine when you left him.'

'Yes. Counting his money.'

Why do I keep on lying? Something tells me that the less I tell everyone, the better. We chatted on a bit more and he informed me that Munro was coming to see me about the decryption of the letters. Finally he stood and shook my hand.

'My sincere apologies, Rief.'

'There's not much I can say, in the circumstances. What happened to Madame Duchesne?'

'She took a train back to Geneva. She's back there now, working away as Agent Bonfire. Worth her weight in gold.'

'Does she know I survived?'

'I'm pretty sure she thinks you're dead, actually. I thought it best not to raise the matter – I didn't want to upset her unnecessarily, you see. She thought she was acting on my orders, after all. She couldn't really be blamed.'

'That's very considerate of you.'

My mother had brought my mail from Claverleigh, including the letter I'd sent myself from Geneva containing the Glockner decrypts. I made fresh copies of all six and gave them to Munro when he came to see me yesterday.

We sat in what used to be the Junior Common Room. There was a foursome playing bridge but otherwise it was quiet. A rainy, fresh day, the first inklings of autumn in the air.

I spread the transcripts on the table in front of us. Munro looked serious.

'What's disturbing me is that this man seems to know everything,' he said. 'Look – construction of two gun spurs on the Hazebrouk–Ypres railway line . . .' He pointed to another letter. 'Here – the number of ambulance trains in France, where the ammunition-only railheads are . . .'

'Something to do with the railway organization?'

'You'd think so – but look at all this stuff about forage.'

'Yes,' I said. 'I don't get that.'

'There's one horse for every three men in France,' Munro said. 'Hundreds of thousands – and they all have to be fed.'

'Ah. So, follow the forage trail and you'll find the troop build-up.'

Munro mused on. 'Yes, where is he? Ministry of Munitions? Directorate of Railway Transport? Quartermaster-General's Secretariat? General Headquarters? War Office? But look at this.' He picked up letter number five and quoted, '"Two thou refrig vans ordered from Canada." Refrigerated vans. How can he know that?'

'Yes. What are they for?'

'You want your meat fresh in the front line, don't you, soldier?'

Munro smoothed his neat moustache with the palp of his forefinger, thinking hard. Then he turned and looked at me with his clear enquiring gaze.

'What do you want to do, Rief?'

'What do you mean?'

'Do you want to return to your battalion? They're still in Swansea – but you can't keep your rank. Or you can have an honourable discharge. You've more than done your duty – we recognize that and we're very grateful.'

It didn't take much thought. 'I'll take the honourable discharge, thank you,' I said, knowing I couldn't go back to the 2/5th E.S.L.I. 'I should be out of here in a couple of weeks,' I added.

Then he stiffened, as though he'd just thought of something.

'Or you could do one more job for us, here in London. What do you say?'

'I really think I've more than –'

'I'm phrasing it as a question, Rief, to allow you to reply in the affirmative.' He smiled, but it was not a warm smile. 'You'll stay a lieutenant, same pay.'

'Well, when you put it like that – yes. As long as I don't get shot again.'

Just at that moment some catering staff came in and began to lay the long table for lunch, with much clattering of plates and ringing of silverware.

'Do you fancy a spot of lunch?' I asked Munro.

'I don't fancy hospital gruel,' he said. 'Can we go to a pub?'

We walked through the college and out of the rear entrance on to Walton Street.

'I've never been in this college,' Munro said. 'Though I must have walked past it a hundred times.'

'What college were you in?' I asked him, not surprised to be not surprised that he'd been an Oxford undergraduate.

'Magdalen,' he said. 'Other side of town.'

'Then you joined the diplomatic service,' I said.

'That's right, after my spell in the army.' He glanced at me. 'What was your college?'

'I didn't go to university,' I said. 'I started acting straight after my schooldays.'

'Ah, the University of Life.'

The pub was called The Temeraire and its sign was a lurid misrepresentation of Turner's masterpiece. It was small and wood-panelled with low tables and three-legged stools and prints of old ships-of-the-line on the walls. Munro fetched two pints and ordered himself a veal-and-ham pie with mashed potatoes and pickled onions. I said I wasn't hungry.

'There's a big attack due,' Munro said, sprinkling his pie and mash with salt and pepper. 'In a matter of days, in fact. Supporting a French offensive. In the Loos sector.'

I spread my hands and looked at him with some incredulity. 'For heaven's sake,' I said. 'I suggested strongly that we stopped all operations. I urged that we stopped. They'll be waiting for us – look at the last two Glockner letters. You can pinpoint the area yourself.'

'If only it were that easy. The French are being very insistent.' He smiled thinly, unhappily, obviously feeling the same way I was. 'Let's hope for the best.'

'Oh, we can always do that. Costs nothing, hope.'

Munro made a rueful face, said nothing and tackled his pie. I lit a cigarette.

'There's one thing our correspondent missed,' Munro said. 'Curious. We're going to use poison gas at Loos – though we refer to it as the "accessory".'

'Well, they did it to us at Ypres,' I said, carefully. 'All's fair in love and war.' I was wondering why he was telling me this. Was it some kind of test?

'I wonder why he missed it,' Munro went on. 'Maybe it'll help us locate him.' He took a sip of his beer. 'Have a week's leave when you get out of hospital. Then I want you to meet someone in London. We need to plan our course of action.'

'So I'm still to remain a lieutenant.'

'Absolutely.' Then he said, trying to make it sound throwaway. 'You never told me what the cipher-text was.'

'I told Massinger and Madame Duchesne.'

'Oh yes, a German bible. But that obviously wasn't the truth.'

It's always dangerous to forget how clever Munro is, I now realize as I write this account up. He seems at times so boringly proper – the career soldier, the career diplomat, a neat and tidy man secure in his status and ever so slightly smug and superior, though he tries not to let it show. But not at all – that's what he wants you to think. I don't really know why – maybe because he had tried to test me with news about the 'accessory' – but I decided to test him, in turn.

'I decided not to tell them,' I said. 'In fact it was the libretto of an obscure German opera.'

'Oh yes? Called?'

I watched his face very carefully.

'*Andromeda und Perseus.*'

He frowned. 'Don't think I know it,' he said with a vague smile.

'No reason why you should, I suppose. By Gottfried Toller. Premiered in Dresden in 1912.'

'Ah, modern. That explains it. I was thinking of Lully's *Persée*.'

I felt a chill creep through me and I decided there and then not to trust Munro any more, however much I was naturally inclined to like him. Anyone living in Vienna in 1913 would have known about Toller's *Andromeda*. Anyone – certainly someone who was familiar with Lully's *Persée*. Why was he lying? Why were we both smilingly lying to each other? We were on the same side.

'Did Glockner give you his libretto?'

'Yes. In return for the money.'

'What happened to it?'

'I lost it. In all the fuss over the shooting. It was left behind somewhere in the nursing home in Evian, I assume. I haven't seen it since.'

Munro put down his knife and fork and pushed his plate aside.

'Shame. Could you lay your hands on another copy – through your contacts in the theatrical world, perhaps?'

'I could try.'

'Let's have another pint, shall we? Celebrate your speedy recovery.'

2. A Turner Two-Seater with a Collapsible Hood

LYSANDER WAS DISCHARGED FROM Somerville College a week later and decided to take his leave in Sussex as Hamo's guest in the cottage at Winchelsea. Hamo had acquired a motor car – a Turner two-seater with a collapsible hood – and together they went for drives over the Downs and into Kent to Dungeness and Bexhill, to Sandgate and Beachy Head and one epic journey to Canterbury where they stayed the night before motoring home. Lysander punctuated the motor tours with walks of increasing length as he began to feel stronger and his injured left leg showed signs of bearing up. The scar on his thigh was still unsightly, buckled and lurid – a lot of muscle had been cut away in search of the evasive coins – and after his walks, steadily progressing through half a mile, a mile, two miles, he felt the leg stiff and sore. Still, it was the best thing for it, he reckoned, as he felt his love of walking renewing and, as soon as his confidence had grown sufficiently, he threw his stick away with relief.

On his final Saturday before his return to London they motored into Rye for lunch and then went for a walk on Camber Sands. They made their way down a path through the barbed wire and the crude anti-invasion defences on to the beach. The tide was out and the huge expanse of sand seemed like the vestige of an ancient, perfect desert washed up here on the south coast of England, unbelievably flat and smooth. A mile away someone was flying a kite but otherwise they had the great beach to themselves. Lysander stopped – he thought he could hear the rumble of distant explosions.

'That's not from France, is it?' he said, knowing the offensive was due any day now.

'No,' Hamo said. 'There's a range up the coast – training gunners. How's the leg?'

'Getting better. No pain, but I'm still aware of it, if you know what I mean.'

They strode on in silence. There was a coolness lurking in the afternoon air.

'Do you know who I mean by Bonham Johnson?' Hamo asked.

'The novelist?'

'Yes. He lives not far away. Over by Romney. Turns out he's a great admirer of my African book. He's asked me to his sixtieth birthday party.'

'You can drive over.'

'He wants me to bring a guest. In fact he rather specified you – the actor-nephew – I think he's seen you on stage. You up for it? Week tomorrow.'

Lysander thought – it was the last thing he wanted to do but he rather felt Hamo's invitation was more entreating than its casual delivery implied.

'Assuming I have weekends off – yes. Might be interesting.'

Hamo was clearly very pleased. 'Literary types – ghastly. Feel I need moral support.'

'You're the one who's written a book, Hamo.'

'Ah – but you're the famous actor. They won't notice me.'

Lysander went up to London on Sunday evening. The Chandos Place flat was still sublet so he booked himself into a small lodging house in Pimlico – with the grandiose name of The White Palace Hotel – not far from the river. He could walk to Parliament Square in thirty minutes or less. Munro had asked him to meet at a place called Whitehall Court on the Monday morning but had been vague as to who else would be there and what would be discussed.

As it turned out, on the Monday morning, Lysander realized that Whitehall Court was one of those London buildings he'd seen from a distance countless times but had never bothered to identify properly. It looked like a vast nineteenth-century château – thousands of rooms with turrets and mansard roofs, containing a gentleman's club, a hotel and many floors of serviced apartments and offices. It was set back from the river behind its own gardens between Waterloo Bridge and the railway bridge that serviced Charing Cross station.

A uniformed porter checked his name on a clipboard and told him to go up to the top floor, turn left at the top of the stairs, through the door, down a passageway and someone would be waiting. Lysander saw him pick up the telephone on his desk as he made for the foot of the stairway.

That someone turned out to be Munro – in civilian clothes – who showed him into a simple and severely furnished office with a view of the Thames through the windows. Massinger was there waiting, uniformed, and greeted Lysander stiffly, as if he were still guilty for his near-fatal error with his imperfect French. There was a large, leather-topped, walnut desk set back against a wall facing the windows with the chair behind it empty. Someone of greater eminence had yet to arrive.

The three men sat on the available chairs. Munro offered refreshments – tea – and was politely declined. Massinger asked Lysander how he was feeling and Lysander said he felt pretty much back to normal, thank you. A train clattered over the railway bridge from Charing Cross and, as its whistle sounded, as if on cue, the door opened and a grey-haired elderly man in a naval captain's uniform limped in. The clumping sound as he set his right leg down made Lysander think the limb was artificial. He had a mild, smiley manner – everything about him, apart from the wooden leg, seemed unexceptional. He was not introduced.

'This is Lieutenant Rief, sir,' Munro said. 'Who did the splendid job in Geneva.'

'Exceptional,' Massinger chipped in, proprietorially. Switzerland was his territory, Lysander remembered.

'Congratulations,' the captain said. 'So you're the man who found our rotten apple.'

'We haven't quite found him yet, sir,' Lysander said. 'But we think we may know what barrel he's in.'

The captain chuckled, enjoying the metaphor's resonances.

'So, what do we do next?' he said, looking at Massinger and Munro.

'Not really my area,' Massinger said, defensively, and once again Lysander wondered about the hierarchy in the room. The captain was the big chief, clearly, but who was the senior between Massinger and Munro? What autonomy did either of them have, if any?

'I think we have to get Rief into the War Office somehow,' Munro said. 'His best asset is that he's completely unknown – unlike us. Fresh face – a stranger.'

246

The captain was drumming his fingers on his desk top. 'How?' he said. 'He's just a lieutenant. Nothing but bigwigs in the War Office.'

'We set up a commission of enquiry,' Munro said. 'Something very boring. Send in Rief with authorization to ask questions and examine documents.'

'Sir Horace Ede chaired a commission last year on transportation,' the captain said. 'There could be some supplementary matters arising –'

'Exactly. That Lieutenant Rief had to cover and account for.'

'And there's a joint nations' conference coming up which would explain why we have to have everything ship-shape.'

'Couldn't be better.'

Massinger was looking increasingly uncomfortable at being sidelined in this way with nothing to contribute. He cleared his throat loudly and everybody stopped talking and looked at him. He held up both hands in apology. Then took out his handkerchief and blew his nose.

'How long would you need, sir?' Munro asked.

'Give me a couple of days,' the captain said. 'The higher the authorization the easier it'll be for Rief, here.' He turned to Lysander. 'Hold yourself in readiness, Rief. If we want you right at the heart of things then we need to give you some power.'

Massinger finally spoke. 'You don't think we're treading on M.O. 5's toes, do you, sir?'

'This wretched mess all originated out of Geneva,' the captain said with a trace of impatience in his voice. 'It was your show – so it's our show. I'll square things with Kell. He doesn't have any men to spare, anyway.'

Lysander didn't know what they were talking about. He picked at a loose shred of skin on his forefinger.

'Right, let me get on to it,' the captain said. 'We'd better give our rotten apple a codename so we can talk about him.'

'Any preferences?' Munro asked.

Lysander thought quickly. 'How about Andromeda?' he said, his eyes fixed on Munro. Munro's face didn't move.

'Andromeda it is – so let's find him, fast,' the captain said, and rose to his feet. The meeting was over. He crossed the room to Lysander and shook his hand. 'I saw your father play Macbeth,' he said. 'Scared me to bits. Good luck, Rief. Or should I say welcome aboard?'

3. The Annexe on the Embankment

MUNRO TOLD HIM TO go away and enjoy himself for a few days until he was called for. Once everything had been set up he would be briefed and given precise instructions. So he returned to the White Palace Hotel in Pimlico and tried to keep himself distracted and amused even though he was aware of a steadily increasing undercurrent of uneasiness flowing beneath the surface of his life. Who was this all-powerful captain-figure? What role and sway did he enjoy? To what extent, if at all, could he rely on Munro and Massinger? Could he trust either of them? And why had be been selected, once again, to do his duty as a soldier? Perhaps he'd gain some answers in the coming days, he reflected, but the complete absence of answers – even provisional ones – was troubling.

He went to his tailor, Jobling, and had a small buttonhole fitted for his wound-stripe – an inch-long vertical brass bar worn on the left forearm – sewn into the sleeves of his uniform jackets. Jobling was obviously moved when he told him the nature of his injuries. Three of his cutters had joined up and two had already died. 'Don't go back there, Mr Rief,' he said. 'You've done your bloody bit, all right.' He also adjusted the fit of his jacket – Lysander had lost weight during his convalescence.

He went to see Blanche in *The Hour of Danger* at the Comedy. Backstage in her dressing room she didn't allow him to kiss her on the lips. He asked her to supper but she said she couldn't go as she was 'seeing someone'. Lysander asked his name but she wouldn't tell him and they parted coolly, not to say acrimoniously. He sent her flowers the next day to apologize.

He quickly organized a small dinner party in a private room at the Hyde Park Hotel for four of his actor friends with the precise intention of finding out the name of Blanche's new beau. Everybody knew and, to his alarm, it turned out to be someone he was slightly acquainted with as well – a rather successful playwright that he'd read for called James Ashburnham, a man in his late forties, a widower. A handsome older man with a reputation in the theatre as something of a philanderer, Lysander thought, feeling betrayed, though a moment's reflection made him realize he had no right to the emotion – he was the one who had broken off their engagement, not Blanche. As Blanche had reminded him, they had decided to remain friends, that was all, consequently her private life was her concern alone.

Of course, being rejected for someone else made him feel hurt and his old feelings for Blanche re-established themselves effortlessly. She was an extremely beautiful, sweet young woman and whatever they had shared together couldn't be simply tossed aside that easily. What was she doing having an affair with a middle-aged playwright old enough – well, almost – to be her father? He was surprised at how agitated he felt.

On the Friday morning there was a knock at his door and Plumtree, the young chambermaid, told him there was a gentleman to see him in the back parlour. Lysander went downstairs with some trepidation – it was underway, the play was about to start again – orchestra and beginners, please. Fyfe-Miller was waiting for him, smart in a commander's uniform, with a file of papers under his arm. He locked the door and spread them on the table. He and Munro had analysed the variety of information in the Glockner letter decrypts and were convinced they could only have come from one department in the War Office – the Directorate of Movements. This department was currently housed in an annexe to the War Office on the Embankment in a building near Waterloo Bridge. Lysander was to report there at once to the director, one Brevet Lieutenant-Colonel Osborne-Way, who would ensure that Lysander was provided with his own office and a telephone. He was expected this afternoon – there was no time to waste.

'Can't it wait until Monday?' Lysander asked, plaintively.

'There's a war on, Rief, in case you hadn't noticed,' Fyfe-Miller said, not smiling for once. 'What kind of attitude is that? The sooner we find out who this person is, the safer we shall all be.'

At two-thirty that afternoon, Lysander stood across the street from the seven-storey building that housed the Directorate of Movements. He was standing approximately half way between Waterloo Bridge and the Charing Cross Railway Bridge. Cleopatra's Needle was a few yards away to his left. The phrase 'searching for a needle in a haystack' came pessimistically into his head. The Thames was at his back and he could hear the wash of water swirling round the jetties and the moored boats as the tide ebbed. He was smart in his new uniform with his brass wound-bar and with highly polished, buckled leather gaiters encasing his legs from knee to boot. He took his cap off, smoothed his hair and resettled it on his head. He felt strangely nervous but he knew that, above all, he now had to act confident. He lit a cigarette – no hurry. He heard a flap of wings and turned to see a big black crow swoop down and settle on the pavement two yards from him. Big birds, up close, he thought – size of a small hen. Black beak, black eyes, black feathers, black legs. 'City of kites and crows,' Shakespeare had said about London, somewhere. He watched as the bird made its hippity-hoppity way towards half a discarded currant bun in the gutter. It pecked away for a while, looking around suspiciously, then a motor car passed too close and it flew off into a plane tree with an irritated squawk.

Lysander realized he could think of three or four symbolic, doom-laden interpretations of this encounter with a London crow but decided to investigate none of them further. He threw his cigarette into the Thames, picked up his attaché case and, watching out for the speeding traffic, made his way across the Embankment to the Annexe's front door.

Once he'd presented his credentials, Lysander was taken by an orderly up to the fourth floor. They pushed through swing doors into a lobby with two corridors on either side. On the wall were lists of various departments and meaningless acronyms and small arrows indicating which corridor to take – DGMR, Port & Transport Ctte, Railway and Road Engineering, DC (War Office), Ordnance (France), Food Controller (Dover), DART (Mesopotamia), ROD (II), and the like. Lysander and the orderly turned right and walked down a wide linoleum-floored passageway with many doors off it. The sound of typewriters and ringing telephone bells followed them all the way to a door marked 'Director of Movements'. The orderly knocked and Lysander was admitted.

The Director of Movements, Brevet Lt.-Colonel Osborne-Way (Worcester Regiment) was not at all pleased to see him, so Lysander recognized in about two seconds. His manner was unapologetically brusque and cold. Lysander was not offered a seat, Osborne-Way did not attempt to shake his hand, nor return his salute. Lysander handed him over his magic laissez-passer to the kingdom of the Directorate – a sheet of headed notepaper signed by the Chief of the Imperial General Staff himself, Lieutenant-General Sir James Murray, KCB, that said that 'the under-named officer, Lieutenant L.U.Rief, is to be afforded every possible assistance and access. He is acting under my personal instructions and is reporting directly to me.'

Osborne-Way read this missive several times as if he couldn't believe what was actually written down in black and white. He was a short man with a grey toothbrush moustache, and large puffy bags under his eyes. There were seven telephones in a row on his desk and a camp bed with a blanket was set up in the corner of his office.

'I don't understand,' he said, finally. 'What's it got to do with the C.I.G.S., himself? Why's he sending you? Doesn't he realize how busy we are here?'

As if to illustrate this claim two of the telephones on his desk began to ring simultaneously. He picked up the first and said 'Yes. Yes . . . repeat, yes. Affirmative.' Then he picked up the second, listened for a moment and said 'No,' and hung up.

'This is not my idea, sir,' Lysander said, reasonably. He was affecting a slightly drawling, nasal voice, faintly caddish and bored-sounding, he thought, conscious that this tone would make Osborne-Way like him even less. He didn't care – he wasn't entering a popularity contest. 'I'm just following orders. Some unfinished, supplementary business to Sir Horace Ede's commission of inquiry on transportation. Matter of some urgency given the up-coming all-nations' conference.'

'What do you need from us, then?' Osborne-Way said, handing the letter back as if it was burning his hand.

'I'd like a list of all personnel in the Directorate and their distribution of duties. And I'd be grateful if you'd alert everyone in the Directorate to the fact that I am here and have a job to do. At some stage I will want to interview them. The sooner I'm finished the sooner you'll see the back of me,' he smiled. 'Sir.'

'Very well.'

'I believe I have an office assigned to me.'

Osborne-Way picked up a telephone and shouted, 'Tremlett!' into the mouthpiece.

In about thirty seconds a lance-corporal appeared at the door. He had a black patch over one eye.

'Tremlett, this is Lieutenant Rief. Take him to Room 205.' Then to Lysander he said, 'Tremlett will fetch you any files or documents you need, any person you wish to interview and will provide you with tea and biscuits. Good day.' He opened a drawer on his desk and began removing papers. The meeting was clearly over. Lysander followed Tremlett back along the wide passageway, taking two right-angled turns as they made for Room 205.

'Good to have you aboard, sir,' Tremlett said, turning and giving him a lopsided smile, the portion of his face below the patch not moving. He was a young man in his early twenties, with a London accent. 'I'm on extension 11. Give me a tinkle whenever you need me. Here we are, sir.'

He opened the door to Room 205. It was a windowless box with a dirty skylight. Here was a table, two wooden chairs and a very old filing cabinet. On the table was a telephone. It was not a room one would want to spend many hours in, Lysander thought.

'What's that curious smell?' he asked.

'Disinfectant, sir. Colonel Osborne-Way thought we should give the place a good swab-out before you arrived.'

He told Tremlett to bring him Osborne-Way's list as soon as possible, sat down and lit a cigarette. His eyes were already stinging slightly from the astringency of the disinfectant. The battle lines had been drawn – the Director of Movements had made a pre-emptive strike.

There were twenty-seven members of the Directorate of Movements on the fourth floor of the Annexe, and many clerical and secretarial staff to serve them. Almost all of them were army officers who had been wounded and were unfit for active service. As he looked down the list of names Lysander found himself wondering – which one of you is Andromeda? Which one of you has been sending coded messages to Manfred Glockner in Geneva? Who has access to the astounding detail those letters contained? Where are you, Andromeda? Temporary Captain J.C.T. Baillie

(Royal Scots)? Or temporary Major S.A.M.M. Goodforth (Irish Guards)? . . . He leafed through the typed pages, wondering what had made him choose Andromeda as the name of the traitor in the Directorate. Andromeda – a helpless, naked, beautiful young woman chained to the rocks at the ocean's edge, waiting terrified for the approach of the sea monster Cetus – didn't exactly conform to the stereotypical image of a man actively and efficiently betraying his country. 'Cetus' might have been more apt – but he liked the ring and the idea of looking for an 'Andromeda'. The paradox was more intriguing.

But he quickly became aware as he contemplated Osborne-Way's list that it would not be an easy process. He picked a name at random: temporary Captain M.J. McCrimmon (Royal Sussex Regiment). Duties – 1. Despatch of units and drafts to India and Mesopotamia. 2. Inter-colonial moves. 3. Admiralty transport claims and individual passage claims to and from India. He picked another – temporary Major E.C. Lloyd-Russell (Retired. Special Reserve). Duties – 1. Despatch of units and drafts from India to France (Force 'A') and Egypt (Force 'E'). 2. Union of South Africa contingent. Labour corps from South Africa and India to France. 3. Supervision of Stores Service from the USA and Canada to the United Kingdom. Then there was Major L.L. Eardley (Royal Engineers). Duties – 1. Travelling concessions and irregularities. 2. Issue of railway warrants unconnected with embarkation. 3. General questions concerning railways and canals in the United Kingdom.

And so it went on, Lysander beginning to feel a mild nausea as he tried to take all this amount of work – these 'duties' – on board. He ordered a pot of tea and some biscuits from Tremlett. He thought of himself as a child on the roof of a vast factory peering down through a skylight at all the machinery and the people inside. Who were they? What were they doing? What was being made? All these strange jobs and responsibilities – 'Railway Engineering Services. Accounts for work services. Occupation and rent of railway property. Shipping statistics. Labour Corps to France. Remounts to France. Long-voyage hospital ships. Despatches of stores to theatres of war other than France. Construction of sidings . . .' They went on and on. And this was only one department in the War Office. And there were thousands of people working in the War Office. And this was only one country at war. The Directorate of Movements would have its equivalent in France, in Germany, in Russia, in Austria-Hungary . . .

He began to feel dizzy as he sat there trying to conceptualize the massive scale of this industrial bureaucracy in the civilized world, all directed to the common end of providing for its warring armies. What gigantic effort, what millions of man-hours expended, day after day, week after week, month after month. As he tried to come to terms with it, to visualize in some way this prodigious daily struggle, he found himself perversely glad that he had actually been in the front line. Maybe that was why they employed wounded soldiers rather than civil servants or other professional functionaries. These temporary Captains and Majors in the Directorate of Movements at least knew the physical, intimate consequences of the 'movement of stores' that they ordered.

Lysander personalized it, grimly. When he had thrown that Mills no.5 bomb into the sap beneath the ruined tomb it was the final moment in the history of travel of that small piece of ordnance – a history that stretched back through space and time like a ghoulish, spreading wake. From ore mined in Canada, shipped to Britain, smelted, moulded, turned, filled and packed in a box, designated as 'stores to be transported from the United Kingdom to France'. Perhaps new sidings had been built in a rural railway station in northern France to accommodate the train carrying these stores (and what was involved in constructing a siding, he wondered). And from there it would be transferred to a dump or depot by animal transport whose forage was supplied through Rouen and Havre, also. Then soldiers would carry the boxes of bombs up to the line through communication trenches dug by 'labour from the Union of South Africa'. And then that Mills no. 5 bomb eventually found itself in the kitbag of Lt. Lysander Rief, who threw it into a sap beneath a tomb in no man's land and a man with a moustache and a fair-haired boy struggled to find it in the dark amongst the tumbled masonry, hoping and praying that some defect in its manufacture, or some malfunction caused by its long journey, would cause it not to detonate . . . No such luck.

Lysander found that he was sweating. Stop. That way madness lies. He thought of tips of icebergs or inverted pyramids but then an image came to him from nowhere that seemed to cohere with what he had been imagining more fittingly. A winter bonfire.

He remembered how, on very cold days in winter, when you lit a bonfire the smoke sometimes refused to rise. The slightest breeze would move it flatly across the land, a low enlarging horizontal plume of smoke that hugged the ground and never dispersed into the air as it did with a normal fire on a warmer day. He saw all the monstrous, gargantuan effort of the war as a winter bonfire – yes, but in reverse. As if the drifting, ground-hugging pall of smoke were converging – arrowing in – on one point, to feed the small, angry conflagration of the fire. All those miles of broad, dense, drifting smoke narrowing, focussing on the little crackling flickering flames burning vivid orange amongst the fallen leaves and the dead branches.

Lysander left Room 205 and wandered the corridors of the Directorate, passing other officers and secretarial staff as he went. Nobody paid him any attention, the ringing of the phones and the dry clatter of the typewriter keys a constant aural backdrop. He peered into one room where the door was ajar and saw three officers sitting at their desks all speaking into their telephones. Two women typists faced each other typing, as if duelling, somehow. He walked down the stairs and saw the signs on the other floors –

MOVEMENTS, RAILWAYS AND ROADS
INLAND WATER TRANSPORT (FRANCE)
INSPECTOR-GENERAL (ALL THEATRES)
IRISH RAILWAYS

He stepped out, feeling exhausted and a little overwhelmed, on to the Embankment and took some deep breaths of dirty London air. He stretched, flexed his shoulder muscles, rolled his head around, easing his neck, feeling weak and almost tearful at the magnitude of the task he'd been set. Who the hell was Andromeda? And, when he found him, what would happen then?

4. English Courage

'YOU KNOW,' HAMO SAID over the noise of the engine, 'I never feel nervous about anything in life but I feel strangely nervous today.'

They were in the Turner two-seater motoring towards Romney on Sunday morning, heading for Bonham Johnson's lunch party.

'I know what you mean,' Lysander said, leaning towards him and cupping his hand around his mouth. 'I felt exactly the same the other day when I went into the War Office. First day at school.' He looked around and saw a signpost flash by – Fairfield, 2 miles. 'Let's stop at a pub or a hotel and have a drink first. Dutch courage. Why's it called Dutch courage? English courage is what we need.'

'Excellent idea,' Hamo said. He was wearing a flat leather cap, reversed, and driving goggles. They had the hood of the two-seater down as the day was fine, though breezy. They both wore greatcoats and Lysander had his Trilby tied securely on his head with his scarf.

They found a small pub in Fairfield and ordered whisky sodas at the bar.

Hamo said, 'I'm just terrified that one of these literary types is going to ask me about Shakespeare or Milton.'

'No they won't. You're the one they want to see and meet. You wrote *The Lost Lake*. That's what they'll want to talk about – not Keats and Wordsworth.'

'I wish I had your confidence, my boy.'

'Hamo, you've won the Victoria Cross, for god's sake. They're just a bunch of idle writers.'

'Still . . .'

'No. Do what I do. If I don't feel confident I *act* confident.'

'I'll try. That's exactly what your father would have said. D'you know, I think another whisky would help.'

'Go on, then. Me too.'

Lysander watched his uncle go up to the bar to order another round, feeling a kind of love for him. He looked slim and upright in his dark grey suit, the ceiling light shining off his bald pate like some incipient halo. Hamo's halo. Nice thought.

Bonham Johnson's house – Pondshill Place – was large and imposing – a Victorian farm of cut and moulded red brick and tall groups of chimney-stacks. At one end was a wide bow window looking over a terraced garden that fell gently to a reflecting pool surrounded by closely clipped obelisks of box trees. There was a barn and stable block to one side where the guests' motor cars were to be parked. A farm labourer waved them into the courtyard where there were already a dozen cars in two neat rows.

'Oh good,' Hamo said. 'Looks like a big crowd. I can hide myself.'

The main door to Pondshill Place was opened by a butler, who invited them to 'go through to the saloon'. This was the drawing room with the big curved bay window and was already occupied by upward of twenty people – all very casually dressed, Lysander noticed, glad that he had decided on a suit of light Harris tweed. He saw some men without ties and women in brightly coloured print dresses. He whispered, 'Relax!' to Hamo and they helped themselves to a glass of sherry from a tray held by an extremely pretty young maid, Lysander noticed.

Bonham Johnson was a very stout man with longish thinning hair and a grizzled pointed beard that made him look vaguely Jacobean, Lysander thought. He introduced himself and launched into a fluent and protracted hymn of praise to *The Lost Lake of Africa* – 'Extraordinary, unparalleled.' Even Hamo yielded in the face of this encomium and Lysander happily let Johnson lead him away across the room, hearing him ask, 'Do you know Joseph Conrad? No? You'll have a lot in common.'

Lysander headed back to the maid with the sherry and helped himself to another glass.

'What time is lunch being served?' he asked, fixing her with his eyes. She was strikingly pretty. What was she doing serving Bonham Johnson's guests?

'About one-thirty, sir. Still a few more guests to arrive.'

'This may seem a strange question. But have you ever thought of –'

'Lysander?'

He turned round and for a brief second didn't recognize her. The hair was darker, cut short with a severe straight fringe across the eyebrows. She was wearing a jersey dress with great lozenges of colour blocks – orange, buttercup-yellow, cinnamon. He felt himself shiver, visibly. The shock-effect was palpable, unignorable.

'Hettie . . .'

'I'm so glad you could come. I told Bonham that your uncle would be the best way to lure you here.' She leaned forward and kissed his cheek and he smelled her scent again, for the first time in a year and a half. Now he had tears in his eyes. He closed them.

'So it was all your doing . . .'

'Yes. I had to find a way of seeing you. You're not going to be beastly to me, are you?' she said.

'No. No, I'm not.'

'Are you all right? You've gone quite pale.'

'Is Lothar here?'

'Of course not. He's in Austria.'

This was impossible. He felt he was in some kind of emotion-race, feelings and sensations succeeding each other in a frantic, spinning helter-skelter.

'Can we get out of here?' he managed to say.

'No. Jago would be horribly suspicious. In fact he won't even like me talking to you for very long.'

'Who's Jago?'

'My husband – Jago Lasry.'

Lysander sensed he was meant to react to the name but he had never heard of the man.

Hettie looked at him sardonically.

'Come on, don't play those games with me. Jago Lasry, author of *Crépuscules*. Mmm? Ring a bell? The *Quick Blue Fox and other stories*. Yes?'

'I've been in the army since the war started – very out of touch.'

She moved closer and he was reminded of how small-made and tiny she was – the top of her head reaching his chest. She lowered her voice.

'I'm sitting beside you at lunch but we must pretend to be strangers – almost-strangers, anyway. And I'm not called Hettie any more. I'm Venora.'

'Venora?'

'A Celtic name. I always hated being called Hettie. It seemed fine in Vienna but it's all wrong here. Imagine being Hettie Lasry! See you at lunch.'

She walked away and Lysander, still in awful turmoil, mistily watched her ease her way through the crowd of guests to greet one of the tieless young men. A small wiry fellow, in his late twenties, Lysander supposed, with a dark patchy beard, wearing a maroon corduroy suit. Jago Lasry, author of *Crépuscules*. He saw the man's head turn to seek him out. So Hettie/Venora had been behind this invitation . . . he wondered what she wanted of him. He drained his sherry glass and went back for a refill.

He heard the rest of Hettie's story at lunch – in fits and starts, out of sequence, with many a doubling-back and re-explanation, at his insistence. To his shock he discovered she had been living in England since the beginning of the year. She had left Vienna in November 1914 and had crossed into Switzerland, making her roundabout way back home via Italy and Spain.

'Why didn't you bring Lothar with you?'

'He's much happier in Austria. He's living in Salzburg with one of Udo's aunts. Happy as anything.'

'Have you got a photograph of him?'

'I have, but . . . not here. Jago doesn't know about Lothar, as it happens. Let's keep it between ourselves, if you don't mind.'

She had met Jago Lasry shortly after her return and they had married in May ('Love at first glimpse,' she said), so it transpired, and they were currently living in Cornwall in a cottage owned by Bonham Johnson. Lasry was a protégé of Johnson, who had been very generous with introductions to publishers and editors and the provider of small loans, when required, so Hettie told him. Lysander glanced across the table at Lasry – a skinny, intense man who appeared to eat his food with the same concentration and urgency as he spoke. He suspected Bonham Johnson was more than a little in love with his protégé.

'I told Jago that you and I had met briefly in Vienna,' Hettie said. 'That we were both seeing the same doctor there. Just in case he was suspicious.'

'Bensimon's back in London, you know. I heard from him.'

Hettie looked at him in that strange way she had. A bizarre mixture of sudden interest and what seemed like potential threat.

'Just like the old days, eh?' she said.

'What do you mean?'

She looked away and asked the person next to her to pass the salt. Lysander felt her hand on his thigh under the table and her fingers quickly searching for and finding the bulge of his penis. She gripped him hard through the cloth of his trousers, then ran her fingertips up and down. He reached for his wine glass, as if it would give him support – he thought he might swoon or cry out. She took her hand away.

'I have to see you,' he said, quietly, a little hoarsely, talking into his plate, trying not to look at her, slicing his lamb into small pieces to keep his mind occupied. 'I'm staying in London. A small hotel in Pimlico called The White Palace. They've a telephone.'

'I don't know if I can get up to London. Difficult – but I can try.'

'Send me a postcard – The White Palace Hotel, Pimlico, London, South West.'

Now she had turned to look at him again and he stared into those slightly-too-wide, pale hazel eyes. He realized that seeing her again here was a watershed. He felt he knew himself once more, understood the kind of person he was, what he needed, what he asked of life.

'I promise I'll do my best,' she said. 'Listen. You couldn't lend me some money, by any chance, could you?'

'Surprisingly nice fellow, that Bonham Johnson,' Hamo said. 'Put me completely at my ease. What a fuss I made for nothing – I could tell he was musical at once.'

'Musical?'

'One of us.'

'Ah. Right.'

'What did you need ten pounds for?' Hamo asked, stooping to crank the starting handle of the Turner. 'Lucky I had some cash on me.'

'I had to lend it to that woman I introduced you to. Vanora Lasry.'

'Very generous of you,' Hamo said, clambering on board the

now gently shuddering vehicle. 'To lend all that money to a perfect stranger.'

'That was her, Hamo,' Lysander confessed with relief. 'That was Hettie Bull – the mother of my son.'

'Good god!'

They pulled away out of the stable block and headed back across flat expanses of the marsh towards the main road to Rye. Lysander leaned close and shouted a brief explanation of what had taken place into Hamo's ear. As he listened, Hamo's head shook more regularly in bemusement and sympathy.

'I've got nothing to say to you, dear boy. Not a word of reproach. I know exactly what you're feeling. *La coeur a ses raisons.* Oh, yes!'

They motored along at a steady speed, the light fading, and when they caught glimpses of the Channel as the road took them closer to the coast they saw the setting sun burnishing the sea, like hammered silver. Lysander felt both exhilarated and confused. Meeting Hettie again made him achingly conscious once more of the irrefutable nature of his obsession with her. Obsession – or love? Or was it something more unhealthy – a kind of craving, an addiction?

He and Hamo sat up late, talking, drinking whisky – Lysander taking the opportunity to relate Hettie's story in more detail.

'Are you going to see her again?' Hamo asked.

'Yes. I have to.'

'Are you sure that's wise – now she's married and all that?'

'Very unwise, I'd have thought. But I can't see any alternative, Hamo. I'm sort of in thrall to her.'

'I understand. Oh, yes, I understand.'

Hettie had introduced Lysander to Jago Lasry after lunch was finished and Lysander felt himself being scrutinized, the suspicion and scepticism overt. Hettie linked arms with her husband, trying to emanate uxorious contentment.

'We both had the same doctor in Vienna,' Lysander said, searching for something bland and conventional to say to this coiled, angry, small man.

'Same quack, you mean.'

'I wouldn't go that far.'

'How far *would* you go, Mr Rief?'

'Let's say Dr Bensimon was a great help to me, therapeutically. Made a huge difference.'

'He just fed Vanora drugs.'

'Freud himself used Coca. Wrote a book about it.'

They then had a short, fervid discussion about the demerits of Sigmund Freud and Freudianism. Lysander began to feel increasingly out of his depth as Lasry spoke of Carl Jung and the 4th International Psychoanalytical Conference in Munich in 1913, subjects Lysander knew nothing about. He found himself trying to place Lasry's accent – Midlands, he thought, Nottingham coalfields – but before he could be any more precise Johnson drew Lasry away to meet 'the editor of the *English Review*'. Lysander stood there swaying, exhausted.

'I'd better join him,' Hettie said. 'I can see you've put him in one of his moods.'

'Why didn't you come to me the moment you were back in England?' Lysander said, suddenly aggrieved and hurt.

'I thought it was pointless – thought you'd never forgive me for Lothar. And the police. And all the rest.'

Lysander remembered his travails in Vienna at Hettie's hands, experiencing a sudden vivid recall of his anger and frustration. He wondered why he couldn't sustain these brief, intense rages that Hettie provoked. What was it about her? How did she undermine them so easily?

'I forgive you,' he said, weakly. 'Come and see me in London. Please. We'll sort everything out.'

And what did he mean by that? – he thought as he went up the stairs to his bedroom that night, his head numb and muddy with all the whisky he'd drunk and the swarm of emotions that had persecuted him all day. As he undressed he remembered that the hunt for Andromeda was meant to begin in earnest the next morning. In his troubled half-drunkenness he thought that, actually, in a house in Romney in the heart of Romney Marsh he had met the real Andromeda herself once more, in all her importunate beauty.

Coincidence? What was the Viennese connection in the Andromeda affair, he wondered dozily. If Hettie hadn't accused him of rape, if he hadn't called on Munro at the embassy, if he hadn't artfully engineered his own escape, then his current life would be entirely different. But what was the point of that? The view backward showed you all the twists and turns your life had taken, all the contingencies and chances, the random elements of good luck and bad luck that made up one person's existence. Still, questions buzzed around his brain all night as he tossed and fidgeted, punched and turned his pillows, opened and closed the windows of his room, waiting for sunrise. He managed to sleep for an hour and was up and dressed at dawn, off to the Winchelsea Inn for a pony and trap to take him into Rye. Monday, 27th September, 1915. The hunt was on.

5. Autobiographical Investigations

I BOUGHT A NEWSPAPER this morning on my walk to the Annexe. 'Great offensive at Loos'; 'Enemy falls back before our secret weapon'; 'Significant advances across the whole front despite heavy casualties'. The vapid vocabulary of jingoistic military journalism. It had all started this weekend while I was at Winchelsea and at Bonham Johnson's lunch party as I was sipping sherry, feeling Hettie grip me under the table and arguing about

Freud with her obnoxious husband. There are long faces in the Annexe, however. Here in the Directorate we quickly know when the ambulance trains are full. Provision was made for 40,000 wounded men and already it appears inadequate. Not enough heavy artillery, ammunition dumps insufficiently supplied. Our cloud of poison gas seems to have had the most partial effectiveness – reports have come in complaining that it hung in the air over no man's land or else drifted back into our trenches to blind and confuse our own men waiting to attack. The one thing we can't supply from the Directorate of Movements is a stiff westerly breeze, alas.

Going through Osborne-Way's list it's at once obvious that a significant number of the officers in the Directorate could not possibly have access to all the information in the Glockner letters. However, I've decided as a matter of policy and subterfuge to interview everyone – I don't want to concentrate on any particular group and thereby raise suspicions. Andromeda, whoever he is, mustn't develop the slightest concern over this supplementary enquiry into Sir Horace Ede's Commission on Transportation. So, I've summoned Tremlett and given him the entire list of interviewees. I begin with one Major H.B. O'Terence, responsible for 'Travelling claims by land. Visits of relatives to wounded in hospital in France'. He's going to be a busy man in the coming days and weeks – best to finish with him first.

It has proved to be both a shock and unusually destabilizing to have seen Hettie. All my sex-feelings for her have returned in an instant. Incredible desire. Old images of her naked and what we did with each other. And all my contradictions and confusions about her crowd in as well. Vanora Lasry – I can hardly believe it. And what about Lothar? Your son, your little boy. Again, emotions wax and wane. One second he seems unreal, a product of my imagination, a fantasy – and then, the next, I find myself thinking of this little boy, this baby, living in a suburb of Salzburg with Udo Hoff's aunt. Does Hettie care? Why wouldn't she tell her new husband that he has a stepson? I bought Lasry's book of poems, *Crépuscules*. Modern nonsense in the main. Free verse is both seductive and dangerous, I can see – it can be a licence to be pretentious and obscure. Lasry often abuses it, in my opinion. I take more care.

SEVENTH CAPRICE IN PIMLICO

The dawn created itself
And turned to see what had been lit.

Rubbish, litter, broken glass and a bit
Of green England, unsmirched, a glance
At something beautiful. Behold the dance:
The girls advance,
The boys decline.
Emerging from the Piccadilly Line
I find the tropic odours of Leicester Square
Beguile and mesmerize.
I roam the streets at midnight. The glare
Of gaslights an artificial sunrise.

'*Les colombes de ma cousine*
Pleurent comme un enfant.'

I asked Tremlett to do me a favour and to look up the casualty lists of the Manchester Fusiliers – to check whether a Lt. Gorlice-Law or a Sergeant Foley appeared. He came back with the news that Lt. Gorlice-Law had died of wounds on June 27th and a Sgt. Foley was in a hospital in Stoke Newington. 'He must be blind, sir,' Tremlett said, pointing to his patch. 'That's where they took my peeper out.' So Gorlice-Law died the day after our raid into no man's land . . . I feel I have to try and see Foley and find out exactly what happened that night after I crawled away and left them. Feelings of guilt inexorably creep over me. Was it my fault? No, you fool. You were ordered to bomb that sap to create a diversion. After that the gods of war and luck took over and you were as much subject to their fatal whim as any of the thousands of soldiers facing each other on both sides of the line.

6. Unlikely Suspects

LYSANDER INTERVIEWED THE OFFICERS of the Directorate over the next three days in the cramped and antiseptic quarters of Room 205. All were conducted in the same tone of apologetic tedium and polite routine – he wanted to make no one remotely suspicious or alarmed. He asked for their understanding – he knew he was wasting precious time – and strove to be as amiable as possible, but the men he saw were uniformly wary and resentful – sometimes even contemptuous. Osborne-Way had obviously been at work preparing the ground.

He ended up with a list of six key names, including the Director, Osborne-Way, himself. All these men were capable, theoretically, of reproducing the specific type of information contained in the Glockner letters. Four of them were responsible for 'Movement and control of war material and stores to France'. One dealt with control of ports, one with railway material – 'tanks, road metal, timber, slag and coal'. One was a rare civilian in the Directorate who was solely concerned with the compilation of shipping statistics – so every fact ended at his desk. Apart from Osborne-Way (an unlikely suspect, though Lysander refused to rule him out – unlikely suspects were more suspect in his opinion) the two men who most interested him were a Major Mansfield Keogh (Royal

Irish Regiment) who was the Assistant Director of Movements – Osborne-Way's number two – and a Captain Christian Vandenbrook (King's Royal Rifle Corps) who supervised the 'despatch to France of ammunition, ordnance, supplies and Royal Engineers' stores'.

In principle the Directorate of Movements retained no more responsibility once stores were landed at Le Havre, Rouen or Calais; at that moment the Quartermaster General's department at headquarters in St Omer took over. However, in practice, there were always problems – trains went missing, ammunition found itself in the wrong depots, ships were sunk in the Channel. Significantly, Lysander thought, both Keogh and Vandenbrook had been to France independently on three occasions in 1915 (Osborne-Way had been twice) to liaise with the Director of Railway Transport and his staff and to supervise the construction of marshalling yards and sidings behind the lines. There was ideal opportunity to discover everything the Glockner letters contained.

Keogh was a quiet, earnest, efficient man who seemed consumed by some private sadness. He was civil and prompt with his answers but Lysander felt he regarded him as a mere nothing – a buzzing fly, a crumpled piece of paper, a leaf on the pavement. Keogh looked at him with empty eyes. By contrast, Vandenbrook was the most open and charming of his interviewees. He was a small, lithe, handsome man with perfect, even features and a fair moustache with the ends dashingly turned up. His teeth – he smiled regularly – were almost unnaturally white, Lysander thought. Vandenbrook was the only person he talked to who asked him about himself and who seemed happy to acknowledge that he'd seen him on stage before the war. Lysander knew his past life was common knowledge in the Directorate – he had overheard Osborne-Way refer to him as the 'bloody actor-chappie' more than once – but only Vandenbrook made overt and unconcerned reference to his stage career and Lysander liked him for it.

The War Diary of the Directorate had revealed the facts about

Keogh's and Vandenbrook's trips to France. Tremlett supplied him with the ledger that detailed all the departmental 'travelling claims by land'. Keogh had responsibility for the port of Dover; Vandenbrook for Folkestone. Both men visited the ports every few days, where the Directorate kept branch offices, and their expenses – train tickets, hotels, taxis, porters, meals and refreshments – were docketed, copied and filed. Lysander decided to investigate Keogh first, then Vandenbrook, then Osborne-Way. Save the biggest beast for last.

Lysander saw Keogh come out of the Annexe and walk through to Charing Cross. He followed at a safe distance though he thought it unlikely he'd be recognized. He was wearing a false moustache, a bowler hat and was carrying a briefcase. He had chosen an old dark suit and made it short in the arms to expose the frayed cardboard cuffs of his shirt, looking, he hoped, like one of the thousands of clerical workers who spilled out of the great ministries of state in Whitehall at the end of the working day and began their routine journey homewards by the various means of public transport – omnibus, tram, and Underground and Tube railway. He followed Keogh on to the Underground at Charing Cross and sat at the far end of the compartment from him as they rattled along the District Line and over the Thames to East Putney. He watched Keogh plod up Upper Richmond Road and then turn off into a street of semi-detached brick villas. Keogh went into number 26. From inside the house Lysander could hear the faint barking of a dog, quickly silenced. He saw that the blinds of every window were drawn down. It was still light – perhaps he was one of the few London households that observed a proper blackout against the Zeppelin raids, but there seemed little point in that if your neighbours were lax. A death in the family? . . .

He spotted a woman pushing a pram up the pavement on the other side of the road and so crossed and came up behind her.

Putting on a slight cockney accent he asked if she knew which house Mr and Mrs Keogh lived in.

'I been knockin' on the wrong door, missus, it seems.'

'You want number 26, dear,' she said. 'But don't go asking for Mrs Keogh, though.'

'Why's that, then?'

'Because she died two months ago. Diphtheria. Very sad, terrible shame. Lovely young woman. Beautiful.'

Lysander thanked her and walked away. So, a recent widower – that explained the vacant, indifferent stare. Did that rule him out? Or did the meaningless death of a beautiful young wife provoke feelings of nihilism and rage against the world? He would have to find out more about Major Keogh. In the meantime he would turn his attention to Captain Christian Vandenbrook.

Vandenbrook was rich enough to take a taxi home from work. Lysander sat in the back of a cab at the end of the afternoon outside the Annexe, watched Vandenbrook flag down a passing taxi and followed it to his club in St James's. Two hours later he emerged, hailed another cab and was driven home to Knightsbridge to a large white stucco house in an elegant sweep of terrace off the Brompton Road. Vandenbrook was doing very well for a captain in the King's Royal Rifle Corps.

Lysander dismissed his taxi and walked up and down the smart crescent of large houses. Through a window he caught a glimpse of Vandenbrook accepting a cut-crystal tumbler from a silver tray held by a butler. Staff, as well. Twenty minutes later another taxi pulled up and a couple – dressed for dinner – descended and rang the doorbell. Lysander returned to his small hotel in Pimlico, conscious that someone with Vandenbrook's manifest privileges had no real need to turn traitor. Osborne-Way was next.

At the hotel he found he had a postcard, sent from St Austell,

Cornwall. It read, 'Arriving Friday evening. Have booked room at White Palace, Pimlico. Vanora.'

Tremlett fetched him the ledger of 'Travelling claims by land' and stood there waiting for further instructions as Lysander flicked through the pages.

'Colonel Osborne-Way hasn't filed any expenses claims.'

'No, sir. He sends his direct to the War Office. He was on the General Staff – seconded here, like.'

'Seems odd. Can we get them?'

Tremlett sucked his teeth.

'We can try but it might take a while. We may need you to go yourself with your magic letter.'

'Thanks, Tremlett, that'll be all for the moment.'

He looked through Keogh's claims and noted the dates he'd been to Dover over the past months; then he turned to Vandenbrook and collated their respective journeys – some days they tallied, some days they didn't. However, he noticed that Vandenbrook very rarely stayed in Folkestone – his accommodation claims were for hotels in Deal, Hastings, Sandwich, Hythe and once in Rye. Probably keen to get some golf in, Lysander thought, leafing through the dockets, or else wanted to be away from the Directorate organization – sensible man.

There was a knock on his door. Lysander put the bottle of champagne back in the ice-bucket and crossed the room, trying to stay calm, and opened the door. Hettie stood there, smiling, as if this encounter were the most natural and normal in the world.

'What a funny little hotel you chose,' she said, stepping in.

'My room's minute.' Lysander closed the door behind her, feeling as if his chest were stuffed with hot, rough wool – an ill, constrained breathlessness stopping him speaking. He sensed a weakness flow through him, as though his knees might buckle and he'd fall to the floor.

'Aren't you going to give me a kiss?' Hettie said, unpinning her hat and throwing it on to a chair. 'Let's take our clothes off now – then we can drink our champagne.'

'Hettie, for heaven's sake –'

'Come on, Lysander. Race you.'

They kissed. He felt his lips on hers and then her tongue in his mouth. They undressed and Lysander opened the champagne and poured it. He noticed Hettie had kept her hosiery on and her high-heeled shoes and her jewellery. Jet beads at the neck, a cluster of ivory bracelets.

'Why are we doing this?' he asked, faintly. 'This way.'

'Because I *know* you, Lysander. Remember?' she said, almost scoldingly. 'Because I know what you like.' She strode around the room, unselfconsciously, checked that the curtains were properly drawn. 'It's exciting, isn't it? To be naked in a hotel room in Pimlico drinking champagne . . .' She glanced down at him. 'My – you seem to agree.'

She came over to him and he touched her breasts and drew her close. Again, oddly, he felt like weeping – as if some form of destiny were being fulfilled, here in this unassuming room; that he was here with Hettie in his arms, once more. This was the problem with her, he acknowledged – or, rather, this was *his* problem with Hettie – it was like being with no other woman. He had never felt this need, this strongly, with anyone else.

She kissed his chest and he put his arms around her. She hugged her small body against his.

She raised her face and whispered, 'I've missed you.' Then she took him in her hand and led him compliantly to the bed.

7. The Dene Hotel, Hythe

THE DIRECTORATE OF MOVEMENTS had opened and maintained branch offices in Dover and Folkestone since the end of 1914, the easier to supervise the loading and despatch of the millions of tons of stores that were sent out to France each week. They were staffed mainly with former port authority officials and clerical workers but, every few days, Keogh and Vandenbrook would make a routine journey to oversee the office work or, more likely, sort out problems.

Looking through the departmental memoranda on Monday Lysander saw that two cargo vessels had collided in the Channel, one of them sinking with the loss of '600 black labour drowned (approx.)'. Osborne-Way had added a note in the margin in his small crabbed schoolboy's hand, 'Attn. Capt. VdenB.' Lysander asked Tremlett where Vandenbrook was and he came back with the information that he had not come into the Annexe that morning but had gone straight to Folkestone to 'sort out the steaming mess'.

Lysander told Tremlett to have a railway pass made out for him and he caught a train to the coast from Victoria before noon. At Folkestone he negotiated with a taxi-driver who grudgingly agreed to stay with him until midnight for £5 cash. Lysander thought of the soldiers in the trenches earning their eighteen pennies a day for their unique version of the diurnal grind. Still, the mobility might be essential – he had a feeling Vandenbrook wouldn't be spending the night in Folkestone.

He had the taxi park a little way up the street from the Directorate offices in Marine Parade and settled down to wait. It turned out to be a long one, Vandenbrook not emerging until seven o'clock that evening. A motor car drew up and he climbed in. They headed out of town, going west along the main coast road towards Hythe. Vandenbrook was dropped off at the front door of the Dene Hotel – a neat brick and hung-tile, two-storey building with a garage at the rear and a modern extension, just off the high street on the lower slopes of the hill that led up to Hythe's principal church, St Leonards. The car drove away, returning to Folkestone. After five minutes, Lysander followed him in.

The reception lobby was a low, beamed area with doors off to a saloon bar and a dining room and a fine curved oak staircase that led to the bedrooms on the first floor. Far more comfortable than the Commercial Hotel, Folkestone, he was sure, and where Directorate staff usually stayed, so Tremlett had informed him. Lysander saw fresh flowers in a bowl on the reception desk and read the posted menu outside the dining room where he noted a simple but classic choice of English dishes – a roast, a saddle of lamb, devilled kidneys, Dover sole. He felt suddenly hungry – no wonder Vandenbrook preferred to find his own lodgings.

He went into the bar and chose a seat where he had a view of the lobby through the glass-paned door. He ordered a whisky and soda and thought he'd wait until Vandenbrook came down for dinner and surprise him. They would have a laugh about it and at least he'd eat a decent meal before he caught the last train back to London.

He sipped his whisky and lit a cigarette, his mind turning inevitably towards Hettie and the night they'd spent together. She could only stay until morning, she had said, as she had to meet Lasry in Brighton, where they were going to look for somewhere to live – Cornwall was beginning to pall, so far away, and Bonham Johnson was urging them to be closer to London. She promised Lysander that she would come back to London for several days as soon as she could think up an excuse that would appease her suspicious husband. Lysander thought he might rent a small service apartment in a mansion block somewhere central where they could safely spend time together – he was growing tired of hotel life, anyway, and god knew how long he'd be stuck in the Directorate of Movements, searching for Andromeda. He wasn't anticipating his investigation of Osborne-Way with any great pleasure. He'd have to be exceptionally cautious, take real pains not to be –

His mother walked into the hotel.

His first instinct was to rush out into the lobby and surprise her, but something made him shrink back in his seat. She was wearing a fur coat and one of the new, fashionably smaller hats. She spoke to the receptionist and a porter was called and sent away. Luggage? Was she staying the night? The mâitre d' emerged from the dining room and shook her hand, obsequiously. She must be known here . . . She was led away towards the dining room and out of his line of sight.

Lysander would have liked to put this encounter down as one of life's many coincidences. Coincidences – the most extraordinary coincidences – happened all the time, he knew, and in a manner that would make the laziest farceur blush. But life's strange congruences were not applicable here – every suddenly aching bone in his body was telling him that this was no accidental coming-together of the respective orbits of Vandenbrook, Rief and Anna, Lady Faulkner. Then he saw Vandenbrook come down the stairs, cigarette in hand, and turn into the dining room. He knew instantly that he was going to his mother's table, that this rendezvous had been planned, but decided to wait five minutes before he sought his 'ocular proof'. He strolled out of the bar and pretended to consult a map of Hythe conveniently hung to one side of the dining-room door. It was ajar and he could see at an angle into the salon. There was a fireplace and a dozen tables, half of them occupied. And there in the corner was his mother, accepting a glass of wine poured by the sommelier, and there across the table from her was Christian Vandenbrook. They toasted each other – they seemed familiar and relaxed – clearly this was not their first introduction. As they talked and consulted the menu, Lysander saw that they were displaying all the timeworn and conventional feints and poor disguises of lovers meeting in a public place and hoping the real nature of their relationship would be invisible.

8. The Colonel's Daimler

'I NEED A MOTOR car, Tremlett,' Lysander said. 'I have to do a tour of the south-east. Does the Directorate have transport?'

'There is Colonel Osborne-Way's motor, sir. A Daimler. Sits in the garage for weeks at a time.'

'That'll do nicely.'

'I think we'll have need of your magic letter, however, sir.'

It turned out to be a big, new, maroon-and-black, 1914-model, seven-seater Daimler that had been ordered and paid for straight from the Daimler works in Coventry by the director of a chemical firm in Leipzig. It had been seized by the authorities at the outbreak of war before it could be shipped to Germany, but how it had ended up as Osborne-Way's personal vehicle was something of a mystery. It was ideal for Lysander's purposes, however, and Tremlett quickly and enthusiastically volunteered to act as chauffeur. Armed with copies of the relevant claims, the two of them headed off the next day – Lysander reclining grandly in the rear on mustard-yellow kid-leather seats – on a circuit of all the hotels on the Kent and Sussex coast that Christian Vandenbrook chose to frequent.

One night in Ramsgate drew a blank, but Sandwich, Deal and Hythe confirmed the pattern. They were all small, relatively expensive hotels with ardent recommendations from the better guidebooks. The hotel registers revealed that whenever Captain Vandenbrook was booked in so too was Lady Faulkner. She didn't stay with him in Rye, nor in Hastings, however – perhaps a little too close to home, Lysander thought. All in all, over a period from September 1914 to this latest October encounter, they had spent the night in the same hotel nine times. He would not have been surprised to find similar evidence in London – they were bound to have met there also, she went up to town two or three times a month – but Vandenbrook could hardly present a claim for a night in a London hotel to the Directorate's accounts department.

An affair of over a year, then, Lysander considered, and one that had begun while Crickmay Faulkner was still very much alive. The thought of his mother with Vandenbrook, carnally, made him uneasy and disturbed – made him instantly think of her differently, as if she had suddenly become someone entirely separate from the woman he knew and loved. But of course she wasn't old, he told himself, she had other roles in life beyond that of his 'mother'. She was an extremely attractive mature woman, cultured, vivacious, confident. Vandenbrook himself – sophisticated, charming, handsome, amusing, rich – was exactly the sort of man she would be attracted to. He could see that, understand that, all too clearly. He tried not to condemn her for it.

In Hastings, at the Pelham Hotel, the last hotel on their itinerary, the staff had been particularly helpful and concerned. Vandenbrook had stayed there four times and must have been a heavy tipper, Lysander thought. The young receptionist was full of anxious enquiries.

'I do hope everything was to Captain Vandenbrook's satisfaction. We'd be most upset if he was in any way displeased.'

'Not at all. Routine enquiry.'

'Has something gone wrong, sir?'

'Well,' Lysander improvised, 'something's gone missing – we're just retracing the captain's movements over the last few weeks and months.'

'Are you a colleague?' the receptionist asked. She was young, eighteen or nineteen, and had arranged her hair in a curious low swipe over her forehead that was not particularly flattering, Lysander thought, it made her look a bit simple, though she evidently wasn't. He suspected she had been subjected to the full Vandenbrook charm on many occasions.

'Yes, I am. We work together in London.'

'Please do tell him that his envelopes were all collected as specified. Never more than two days later.'

'I will, thank you.'

He said goodbye, promised to pass on the affectionate good wishes of the staff of the Pelham Hotel, Hastings, to the captain and tried to walk casually back out to the street. Tremlett was smoking by the Daimler, cap pushed to the back of his head. With his eye patch he looked unusually slovenly. He threw away his cigarette as Lysander strode up to him and readjusted his cap.

'Back to London, sir?'

'Back to Hythe.'

'Thought we were done for the day, sir.'

'The devil's work is never done, Tremlett. Quick as you like, please.'

They drove back up the coast to Hythe and returned to the Dene Hotel. Lysander walked into reception, experiencing the curious sensation of his life repeating itself. This was his third visit to the Dene Hotel in forty-eight hours.

'Good evening, sir. Welcome back.'

'I was just wondering . . . Did Captain Vandenbrook leave anything – in his room, perhaps?'

'Oh, you mean the envelope. I should have said this morning. Usually a porter from the station collects it.'

The receptionist reached under his counter and drew out a large buff manila envelope. On the front was written, 'Capt. C. Vandenbrook – to be collected.'

Lysander thanked the clerk and went into the saloon bar. It was quiet – one old man smoking a pipe in a corner and reading a newspaper. Lysander felt a coldness fall from the nape of his neck over his shoulders and back, as if he were standing in an icy draught. Mysteriously, the wound in his thigh began to ache, suddenly, a kind of burning. He knew what the envelope would contain. He ripped it open with his thumb and began to read.

'145 thou six inch howitz shells to Béthune. 65 wagons-under-load at Le Mans. Repair of telegraph lines Hazebrouk, Lille, Orchies, Valenciennes. New standard gauge line Gezaincourt-

Albert. Gun spur engineer store depots Dernancourt. 12 permanent ambulance trains Third Army Second Army.'

He turned to the next page. It went on and on. He carefully placed the three sheets of paper back into the envelope, folded it longways and slipped it in his jacket pocket. He ordered a large brandy and tried to empty his mind. He concentrated on one fact alone, it was enough – for the moment further speculation was a waste of time. He had found his Andromeda.

9. Autobiographical Investigations

I DECIDED, FOR THE moment, to tell no one and do nothing. Something was violently and differently wrong here – not least the presence of my mother. I had opened the envelope expecting to see the usual columns of figures as in the previous six Glockner letters, but instead saw pages of close-written factual prose – all the raw intelligence that Vandenbrook's role in the Directorate could provide. Not for the first time in this whole affair I felt myself wantonly adrift – seeing a few details but making no connection – and also consumed with the feeling that invisible strings were being pulled by a person or persons unknown and that I was attached to their ends. I needed time to take this new information in, time to deliberate, and I realized I had to be very careful over what my own future movements and decisions were. Perhaps it was the moment for me to go on the offensive, myself. Certain facts needed to be established before I could return to Munro and Massinger with my astounding discoveries. The first course of action was to confront Vandenbrook and see what explanation he would fabricate about the contents of his envelope. Then there was the urgent need to have a conversation with my mother.

★ ★ ★

John Bensimon's beard has turned quite grey since I last saw him in Vienna. He's put on some weight also, yet there's something strangely diminished about him, I feel, though on reflection it was perhaps the fact that it was England where we eventually met again that was responsible. To be a psychoanalyst practising in Vienna, with your smart consulting rooms just a few blocks away from Dr Freud's, was a more dramatic and self-enhancing state of affairs than showing your patient into a converted bedroom at the back of a terraced house in Highgate.

Bensimon seemed genuinely pleased to see me, I sensed – perhaps I came trailing clouds of his former glory – and he shook my hand warmly, even though I had knocked on his front door unannounced at the end of the afternoon. He introduced me to his wife, Rachel – a demure, timid woman – and his twin daughters, Agatha and Elizabeth, before he showed me up to his study with a view through the windows of the sooty backs of terraced houses and the long thin gardens that trailed scruffily from them, containing the usual assortment of various-sized, dilapidated sheds that haunt the cluttered ends of these city plots, with their blistered tar-paper roofs, broken windows and creosoted weatherboarding, washing lines and brimming rainwater barrels.

He still had his desk, his turned-away couch and armchair and, I was glad to see, the silver African bas-relief from Wasagasse.

'Not quite the same,' he said, as if reading my thoughts. 'But we must try to do the best with what we have.'

'How's business?' I asked.

'Slow, let's say,' he conceded with a rueful smile. 'People in England haven't yet realized how much they need us. It's not at all like Vienna.' He offered me the couch or the armchair. 'Is this a social visit, or can I help you professionally?'

I told him that I wanted to reinstate our old relationship – perhaps a weekly consultation, I said, going to the armchair. I sat down and focussed on the familiar fantastic beasts and monsters, for a moment enjoying the illusion that I was still in 1913 and nothing had happened to me since. In a very real sense, the disturbing thought came to me, I had changed enormously, irrevocably – I was a different person.

'Is it the old problem?' he asked. 'I still have all your files.'

'No, that seems well and truly solved, happily,' I said. 'My new problem is that I can't sleep at night. Or, rather, that I don't want to sleep at night because I always seem to dream the same dream.'

I told him my dream – the recurring jumbled experience of my night in no man's land that always culminated with my bombing of the sap and the image of the two torchlit faces looking up at me – the man with the moustache and the fair-haired boy.

'What happens next?' he asked.

'I wake up. Usually my face is wet with tears, though I don't recall weeping in the dream. I'm taking chloral hydrate – it's the only thing that makes me sleep the night through.'

'How long have you been taking that?'

'Some months – since Switzerland,' I said without thinking.

'Oh, you've been to Switzerland. How interesting. Were you there long?'

'A matter of days.'

'Right.' Discreet silence. 'Well, we'd better take you off the chloral – its long-term consequences can be rather drastic.'

'What do you mean?'

'You can become over-dependent on it. Its effects can be disturbing. You can – how shall I put it? – you begin to lose your grip on reality.'

'Whatever reality is . . . Sometimes I want nothing more than to lose my grip on reality. I just want to get to sleep at night.'

'That's what everyone says. And then . . .'

'Well – perhaps we could try hypnosis once more.'

'Actually, I think this is a perfect opportunity for Parallelism. But let's take you off the chloral first.'

He wrote me out a prescription for another 'somnifacient' and told me that his fee in England was two guineas an hour. We made an appointment for the following week. Cheap at the price, I thought, suddenly hugely relieved that I'd come to see him. I believed that Dr Bensimon could cure me of anything. Well, almost anything.

Talking of which, I told him as I left that I had seen Hettie Bull again and his face darkened.

'It's none of my business, but I'd have nothing to do with that young woman, Mr Rief,' he said. 'She's very dangerous, very unstable.'

This evening I was leaving the Annexe when I heard a shout, 'Rief! I say! Over here!' I looked round to see a man standing on the other side of the Embankment, leaning on the river wall. I crossed the roadway and saw that it was Jack Fyfe-Miller – but dressed as a stevedore in a flat cap with a scarf at his throat, moleskin trousers and heavy boots. We shook hands and I looked him over, professionally.

'Almost convincing,' I said. 'But you need some dirt under your nails – rubbed into your cuticles. You've got the hands of a curate.'

'The expert speaks.'

'Black boot polish,' I advised. 'Lasts all day.'

'Where're you headed?' he asked, staring at me with his usual strange intensity.

'Walking back to my hotel.'

'Ah, hotel life. Lucky for some.'

'There's nothing special about it. A small hotel in Pimlico – very average.'

'Have you got a girl, Rief?'

'What? No, not really. I used to be engaged to be married, once upon a time . . .'

'When I find my girl I'll get married – but she has to be spot-on right for me. Hard, that.'

I was inclined to agree, but said nothing as we walked along in silence for a while, Fyfe-Miller doubtless preoccupied with thoughts of his spot-on girl. From time to time he kicked at the fallen leaves on the pavement with his hobnails like a sulky adolescent, scuffing the stone and sending sparks flying. We walked under the railway bridge that led to Charing Cross and up ahead I saw the grand château-esque rooftops of Whitehall Court. I wondered if that was where he had come from, and perhaps the sight of the building and memories of our last meeting there stirred him as he suddenly became animated again and stopped me.

'Any sign of Andromeda? Any news?' he asked abruptly.

'Ah, no. But I think I'm getting close.'

'Getting close, eh?' he smiled. 'Hard on Andromeda's trail.'

Not for the first time I wondered if Fyfe-Miller were entirely sane.

'It's a question of narrowing the investigation down,' I said, playing for time. 'Analysing exactly who had access to that particular information.'

'Don't take too long, Rief, or your precious Andromeda may fly the coop.' At which point he took his hat off, gave me a mocking theatrical bow and then turned back the way we had come, shouting at me, over his shoulder, 'Boot polish under the fingernails, I'll remember that!'

I wandered back to The White Palace thinking about what he had said. It was a fair point, actually – I couldn't take my own sweet time – Vandenbrook could easily grow suspicious. Was this some kind of a warning I'd been given? Had Munro and Massinger ordered Fyfe-Miller to turn up the pressure on me? . . . I bought the *Evening News* and read that Blanche Blondel had opened at the Lyceum the previous night in *The Conscience of the King* to triumphant acclaim. Blanche – perhaps I'd pop in a note at the stage door . . . Fyfe-Miller had inadvertently reminded me of her and I thought it might be a good moment to see her again.

10. The History of Unintended Consequences

LYSANDER DID SOME QUICK research on Christian Vandenbrook's life and background. Vandenbrook had been caught up in the mass retreat from Mons in the first hectic weeks of the war and had been knocked unconscious by an artillery explosion that left him in a coma for three days. He suffered thereafter from periodic bleeding from the ears and his sense of balance left him for some months. He was declared unfit for active service and joined the General Staff in London. Lysander wondered how this agreeable move had come about, then he discovered that Vandenbrook's father-in-law was Brigadier-General Walter McIvor, the Earl of Ballatar, hero of the Battle of Waitara River in the Maori Wars in New Zealand. Vandenbrook was married to the earl's younger child, his daughter, Lady Emmeline, and they had two daughters themselves, Amabel and Cecilia. A very well-connected man, then, married into wealth and prestige. That explained how he achieved the grand house in Knightsbridge and the other quietly munificent trappings of his life on a captain's pay. But did it explain why he should choose to betray his country? Or why he was having an affair with Anna, now the dowager Lady Faulkner? Obviously the sooner he confronted Vandenbrook the sooner answers to these questions might ensue.

But he felt a kind of inertia seize him as he wondered what the outcome of these next actions and investigations would be – and felt the near-irresistible urge to procrastinate. He knew that the moment he laid out his evidence in front of Vandenbrook everything would change – not just for Vandenbrook but for himself, also. And, perhaps, for his mother. But all history is the history of unintended consequences, he said to himself – there's nothing you can do about it.

At the end of the day Lysander strolled along the Directorate's corridors towards Vandenbrook's office, feeling more than somewhat nervous and on edge. Vandenbrook was dictating a letter to his secretary and waved him to a chair. There was a green plant in a worked brass pot in one corner, a Persian rug on the floor, and on the wall hung a nineteenth-century portrait of a whiskered dragoon with his hand on the pommel of his mighty sabre.

'– Whereupon,' Vandenbrook was saying, 'we would be most grateful for your prompt and detailed responses. I have the honour to remain, obedient servant, etcetera, etcetera. Thank you, Miss Whitgift.' His secretary left.

'Applying leather boot to lazy arse,' he said to Lysander with a wink. 'What can I do for you, Rief?'

'I wonder if we might have a discreet word, in private.'

'"Discreet"? "Private"? Don't like the sound of that, oh, no,' he said with a chuckle, taking his overcoat off the back of the door. 'I'm heading home – why don't you come with me? That way we can have a proper drink and still be "private".'

They took a taxi back to Knightsbridge, Vandenbrook explaining that his wife and daughters had gone to the country – 'to Inverswaven,' he said, as an aside, as if Lysander should know where and of what he was talking. Lysander nodded and safely said, 'Lovely time of year.' He was feeling surprisingly tense but was acting very calm, and he thanked his profession once again for the trained ability to feign this sort of ease and confidence even when he was suffering from its opposite. He offered Vandenbrook a cigarette, lit his and his own with a flourish, flicked the match out of the window and kept up – in a loud, sure voice – a banal flow of conversation about London, the weather, the traffic, the last Zeppelin raid, how the blackout was a risible farce – 'What's the point of painting the tops of street lights black? It's the pool of light they cast that you see from up in the air. Farcical. Risible.' Vandenbrook picked up the mood and the two of them bantered their way west across London. Vandenbrook asked him what he recommended at the theatre. Lysander said he simply had to see Blanche Blondel in *The Conscience of the King*. Vandenbrook said he would pay good money to hear Blanche Blondel read an infantry training manual – and so the two of them chatted on until they found themselves in Knightsbridge in no time at all.

Vandenbrook's butler served them both brandy and sodas and they settled down in the large drawing room on the first floor. It was a little over-furnished, Lysander thought, a grand piano taking up rather too much of one corner of the room and thereby making the rest of the furniture seem jammed together. There were many vases filled with flowers, he saw, as if someone were seriously ill upstairs, and heavy gilt-framed paintings on the walls of Highland scenes in various seasons – perhaps painted around Inverswaven, he surmised.

'I think you'd better have your discreet word with me,' Vandenbrook said, not smiling for once. 'The suspense is affecting my liver.'

'Of course,' Lysander said, standing and taking the envelope out of his inside pocket, unfolding it and handing it to Vandenbrook. 'This was yours – "Capt. C. Vandenbrook – To be collected."'

He could see his shock, suddenly visibly present. His lips pursed, the tendons on his neck flexed, his Adam's apple bobbing above the knot of his tie.

'There are some sheets of paper inside,' Lysander added.

Vandebrook drew the pages half out, glanced at them and shoved them back in again. His eyes turned, to fix themselves on the painting above the fireplace – a stag on some moorland hill, mists swirling.

'Where did you get this?' he asked, his voice suddenly a little shrill.

'Where you left it – the Dene Hotel, Hythe.'

Vandenbrook hung his head and began to sob – a low keening sound, like an animal's pain. Then he began to shake and rock back and forward. Lysander saw his tears fall on to the manila envelope on his lap, staining it. Then Vandenbrook toppled off his chair, slowly, and fell face forward, pressing his brow into the pile of the carpet, making a grinding, moaning noise as if some deep agonizing internal ache were forcing the sound from between his clenched teeth.

Lysander was shocked, himself. He hadn't seen a man collapse so abjectly and so suddenly ever before. It was as if Vandenbrook had become instantly dehumanized, changing into a form of atavistic suffering unit that precluded any reasoning, any sentience.

Lysander helped him to his feet – now absurdly conscious of their situation, two uniformed English officers in a Knightsbridge drawing room, one a spy-hunter and the other the sobbing spy he had hunted and caught – and yet every instinct in him was concerned and humane. Vandenbrook was a man *in extremis*, gasping and snuffling, hardly able to stand.

Lysander sat him down and found some crystal decanters in an unlocked tantalus on a table beside the grand piano and poured him an inch-deep draught of some amber fluid. Vandenbrook took a gulp, coughed loudly and seemed to compose himself, his breathing more measured, his sobbing ceased. He wiped his eyes on his sleeve and stood up, taking some paces towards the fireplace and back. It struck Lysander that, should Vandenbrook attack him, he had no defensive weapon to hand – but Vandenbrook seemed docile, cowed: no threat at all.

He sat down again, smoothed his jacket, smoothed his hair and cleared his throat.

'What're you going to do?' he asked, his voice still quavery and frightened.

'I have to give you up. I'm very sorry.'

'That's why you appeared at the Directorate, didn't you? To find me.'

'To find whoever was passing information to the enemy.'

Vandenbrook started to sob quietly again.

'I knew this would happen,' he said. 'I knew someone like you would come one day.' He looked Lysander full in the face. 'I'm not a traitor.'

'We'll let the courts decide –'

'I'm being blackmailed.'

He asked Lysander to follow him and they went up half a flight of stairs to a small mezzanine room off a landing. This was his 'study', Vandenbrook explained – some bookshelves, a small oak partners' desk with many narrow drawers and a green-shaded reading lamp. In a corner was a large jeweller's safe, the size of a tea-chest. Vandenbrook crouched by it and turned its combination. He opened the door, reached in and removed an envelope, handing it to Lysander. The address said simply, 'Captain Vandenbrook, Knightsbridge'.

'It's always put through the letterbox,' Vandenbrook explained, 'in the middle of the night.'

Lysander lifted the flap and drew out a photograph and two pages of grubby, typewritten paper. The photograph was of a young girl – ten or eleven, he thought, staring blankly at the camera. Her hair was thick and greasy and the cotton blouse she wore seemed too big for her. Around her neck, incongruously, was a single rope of fine pearls.

'I have a problem,' Vandenbrook said, weakly. 'A personal failing, a vice. I visit prostitutes.'

'You're saying this girl is a prostitute?'

'Yes. So is her mother.'

'How old is the girl?'

'I'm not sure. Nine. Eleven . . .'

Lysander looked at Vandenbrook as he stood by his big safe, hunched, swaying, looking at the floor.

'Good god,' Lysander said flatly. 'This girl is younger than your daughters.'

'It's not something I take any pride in,' Vandenbrook said, his voice regaining some of its old arrogance. 'It's a terrible weakness in me. I confess – fully.' He opened a cigarette box on his desk, took out and lit a cigarette.

'Have you ever been to the East End of our great city?' Vandenbrook asked. 'Down by Bow and Shoreditch, those sort of places. Well, if you've got a little bit of spare cash you can get anything you want. Little boys and little girls, dwarfs and giants, freaks of nature, animals. Anything you can imagine.'

'Tell me about the blackmail.'

'I used to visit this girl – with her mother's compliance – once a month or so,' he said. 'I became fond of her. She was unusually unconcerned by what I asked her to . . .' He stopped himself. 'Anyway, out of affection for her I gave her a pearl necklace. That was my mistake. It was in a box, there was the jeweller's name, it was traced back to me. Her mother, a conniving, evil person – she wrote the deposition – now knew my name and who I was.' He sat down on the edge of the desk, suddenly looking exhausted. 'About a year ago, the end of last year, 1914, this envelope arrived with precise instructions. I was to pass on all the information I was party to at the Directorate. Everything I knew – movement of stores, munitions, construction of railway branch lines, and so on. If I didn't comply then this photograph and the girl's testimony would be sent to the Secretary of State for War, my commanding officer, my wife and my father-in-law.' He gave a weak smile. 'I assume you know who my father-in-law is.'

'Yes, I do.'

'Then you'll understand. A little. So I wrote down what I could find out and, as directed by the instructions, left the envelope to be collected by a person unknown in a particular hotel.'

'The same hotel?'

'Various hotels on the south coast. No doubt you've visited them all.'

Lysander looked at the girl's blank face and read a few lines of the deposition. 'The captin use to come and akse me to sit on his nee . . . He took my close off and then he told me to opin my legs as wide as I could . . . Then he woud wash me with a flannel and warm water and tell me to . . .'

Vanderbrook looked at him as he scanned the page, his eyes

dead, the dashing uptilted blond moustache like a bad prop, the affectation of a different man altogether.

'Did you try to find this woman and her daughter?'

'Yes, of course. I hired a private detective agency. But they were long gone from their usual haunts. They obviously sold me on. To someone. Who may have sold me on again. Many men are trapped in this way. You wouldn't believe it. There's a whole trade in this blackmail, passed along, from one person to another –'

'Many?'

'We're all capable of anything,' he said. 'Given the means and the opportunity.'

'The pervert's quick and easy excuse,' Lysander replied, coldly. 'Since time immemorial.'

'I don't excuse myself, Rief, as it happens. I hate myself, I loathe my . . . my sexual inclinations . . .' he said with real feeling. 'Just spare me your sanctimonious moral judgement.'

'Continue with your story.'

'Whenever a copy of this photograph and the witness statement arrived it was a sign that I should supply more information. I was also told which hotel I should leave it at. Another one came two weeks ago. The Dene Hotel, Hythe – the one you have.'

'How do you encode it?'

'What're you talking about?'

'Your previous letters were all in code. This one wasn't.'

'What code? I just write down the facts and figures and leave them at the hotel.'

Lysander looked at him, feeling a new panic. Somehow he knew at once Vandenbrook wasn't lying. But then he checked himself. The man did nothing but lie, it was his *raison d'être*. However, he thought on, furiously investigating the ramifications of this news – if Vandenbrook didn't transform the data into code then who did? If Vandenbrook was lying, then why did he not encode the last letter? There must be another Andromeda – or else

Vandenbrook was playing another game with him. He began to feel his brain cloud.

'What should I do, Rief?'

'Do nothing – go to work, act as normal,' Lysander said, thinking – this would buy him some time. He needed more time now, definitely, the complications were multiplying rapidly.

'What's going to happen to me?' Vandenbrook asked.

'You should hang as a traitor, if there's any justice – but perhaps you can save yourself.'

'Anything,' he said fiercely. 'I'm a victim, Rief. I didn't want to do this but if my . . . my peccadillo was to become known . . . I just couldn't face that, you see. The shame, the dishonour. You've got to help me. You've got to find out who's doing this to me.'

Lysander folded up the deposition and the photograph and slipped them inside his jacket pocket.

'You can't take that,' Vandenbrook said, outraged.

'Don't be stupid. I can do anything I like as far as you're concerned.'

'Sorry. Sorry. Yes, of course.'

'Go to work as usual. Try to act normally, unaffectedly. I'll contact you when I need you.'

11. The Sensation That Nothing Had Changed

IT WAS STRANGE BEING in the Green Drawing Room again, Lysander thought, walking around, letting his fingertips graze the polished surfaces of the side tables, picking up a piece of sheet music and laying it on a window seat. Again, he felt this sensation that nothing had changed and indulged it, letting it linger in him. He was still an adolescent, the century was new, they had just moved to Claverleigh and in a minute or two he would see his mother come into the room, younger, pretty, frozen in time, years back. But he knew how fast the world was spinning, faster than ever. Time was on the move in this modern world, fast as a thoroughbred racehorse, galloping onwards, regardless of this war – this war was just a consequence of that acceleration – and everything was changing as a result, not just in the world around him but in human consciousness, also. Something old was going, and going fast, disappearing, and something different, something new, was inevitably taking its place. That was the concept he should keep in mind, however much it disturbed him and however he found he wanted to resist it. Perhaps he should bring it up with Bensimon – this new obsession he had with change and his resistance to it – and see if he could make any sense of his confusion.

His mother swept through the door and kissed him three times on both cheeks in the continental manner. She was wearing a pistachio-green teagown and her hair was different, swept up on both sides and held in a loose bun at the back of her head, soft and informal.

'I like your hair like that,' he said.

'I like that you notice these things, my darling son.'

She went to the wall and turned the bell handle.

'I need tea,' she said. 'Strong tea. English fuel.'

He had one of those revelations and understood at once why a man would be irresistibly drawn to her – the casual, ultra-confident beauty coupled with her vivacity. He could understand why a Christian Vandenbrook would be ensnared.

Tea was served by a maid and they sat down. She stared at him over the top of her held teacup, her big eyes looking at him, watchfully.

'Do you know, I haven't seen you for ages,' she said. 'How are you? Fully recovered? I must say I do like you in your uniform.' She pointed. 'What're these?'

'Gaiters. Mother – I have to ask you a few rather pointed questions.'

'Me? "*Pointed*"? My goodness. On you go.'

He paused, feeling on the brink again, as if he were about to initiate a causal chain that could lead anywhere.

'Do you know an officer called Captain Christian Vandenbrook?'

'Yes. Very well. I deal with him all the time about Fund business.'

The Fund, Lysander thought, of course. The Claverleigh Hall War Fund. He relaxed ever so slightly – perhaps there was nothing in it after all.

'Did you see him at the Dene Hotel in Hythe three nights ago?'

'Yes. We had an appointment for dinner. Lysander, what's all this –'

'Forgive me for being so blunt and horribly obtuse and impolite but . . .' he paused, feeling sick. 'But – are you having an affair with Captain Vandenbrook?'

She laughed at that, genuinely, but her laughter died quickly.

'Of course not. How dare you suggest such a thing.'

He saw the real anger in her eyes and so closed his as he pressed on.

'You stayed in the same hotel as Captain Vandenbrook nine times in the past year.'

He heard her stand and he opened his eyes. She was looking out on the park through the high, many-paned window. It was drizzling, the light was fading – silvery, tarnished.

'Are you spying on me?'

'I'm spying on *him*. I was following him and I saw him meet you.'

'Why on earth are you spying on Captain Vandenbrook?'

'Because he's a traitor. Because he's been sending military secrets to Germany.'

This shocked her, he saw. She swivelled and stared at him alarmed.

'Captain Vandenbrook – I don't believe it . . . Are you sure?'

'I have the evidence to hang him.'

'I can't . . . How . . .' Her voice trailed off and then she said, incredulously, 'All we talk about is blankets, ambulances, pots of honey, village fêtes and nurses – how to spend the money I raise. I can't believe it.'

'Do you know that every time he meets you he leaves an envelope at the hotel to be collected?'

'No, of course not.'

'He's never asked you to deliver one of these envelopes?'

'Never. Honestly. Look, I met him because the War Office appointed him as the officer to liaise with the Fund when I started everything up. He was incredibly helpful.'

'He's a charming man.'

'He's even been here. Two – no, three times. We've had meetings here. Crickmay met him. He dined with us.'

'Here? He never mentioned it to me.'

'Why would he? I never mentioned you to him. I assume he hasn't the faintest idea that you're my son. That the man with the evidence to hang him is my son,' she added, a little bitterly. 'Or even that I have a son. For heaven's sake – all we talked about was the Fund.'

Lysander supposed that if you are an attractive woman in your very early fifties you don't advertise the fact that you have a son who is almost thirty. And it was true – nothing in Vandenbrook's demeanour, no sly implication or hint, had ever given away that he knew his mother was Lady Faulkner.

'Do you think I might have a drink?' he asked.

'Excellent idea,' she said and rang the bell for the footman who duly brought them a tray with two glasses, a bottle of brandy and a soda siphon. Lysander made their drinks and gave his mother hers. He took big gulps of his. Despite all the denials and the plausible explanations he had a very bad feeling about this connection with Vandenbrook. It was not a coincidence, he knew – there would be consequences. Fucking consequences, again.

'May I smoke?'

'I'll join you,' she said. Lysander took out his cigarette case, lighting his mother's cigarette and then his own.

'Why are you spying on Vandenbrook?' she asked. 'I mean, why you in particular.' She stubbed her cigarette out – she was never much of a smoker. 'You're a soldier, aren't you?'

'I'm attached to this department in the War Office. We're trying to find this traitor. He's causing terrible damage.'

'Well, you've found him, haven't you?'

'Vandenbrook is only handing over information because he's being blackmailed, it seems. So he claims.'

'Blackmailed for what?'

'It's very . . . unpleasant. Very shaming.' Lysander wondered how much to tell her. 'He'd be ruined, totally, if it ever came out what he'd done – marriage, career, family. He'd go to prison.'

'Goodness.' He saw that the vagueness of his reply was more disturbing than anything explicit. She looked at him again. 'So who's blackmailing him?'

'That's the problem – it looks very much as if you are.'

12. Autobiographical Investigations

PERHAPS I SPOKE TOO unthinkingly, too bluntly. She seemed very shaken all of a sudden – not incredulous, any more – as if the shocking but irrefutable logic of the set-up had struck her just as it had struck me. I made her another brandy and soda and told her to go over everything again for me, once more. It started with the first meeting with Vandenbrook at the War Office in September 1914 and subsequent regular contact followed as the Claverleigh Hall War Fund began to generate significant amounts of money. He first came to Claverleigh in early 1915 shortly after his transfer to the Directorate of Movements.

'Why didn't he pass on the War Fund to someone else? The work in the Directorate is frantic.'

'He asked if he could stay on board if he could,' she said. 'He was very impressed by what we were doing, he said, and very concerned that any hand-over to someone else would be detrimental. So I agreed without hesitation. I was very happy – we got on very well – he was extremely efficient. In fact I think I even suggested we meet when he came to Folkestone on business – just to make it easier for him. The first hotel I stayed in was at Sandwich. I offered to motor over.'

'Did you meet him in London?'

'Yes. Half a dozen times – when I went up to town.' She paused. 'I won't deny I enjoyed our meetings . . . Crickmay wasn't well and for me these nights away were, you know, a little escape. Of course, he's an attractive, amusing man, Captain Vandenbrook. And I think we both enjoyed the . . . The mild flirtation. The mildest. But nothing happened. Never. Not even after Crickmay died.'

'I completely understand,' I said. 'I believe you. I'm just trying to see things from his point of view.'

'It's because I'm Austrian, of course,' she said, flatly, almost sullenly. 'I've just realized – that's the key. That's why they'll suspect me. Instantly.' He felt the depression seize her, almost physically, as her shoulders seemed to bow. 'When they connect me with him . . . The Austrian woman.'

'I'm half Austrian too, remember,' I said, worriedly. 'Everything's too neat, too pat . . .'

'What're you going to do?'

'Nothing yet – I have to dig a little more.'

'What about me?'

'Carry on as if nothing has happened.'

She stood up, new anxiety written on her face. She seemed as troubled as I'd ever seen her.

'Have you told anyone about Vandenbrook and what you discovered?'

'No. Not yet. I don't want the rest of them blundering in. I have to be very careful what I say.'

She went over to the window again – it was now quite dark and I could hear the nail-tap of steady rain on the glass.

'You're making things worse for yourself by not telling anyone,' she said, quietly and steadily. 'Aren't you?'

'It's complicated. Very. I don't want you involved in this mess,' I said. 'That's why I need a bit more time.'

She turned and held out her arms as if she wanted to be embraced so I went to her and she hugged herself to me.

'I won't let you be dragged down by this,' she said softly. 'I won't.'

'Mother – please – don't be so dramatic. Nobody's going to be "dragged down". You've done nothing – so don't even think about it. Whoever's blackmailing Vandenbrook has been very clever. Very. But I'll find a way, don't worry. He can be outsmarted.'

'I hope so.' She squeezed my shoulders. I enjoyed having her in my arms. We hadn't held each other like this since my father had died. I kissed her forehead.

'Don't worry. I'll get him.'

I hoped I sounded confident because I wasn't, particularly. I knew that as soon as I told the Vandenbrook story to Munro and Massinger then everything would emerge rapidly and damagingly – the Fund, the meetings, the hotels, the dinners. To my alarm, as I began to think through this sequence of events, I thought I could see a way in which even I could be implicated. Which reminded me.

'I'd better go,' I said, releasing her. 'I just need one thing. You remember I gave you that libretto, the one with the illustration on the cover of the girl. *Andromeda und Perseus.*'

'Oh, yes,' she said, with something of her old wry cynicism returning. 'How could I forget? The mother of my grandchild with no clothes on.' She moved to the door. 'It's in my office.' She paused. 'What's the news of the little boy?'

'Lothar? He's well, so I'm told – living with a family in Salzburg.'

'Lothar in Salzburg . . . What about his mother?'

'I believe she's back in England,' I said evasively.

She gave me a knowing look and went to fetch the libretto. I glanced at my wristwatch – I was still in good time to catch the last train to London from Lewes. But when my mother came back in I could see at once she was unusually flustered.

'What is it?' I said. 'What's wrong?'

'It's the strangest thing. Your libretto – it's missing.'

Sitting in the Lewes–London train. Brain-race, thought-surge. Her office is a study on the top floor where she does her charity administration. Two desks for secretaries, a couple of white wooden bookshelves with a few books and a mass of files slid into them. She said she was convinced this was where she'd put the libretto. We searched – nothing. Books go missing, I said, it wasn't important. It was a book I gave to her almost eighteen months ago, after all. Anything could have happened to it.

As I write this, a man sitting opposite me is reading a novel and, from time to time, picking his nose, examining what he has mined from his nasal cavities and popping the sweetmeat into his mouth. Amazing the secrets we reveal about ourselves when we think we're not being observed. Amazing the secrets we can reveal when we know we are.

Back in my room at The White Palace I find a small bundle of post is awaiting me. One envelope contains a list from a letting agency of four furnished mansion flats, available for short lease, in the Strand and Charing Cross area. I'm excited by the prospect of having my own place, again – and of Hettie being able to stay with me there, incognito and unembarrassed. Another telegram, to my surprise, is from Massinger. He suggests a rendezvous in a Mayfair tearoom at four o'clock tomorrow. The Skeffington Tearooms in Mount Street.

Later. I've spent the last hour drinking whisky from my hip-flask and writing down lists of names in various configurations and placements, joining them with dotted lines and double-headed arrows, placing some in parentheses and underlining others three times. At the end of this fruitless exercise I still find myself wondering why Massinger could possibly want to talk to me.

13. 3/12 Trevelyan House, Surrey Street

LYSANDER CHOSE THE SECOND of the four furnished flats he was shown by the breathless, corpulent man from the letting agency. It was on the third floor of a mansion block in Surrey Street, off the Strand, called Trevelyan House: one bedroom, a small sitting room, a modern bathroom and a kitchen – though the kitchen was no more than a cupboard with a sink and an electric two-ring heater and a bleak view of the white ceramic bricks of the central air-well. In truth, any of the flats would have served his rudimentary purpose perfectly well but there was something newer about the curtains, the carpets and the furniture in number 3/12 that was immediately appealing – no greasy edge to the drapery, no flattened worn patch before the fire or cigarette burns on the mantelpiece. All he needed now, he felt, was something bright and primary coloured – a painting, a couple of new lampshades, cushions for the sofa – to make it more personal, to make it his rather than everybody's.

He signed the lease, paid a month's deposit and was given two sets of keys. He had his linen and his household goods from Chandos Place in store and would hire a porter to bring them around to Trevelyan House right away. He could walk to the Annexe from here in under ten minutes, he reckoned – another unlooked-for bonus in his and Hettie's 'love nest'. He felt the old excitement mount in him at the prospect of seeing her again – at the prospect of being naked in a bed with her again – and noted how the promise of unlimited sensual pleasure blotted out all rational, cautious advice that he might equally have given himself. Hettie – Vanora – was a married woman, now; moreover, her new husband was a jealous and angry man. Hoff and Lasry: two men with fiery, irrational tempers, quick to take the slightest offence – what drew Hettie to these types? Also, the current complications of Lysander's own life should have dictated against the introduction of new circumstances that would add to them. 'Gather ye rosebuds while ye may,' he said to himself, as if that old adage took care of all sensible matters. He had a new home and, perhaps more importantly, only he knew its address.

The Skeffington Tearooms in Mount Street were unabashed about their striving for gentility, Lysander saw as he approached. Elaborately worked lace curtains screened the tea-drinkers from the curious gaze of passers-by; the name of the establishment was written in black glass in a very flourished white copperplate, tightly coiled curlicues ending in gilt flowerlets or four-leafed clovers. A serving maid in a tiny bonnet and a long white pinny was sweeping the pavement outside. It didn't seem a Massinger type of place at all.

Inside was a single large long room lit by crystal chandeliers and lined on three walls by semi-circular maroon velour Chesterfield booths. Two rows of highly polished tables with neat doilies and a centrally placed flower arrangement filled the rest of the area. The hushed tinkle of silverware on crockery and a low murmur of discreet conversation greeted him. It was like entering a library, Lysander felt, with a library's implicit prohibitions against unnecessary noise – quiet footsteps, please, coughs and sneezes to be muffled, no laughter at all.

An unsmiling woman with a pince-nez checked that Massinger's name had been entered in the ledger and a summoned waitress led him across the room to a booth in the far corner. Massinger sat there, smoking, wearing a morning suit, of all things, and reading a newspaper. He looked up to see Lysander and did not smile, merely holding up the newspaper and pointing to a headline. 'English County Cricket to be abandoned in 1916.'

'Terrible business, what?' Massinger said. 'Where does that leave us? Shocking.'

Lysander agreed, sat down and ordered a pot of coffee – he didn't feel like tea; tea was not a drink to share with someone like Massinger.

'What do you want to see me about?' he asked as Massinger crushed his cigarette dead – with conspicuous force – in the ashtray, smoke snorting from his nostrils.

'I don't want to see you, Rief,' he said, looking up. He gestured. 'She does.'

Florence Duchesne stepped up to the table, as if she had suddenly materialized.

Lysander felt a lurch of instinctive alarm judder through him and had the immediate conviction that she was about to pull a revolver from her handbag and shoot him again. He stared at her – it was Florence Duchesne but a different woman from the one he'd last seen on the steamer on Lac Léman. The black weeds and the veil were gone. She had powder and lip rouge on her face and was wearing a magenta 'town suit' with a cut-away jacket and a hobble skirt and a little fichu at the neck of her silk blouse. She had a velvet Tam o' Shanter set on a slant on her head in a darker purple than the suit. It was as if Madame Duchesne's fashionable twin sister had walked in, not the melancholy widow who lived with the postmaster of Geneva.

She slipped into the booth beside him and, despite himself, Lysander flinched.

'I had to see you, Monsieur Rief,' she said in French, 'to explain and, of course, to apologize.'

Lysander looked at her, then Massinger, then back at her again, quite disorientated, unable to think what he could possibly say. Massinger stood up at this juncture and distracted them.

'I'll leave you two to talk. I'll see you later, Madame. Goodbye, Rief.'

Lysander watched him stride across the room to collect his top hat – he looked like a superior shop assistant, he thought. He turned back to Florence Duchesne.

'This is very, very strange for me,' he said, slowly. 'To be sitting here with someone who's shot me three times. Very strange . . . You were trying to kill me, I suppose.'

'Oh, yes. But you must understand that I was convinced you were working with Glockner. I was convinced you had killed Glockner also. And when you lied to me about the cipher-text – it seemed the final clue. And Massinger had ordered me not to take any risks – said you were possibly a traitor, even. Was I meant to let you step ashore at Evian and vanish? No. Especially with all the suspicions I had – it was my duty.'

'No, no. You were absolutely in the right.' The irony in his voice made it unusually harsh, like Massinger's throaty rasp. He recalled Massinger's schoolboy French blunder. She bowed her head.

'And yet . . .' She left the rest unspoken.

'I wonder if they serve alcohol in a place like this?' he asked, rhetorically. 'Probably not, far too plebeian. I need a powerful drink, Madame. I'm sure you understand.'

'We can go to a hotel, if you like. I do want to talk to you about something important.'

They paid and left. At the door to the tearoom she collected a dyed black musquash coat with a single button at the hip. Lysander held it open for her as she slipped her arms into the sleeves and smelled the strong pungent scent she wore. He thought back to their supper on the terrace of the Brasserie des Bastions in Geneva and how he'd noticed it then – thinking it an anomaly – but now he realized it was a trace of the real woman. A little clue. He glanced at her as they walked along the road in silence, heading for the Connaught Hotel.

They found a seat in the public lounge and Lysander ordered a large whisky and soda for himself and a Dubonnet for her. The drink calmed him and he felt his jumpiness subside. It was always amazing how one so quickly accustomed oneself to the strangest circumstances, he thought – here I am having a drink with a woman who tried to assassinate me. He looked across the table at her and registered his absence of anger, of outrage. All he saw was a very attractive woman in fashionable clothes.

'What're you doing in London?' he asked.

'Massinger has brought me out of Geneva. It was becoming too dangerous for me.'

She explained. Her contact in the German consulate – 'the man with the embarrassing letters' – had been arrested and deported to Germany. It would only be a matter of time before he gave her name up. 'So Massinger pulled me out, very fast.'

'I assume you're not a widow.'

'No. But it's a most effective disguise, I assure you. I've not been married, in fact.'

'What about your brother?'

'Yes, he's really my brother – and he's the postmaster in Geneva.' She smiled at him. 'Not everything is a lie.'

The smile disarmed him and he found himself unreflectingly taking in her looks – her strong curved nose, her clear blue eyes, the shadowed hollow at her throat between her collar-bones. He could forgive her, he supposed. In fact it was very easy – how absurd.

'How are you?' she asked. 'I mean, after the shooting.'

'I have seven scars to remember you by,' he said, showing her the stigma in his left palm. 'And my leg stiffens up sometimes,' he tapped his left thigh. 'But otherwise I'm pretty well. Amazingly.'

'Lucky I'm a bad shot,' she said, smiling ruefully. 'I can only say sorry, again. Imagine that I'm saying sorry to you all the time. Sorry, sorry, sorry.'

Lysander shrugged. 'It's over. I'm alive. You're here in London.' He raised his glass. 'I'm not being facetious – despite everything, I'm very pleased to see you.'

She seemed to relax finally – expiation had occurred.

'And you remembered I liked Dubonnet,' she said.

They looked at each other candidly.

'You like Dubonnet and you don't drink champagne.'

'And you used to be a famous actor.'

'An actor, certainly . . . You said you wanted to tell me something.'

She looked more serious now.

'My contact at the consulate told me an interesting detail – I obliged him to tell me an interesting detail – before he was arrested and taken away. They were paying funds to the person who sent the letters to Glockner. A lot of money, transferred through Switzerland.'

'I imagined money was the reason. Was there a name?'

'No.'

'You're sure?'

'This is all he said. But the money they sent was a lot. Already over two thousand pounds. It seems a lot for one man. I thought – maybe there is a cell. Maybe there are two, or three . . .'

Lysander wasn't surprised to have this confirmed but he feigned some perplexity – frowning, tapping his fingers.

'Have you told this to anyone else?'

'Not yet. I wanted to tell you first.'

'Not Massinger?'

'I think with Glockner dead he feels the matter is closed.'

'Could you keep this to yourself for a while? It would help me.'

'Of course.' She smiled at him again. 'Very happy to oblige, as they say.'

He sat back and crossed his legs.

'Are you going to stay in London now?'

'No,' she said. 'Massinger wants to put me into Luxembourg – to count troop trains. He wants me to become the special friend of a lonely old station master.'

'*La veuve Duchesne*, once more.'

'It's very effective – instant respect. People keep their distance. No one wants to trouble you in your terrible grief.'

'Why do you do it?'

'Why do *you*?' She didn't bother to let him reply. 'Massinger pays me very well,' she said, simply. 'I appreciate money because at one stage in my life I was without it. Completely. And life was not easy . . .' She put her glass down and turned it this way and that on its coaster. They were silent for a moment.

'How do you find Massinger?' she asked, still looking down.

'Difficult. He's a difficult personality.'

Now she looked him in the eye.

'I find it difficult to trust him entirely. He changes his mind – a lot.'

Was this a subtle warning, Lysander wondered. He decided to remain neutral.

'Massinger's worried about his job, his role. They want to shut down Geneva and Switzerland – concentrate on Holland.'

'I'm going to Luxembourg via Holland. I have to meet a man called Munro.'

'Munro runs Holland – I think. There's some rivalry, inevitably.'

'I could have gone to Luxembourg from Switzerland very easily. Do you think that's significant?'

'I don't know,' he said, honestly. He reflected that they shouldn't actually be talking to each other like this but he felt her constant doubts and suspicions were exactly like his. You thought you had possession of key facts, of certainties, but they disappeared and were facts and certainties no more.

'I'm just like you,' he said. 'Following instructions. Trying to think ahead. Be aware of potential problems. Trying not to slip

306

up.' He smiled. 'Anyway, I wish you luck. I'd better go.' He rose to his feet and she did the same. She took a card out of her bag and handed it to him.

'I expect to be in London a few more days,' she said. 'It would be nice to see you again. I remember our dinner in Geneva – *un moment agréable.*'

He looked at her card – a card supplied by the hotel she was staying at, Bailey's Hotel, Gloucester Road. There was a telephone number.

'I'll telephone you,' he said, not really knowing why – or even if – he should try to see Florence Duchesne one more time. But somehow he didn't want this to seem like a final parting so he held out this prospect, at least, that they would meet again.

At the front door, outside on the pavement, they made their farewells. She was going to explore, she said, this was her first visit to London. They shook hands and Lysander felt the extra pressure as her squeeze on his fingers tightened and she looked him directly in the eye again. Was that a warning – was he to be careful? Or was it a covert reminder that she expected to be telephoned and would like to see him again? Lysander watched her walk away, the cut of her musquash coat making it sway to and fro, and he speculated about different short-term futures, courses of action, of how he had once imagined Florence Duchesne tipsy on champagne, naked, laughing . . . it didn't seem such a fantasy any more. He hailed a passing cab and asked to be taken to the Annexe.

He knew he would have to work late that night. Tremlett, with the aid of the magic letter from C.I.G.S., had managed to secure all of Osborne-Way's claims for travel and expenses that he had submitted to the War Office. The proviso for their release was that they could only be out of the building for one night.

Tremlett dumped the heavy ledger on his desk.

'Is Captain Vandenbrook in his office?' Lysander asked.

'Captain Vandenbrook is in Folkestone, sir. Back tomorrow morning.'

That was good, he thought – Vandenbrook carrying on as normal. 'Right,' he said to Tremlett. 'Bring me the War Diary and the travelling-claims-by-land dockets.'

He spent the next two hours going through Osborne-Way's claims and collating them with Vandenbrook's movements but there was no visible overlap. In fact Osborne-Way had been in France on at least two occasions when Lysander was sure that Glockner's letters had been left at hotels in Sandwich and Deal. One thing was clear, however – Osborne-Way had enjoyed himself in France. Nights in expensive restaurants in Amiens; a weekend in Paris at the Hôtel Meurice – on what business? – everything charged to the War Office and the British taxpayer. Frustrated, Lysander wondered if he could score some petty revenge and have Osborne-Way's extravagance brought to the attention of someone senior to him, a quiet word that might have the effect of –

He became aware of loud voices and hurrying feet in the corridor outside Room 205.

Tremlett knocked on the door and peered in. His eye patch was slightly askew.

'We're going up top, sir. Zeppelin coming over!'

Lysander unhooked his greatcoat from the back of the door and followed him out and up the stairs to the roof of the Annexe. Half a dozen people were gathered on the flat area by the lift housing staring westwards where the long lucent fingers of searchlights stiffly searched through the night sky, looking for the dirigible. There was the distant popping of anti-aircraft fire and every now and then a shrapnel star-shell burst high above them.

Lysander looked out over the night city, some seven storeys up from street level. To his eyes it could have been peacetime – motor cars and omnibuses, headlights gleaming, shop fronts lit beneath their awnings, ribbons of streetlamps casting their pearly glow.

Here and there were areas of approximate darkness but it was almost inviting, he imagined, to the captain of this airship somewhere overhead. Where shall I drop my bombs? Here? Or there? And, as if his thoughts had been read, the first searchlight found the Zeppelin and then another two joined it. Lysander's first thought was, my god, so huge – gigantic – and serenely beautiful. It was very high and moving forward steadily – how fast, he couldn't tell. The increasing noise from the artillery fire blocked out the sound of its engines as it seemed to float unaided above them, driven on by night winds rather than its motors.

Another gun, nearer, began to fire – *Pop! Pop! Pop!*

'That's the gun in Green Park,' Tremlett said in his ear, then shouted out into the darkness, 'Give 'em hell, lads!'

More cheers came up from the others on the roof as Lysander looked up at the Zeppelin, awestruck, he had to admit, at the vast lethal beauty of the giant silvery flying machine caught in the crossbeams of three searchlights, now almost overhead, it seemed.

'It's eight thousand feet up,' Tremlett said. 'At least.'

'Where are our planes? Why can't we shoot it down?'

'Do you know how long it takes one of our planes to climb to eight thousand feet, sir?'

'No. Not the faintest.'

'About forty minutes. He'll be long gone. Or else he'll drop ballast and jump up another thousand feet. Easy as pie.'

'How do you know all this, Tremlett?'

'My little brother's in the Royal Flying Corps. Stationed at Hainault. He's always – WOAH! FUCK ME! –'

The first bomb had exploded. Not far from the Embankment – a sudden violent wash of flame, then the shock wave and the flat crack of the explosion.

'That's the Strand,' Tremlett yelled. 'Fuckin' hell!'

Then there was a short series of explosions – *Blat! Blat! Blat!* – as bombs fell swiftly one after the other, Tremlett bellowing his commentary.

'They're going for the theatres! Fuckin' Ada! That's Drury Lane! That's Aldwych!'

Lysander felt a bolus of vomit rise in his throat. Blanche was in a play at the Lyceum. Jesus Christ. Wellington Street, corner of Aldwych. He held his watch up – it would be just about the interval now. He looked up to see the Zeppelin turn slowly, heading northwards, up towards Lincoln's Inn. There were more thumps as bombs fell, out of sight.

'Big fire there!' Tremlett yelled. 'Look, they got the Lyceum!'

Lysander turned and raced through the roof access door and pelted down the stairway. He burst out on to the Embankment – the noise of police bells and fire engines, whistles, shouts, all coming down from the Strand and, in the distance, the sound of even more bombs dropping. He ran up Carting Lane past the Hotel Cecil to the Strand. Here he could see the flames, tall as the buildings, a bright unnatural orange lighting the façades on Aldwych and Wellington Street. Gas, he thought, a gas main's gone up. People were rushing along the Strand towards the source of the fire. He pushed his way through them and sprinted up the slope of Exeter Street. There was a thick dust cloud here and all the street lights had been blown out. He turned the corner to see glass and bricks scattered on the road and the first fuming crater. The earth itself seemed to be burning at its centre and fringes. Three bodies lay huddled at the side of the road, like tramps sleeping. The fire was blazing garishly at the end of the street and he ran towards it. He could see it was at the side of the Lyceum itself, the gas main billowing flames forty feet high. Bells, shouts, screams. A woman in a sequinned gown stumbled out of the darkness past him, whimpering, the frayed stump of her right arm twitching at her shoulder. A man in an evening suit lay on his back, both arms thrown wide, not a mark visible on him.

Half a gable-end had come down here and the way forward was blocked by a wall of tumbled bricks six feet high. He could hear women screaming and the shouts of police in Wellington Street bellowing, 'Keep back! Keep back!' He scrabbled up the brickwork and slipped, bashing his elbow. He tried again on the north side of Exeter Street where he could at least gain some purchase from the opposite façades. Glass shone here, glittering shards of orange-diamond jewels – every window in the street blasted out. He was thinking of the Lyceum, where the dressing rooms were – his father had played there all the time in the eighties. Maybe it hadn't been the interval – Blanche would have been safer on stage – but he hadn't seen the wretched play yet so he had no idea where she would have been.

He hauled his way up the sliding brick wall. At the top the gas flare made his shadow monstrously huge on the building front, flickering and undulating. The crater was immense, ten feet deep. More bodies and bits of bodies were scattered about it – the pub at the corner, The Bell, was ablaze. People went to the pub from the Lyceum at the interval – the bomb had caught it at its fullest. Beyond the blaze he could see the police forming a cordon to keep the appalled but curious onlookers away from the soaring flames of the venting gas main.

He heard bricks falling to the road, a sharp egg-cracking sound, and looked up just in time to see a window embrasure topple outwards and drag down the half wall beneath it. He flung himself out of the way and fell awkwardly down the slope to the pavement, winded. Lights were flashing in front of his eyes as he struggled to regain his breath. He hauled himself to his knees and saw a figure a few yards away across the street, standing still in the shadows, apparently looking straight at him.

'Give us a hand, will you?' Lysander shouted, wheezily.

The figure didn't move. A man with a hat and the collar of his coat folded up – impossible to see anything more with the street lights gone. The man was standing at the right angle of Exeter Street where it turned down to the Strand, where he'd seen the first dead bodies.

Lysander rose to his feet shakily, perturbed, and the figure stayed where it was, apparently staring directly at him. What was going on? Why was he just staring, doing nothing? The gas main flared again and for a moment more light was cast – the figure raised his hand to shield his face.

'I see you!' Lysander yelled – not seeing him but wanting to provoke him, somehow. 'I know who you are! I see you!'

The figure immediately turned and ran around the corner – disappeared.

There was no point in chasing, Lysander thought, and anyway, he had to find Blanche. He climbed up and slithered down the other side of the brick pile and ran up to the stage door of the Lyceum. A policeman was sheltering inside.

'The actors! I've a friend –'

'Can't come in here, sir. Everyone's gathered down on the Strand.'

Lysander realized there was no way through by Wellington Street so he had to go back the way he'd come. He picked his way cautiously up the brick wall and saw now that there were policemen and ambulances collecting the bodies. Safe. He ran past them and down to the Strand heading for Aldwych. There was a big surging crowd here. The Strand Theatre opposite had emptied and the streets were full of well-dressed theatre-goers milling about, smoking and chatting excitedly – bow ties, feathers, silk, jewels. He looked around him. Where were the actors?

'Lysander! I don't believe it!'

It was Blanche, a mug of coffee in one hand, a cigarette in the other. Someone's overcoat was thrown around her shoulders like a cape.

He felt weak finding her like this, unmanned suddenly. He went towards her and kissed her cheek, tasting greasepaint. In the rippling light from the gas main she looked almost grotesque in her white Regency wig – a painted loon with dark, arched eyebrows, a beauty spot and red lips.

'Were you caught in the blast?'

He looked down at himself. He was covered in brick dust, the left knee of his trousers was ripped and flapping, he had no hat, a knuckle was dripping blood.

'No. I was working and saw the bombs and so came looking for you. I was worried . . .'

'Ah, my Lysander . . .'

They hugged each other, held each other close. Her whole body was shaking violently, trembling.

'You can't go home in that state,' he said, softly, taking her hands. 'Come to my flat and tidy up. Have a proper drink. It's two minutes away.'

14. Autobiographical Investigations

BLANCHE HAS GONE. IT'S nine in the morning. She sent to the Lyceum for her clothes. The newspapers say seventeen people died in the raid – the 'Great Raid on Theatreland'. Bizarrely, I owe everything to the pilot of that Zeppelin – my first night in 3/12 Trevelyan House was spent with Blanche. Blanche. Blanche naked with her wide low-slung breasts, her jutting hips, long slim thighs like a boy, her white powdered face, the beauty spot, lipstick kissed away. How she slipped her fingers in my hair, gripping, and held my face above hers, eye to unblinking eye, as I climaxed. Deliverance. Relief. Watching her cross the room naked to find my cigarettes, standing there, pale odalisque, lighting one, then lighting one for me.

Question: who was that man in the shadows watching me?

Only now do I sense the after-shock, feel my nerves set on edge. The Zeppelin, the bombs, the dead bodies, the screams. Seeing Blanche again, being with her, made me push everything else to the back of my mind, including that strange meeting in

Exeter Street – part of the madness and horror of the night. Was somebody trying to frighten me? A warning? Vandenbrook was in Folkestone, in theory – but I can't believe that he'd ever try anything so self-destructive, so against his best interests. I'm his only hope.

I sit here and re-run the seconds' glimpse I had of him sprinting away. Why do I think of Jack Fyfe-Miller? What makes me think that? No – surely mistaken identity. But, this much is clear, someone was waiting outside the Annexe, saw me dash out and followed me as I ran towards the bombs . . .

Last night as we lay in each other's arms we spoke.

ME: I still have the ring – our ring . . .

BLANCHE: What are you trying to say, my darling?

ME: That, you know, maybe we should never have broken off our engagement. I suppose.

BLANCHE: Am I meant to read that as a re-proposal of sorts?

ME: Yes. Please say yes. I'm a complete fool. I've missed you, my love – I've been living in a daze, a coma.

Then we kissed. Then I went and took the ring from the card pocket inside my jacket.

ME: I've been carrying it with me. Good luck charm.

BLANCHE: Have you needed a lot of luck, since we split up?

ME: You've no idea. I'll tell you all about it one day. Oh. Perhaps I should ask. What about Ashburnham?

BLANCHE: Ashburnham is a nonentity. I've banished him from my presence.

ME: I'm delighted to hear it. I just had to ask.

BLANCHE [putting ring on]: Look, it still fits. Good omen.

ME: You won't mind being Mrs Lysander Rief? No more Miss Blanche Blondel?

BLANCHE: It's better than my real name. I was born [Yorkshire accent] Agnes Bleathby.

ME [Yorkshire accent]: Thee learn summat new every day, Agnes, flower. Happen.

BLANCHE: We're all acting, aren't we? Almost all the time – each and every one of us.

ME: But not now. I'm not.

BLANCHE: Me neither. [Kissing renewed fiancé] Still, it's just as well that some of us can make a living from it. Come here, you.

I've drafted out a telegram – I'll call in at a telegraph office on the way to the Annexe. Everything's changed now.

DEAR VANORA SAD NEWS STOP YOUR AUNT INDISPOSED SUGGEST POSTPONE LONDON TRIP STOP ANDROMEDA.

At a halfpenny a word that's probably the wisest seven pennies I've ever spent.

15. A Dozen Oysters and a Pint of Hock

LYSANDER TIMED HIS WALK to the Annexe from Trevelyan House and discovered that, at a brisk pace, it took him slightly more than five minutes. He felt briefly pleased at the economies of time and money such proximity to his place of work would supply, but then abruptly reminded himself that his days in the Annexe must, surely, be nearly over. Matters were coming to a head, and fast – still, he had one more trick left to play.

As he sauntered up the Embankment, past Cleopatra's Needle, about to cross the roadway to the Annexe, he saw Munro coming towards him. Too many impromptu meetings, he thought – first Fyfe-Miller, now Munro. Anxiety must be building in Whitehall Court.

'Well, what a coincidence.'

'Cynicism doesn't suit your open, friendly nature, Rief. Shall we have a coffee before your daily grind begins?'

There was a coffee stall under Charing Cross Railway Bridge. Munro ordered two mugs and Lysander lit a cigarette.

'Quite a raid last night,' Munro said.

'Why can't we shoot down something that big? That's what I don't understand. It's vast. Sitting up there in the sky, lit up.'

'There's only one anti-aircraft gun in London with a range of ten thousand feet. And it's French.'

'Couldn't we borrow a few more from them? The Zeppelins will be back, don't you think?'

'Let others worry about that, Rief. We've got enough on our plate. Actually, I will try one of your "gaspers", thank you.'

Lysander gave him one and he lit it, then spent a minute picking shreds of tobacco off his tongue. He wasn't really a practised smoker, Munro, it was more of an affectation than a pleasure.

'How are you getting on?' he asked eventually.

'Slow but steady –'

'– Wins the race, eh? Don't go too slow. Any suspects?'

'A few. Better not single anyone out, just yet – in case I'm wrong.'

He saw Munro's jaw muscles tighten.

'Don't expect us to tolerate your due caution for ever, Lysander. You're there to do a job, not sit on your arse sharpening pencils. So do it.'

He was suddenly very angry for some reason, Lysander saw, noting the patronizing use of his Christian name.

'I'm not asking for your tolerance,' he said, trying to seem calm. 'I've got to make this enquiry look as boring and routine as possible. You wouldn't thank me if I scared someone off or presented you with the wrong person all for the sake of gaining a day or two.'

Munro seemed visibly to regain his usual mood of thinly disguised condescension as he thought about this.

'Yes . . . Well . . . I understand you sent for Osborne-Way's claims from the War Office.'

'Yes, I did.' Lysander concealed his surprise. How did Munro know this? An answer came to him at once – Tremlett, of course. Munro's eyes and ears in the Directorate of Movements. *Eye* and ears, rather. He would keep Tremlett's divided loyalties very much in mind from now on. 'Osborne-Way potentially knows everything that was in the Glockner letters, he's –'

'You had no right.'

'I had every right.'

'Andromeda's not Osborne-Way.'

'We can't be complacent; we can't risk easy assumptions.'

He could see Munro's anger returning – why was he so on edge and quick-tempered? He decided to change the subject.

'I saw Florence Duchesne the other day.'

'I know.'

'Is she still in London?'

'She's left I'm afraid.'

'Oh. Right. I was rather hoping to see her again.' Lysander felt a brief but acute sadness at this news – maybe something had been lost there. For some reason he thought of her as his only true ally – they seemed to understand each other; they were both functionaries following orders from a source neither of them knew or could identify. Their strings were being pulled – that's what linked them ... He looked at Munro, puffing at his cigarette like a girl. He decided that attack was the best means of defence, now.

'Are you telling me everything, Munro? Sometimes I find myself wondering – what's really going on here?'

'Just find Andromeda – and fast.' He threw some coins on the counter, gave him a hard smile and walked away.

Lysander went back to the Annexe with a plan forming in his head, slowly taking shape. If Munro wanted action, then he would give him action.

Tremlett was waiting for him outside Room 205 and seemed unusually chirpy – 'Nice cuppa tea, sir? Warm the old cockles?' – but Lysander looked at him suspiciously now, wondering what Tremlett might have gleaned from their trip to the south-coast hotels. On reflection it seemed unlikely that he'd make the connection with Vandenbrook; Lysander had never told him what he was doing, making Tremlett wait outside each time. But he was no fool. Would he have passed on the details of their journey to Munro, in any event? Probably – even if he couldn't explain it. Was that what was making Munro and Fyfe-Miller so jumpy? Did they have a sense that he was ahead of them, was unearthing facts that they had no inkling of? ... The unanswered questions piled up and yet again Lysander felt himself sinking in a quagmire of uncertainties. He opened a drawer in his desk and took out a booklet of pre-paid telegraph forms. He'd give them something that would make them think again.

He picked up the telephone and dialled Tremlett's extension.

'Yes, sir.'

'Is Captain Vandenbrook back from Folkestone?'

'I believe so, sir.'

'Would you ask him to step into my office.'

Lysander treated himself to a lunch at Max's oyster bar in Dean Street in Soho. He ordered a dozen oysters and a pint of hock and allowed his thoughts to return pleasingly to Blanche and the night they had spent together. She was tall, almost ungainly under the sheets – sheets that they had spread and tucked in themselves in a kind of frenzy, snatching them from his trunks, delivered by porter that morning – she was all knees and elbows, lean and bony. Her flat wide breasts with tawny nipples. It was obvious she'd had many lovers before him. That way she held his head, his hair gathered in her fists holding him still . . . Where or from whom did that trick come? He had no regrets about spontaneously asking her to take back his ring – though he wondered now, as he emptied oysters down his throat, if he had been too precipitate, over-happy, over-relieved that his old 'problem' hadn't recurred with her. No – it had been as good as with Hettie. Hettie, so different. There was no sense of danger with Blanche, however, it was more a kind of rigour. Refreshing, no-nonsense Agnes Bleathby. It was the end of Hettie, of course. But that was only right as Hettie had let him down shockingly, had betrayed him instantly and without a qualm to save herself despite the fact that she was the mother of their son. Lothar meant little or nothing to Hettie Bull, he realized. Furthermore, he – Lothar's natural father – clearly played no part in her life unless he could be useful to her in some selfish way – the marriage to Jago Lasry was the perfect example. No, Blanche had always been the girl for him. She had asked him back to her mews house in Knightsbridge for supper – her show was cancelled until the damage to the theatre was repaired. He smiled at the idea of Blanche cooking supper for him on his return from the office – a little forerunner of their domestic bliss? For the first time in many months he felt the warmth of security wash through him. Contentment – how rare that feeling was and it was only right that it should be cherished. He ordered another round of oysters and another pint of hock.

He returned to the Annexe in good spirits. He had a course of action to follow and Munro would have his answer soon, however unwelcome it might be. Vandenbrook was poised and ready. Yet again Tremlett was waiting by his door, agitated this time.

'Ah, there you are, sir. I was beginning to think you'd gone for the day.'

'No, Tremlett. What is it?'

'There's a man downstairs insisting on seeing you. Claims to be your uncle, sir – a Major Rief.'

'That's because he *is* my uncle. Send him up at once. And bring us a pot of coffee.'

Lysander sat down with a thump, realizing his head was a little blurry from all the hock, but pleased at the prospect of seeing Hamo. He didn't come up to town often – 'London terrifies me,' he always said – so this was an unfamiliar treat.

Tremlett showed Hamo in and Lysander knew at once something was very wrong.

'What is it, Hamo? Nothing to do with Femi, is it?' The fighting in West Africa was over, as far as he knew – everything had moved to the East.

Hamo's face was set.

'Prepare yourself for the worst possible news, my boy . . .'

'What's happened?'

'Your mother is dead.'

16. Autobiographical Investigations

THERE IS THIS MYTH that death by drowning is the best of all deaths amongst the dozens or hundreds available to us human beings –

that with drowning your end arrives simultaneously with a moment of pure exhilaration. I will hold on to that idea but the rational side of my brain asks who provided this testimonial? Where's the evidence?

When I saw my mother's body in the undertaker's at Eastbourne she did, however, look serene and untroubled. Paler than usual, a slight bluish tinge to her lips, her eyes closed as if she were dozing. I kissed her cold forehead and felt a pain in my gut as I remembered the last time I'd made that gesture, holding her warm in my arms. 'I won't let you be dragged down by this.'

Hamo tells me there is an unopened letter at Claverleigh waiting for me but I don't need to read it to know that it will be her confession. Hamo, in his kindness, bless him, ventured the theory that it might have been some awful accident – a slip, a fall, unconsciousness. But I told him I was convinced it was suicide and the letter would merely confirm that. Her body had been found at dawn on the shingly beach at Eastbourne, left by the retreating tide – the proverbial man out walking his dog at first light – she was fully clothed, all her jewellery removed and one shoe missing.

I find myself, all of a sudden, remembering something Wolfram Rozman said to me – it seems eons ago, back in that impossible, unimaginable world before the war began, before everybody's lives changed for ever – when, having been asked what he would have done if the tribunal had found against him, Wolfram had said – blithely, inconsequentially – that he would have taken his own life, of course. I can bring him into my mind's eye effortlessly – Wolfram standing there in his caramel suit, swaying slightly, tipsy from the celebratory champagne, saying in all seriousness, 'In this ramshackle empire of ours suicide is a perfectly reasonable course of action.' Wolfram – was it just bravado, the swagger of a born hussar? No, I recall, it was said smilingly but with absolute rigid logic: once you understand that – you will understand us. It lies very deep in our being. '*Selbstmord*' – death of the self: it's an honourable farewell to this world. My mother had made her honourable farewell. Enough.

Hugh and the Faulkner family are deeply shocked. I feel my grief burn in me alongside a colder, calmer anger. My mother is as much an innocent victim of this whole Andromeda affair as are those two men I killed in a sap one June night in no man's land in northern France. The causal chain reached out to claim them just as it did Anna Faulkner.

My darling Lysander,

I will not allow myself, or my stupidity, to harm you or endanger you in any way. You should understand that what I am about to do seems an entirely reasonable course of action to me. I have a few regrets at leaving this world but they are wholly outweighed by the benefits my imminent non-being will achieve. Think of it that way, my dear – I am no longer here, that's all. This fact, this state, was going to arrive one day therefore it has always seemed to me that any day is as good as the next. I already feel a sense of relief at having taken the decision. You are now free to move forward with full strength and confidence and with no concerns about your foolish mother. I cannot tell you how upset I was after our last conversation, how you were intent on imperilling yourself, on taking a course of action that was plainly wrong, only to spare me. You were prepared to sacrifice yourself for me and I could not allow that, could not live with that responsibility. What I am about to do is no sacrifice – you must understand that for someone like me it is the most normal of acts in a sane and rational world.

Goodbye, my darling. Keep me alive in your thoughts every day.

Your loving mother.

Images. My mother. My father. How she wept at his funeral, the endless tears. The grim flat in Paddington. Claverleigh. Her beauty. Her singing – her rich mellow voice. That terrible sunlit afternoon in Claverleigh Wood. At meals when she talked the way she would unconsciously tap the tines of her fork on her plate to emphasize the point she was making. That night I saw my father kissing her in the drawing room when they thought I was asleep. The way they laughed when I walked in, outraged. The cameo she wore with the letter 'H' carved in the black onyx. How she smoked a cigarette, showing her pale neck as she lifted her chin to blow the smoke away. The confidence with which she walked into a room as if she were going on stage. What else could I have been with those two as my parents? How can I best avenge her?

Dr Bensimon saw me two hours ago. I telephoned him as soon as I had returned from Eastbourne.

'I wish I could say it was an effort fitting you in at such short notice,' he said. 'But you're my only patient today.'

I lay on the couch and told him bluntly and with no preamble that my mother had killed herself.

'My god. I'm very sorry to hear that,' he said. Then, after a pause, 'What do you feel? Do you feel any guilt?'

'No,' I said immediately. 'Somehow I want to feel guilt but I respect her too much for that. Does that make any sense? It was something she thought about and decided to do. In cold logic. And I suppose she had every right.'

'It's very Viennese,' Bensimon said, then apologized. 'I don't mean to be flippant. Choosing that option, I mean. You've no idea how many of my patients did the same – not spontaneously – but after a great deal of thought. Calm, rational thought. Have you any idea what made her do it?'

'Yes. I think so. It's connected with what I'm doing myself . . .' I thought again. 'It's to do with this war and the work I'm doing. She was actually trying to protect me, believe it or not.'

'Do you want to talk about her?'

'No, actually, I want to ask you about something – about someone else. Do you remember that first day we met, in Vienna, at your consulting rooms?'

'The day Miss Bull was so insistent. Yes – not easily forgotten.'

'There was another Englishman present, from the Embassy – a military attaché – Alwyn Munro.'

'Yes, Munro. I knew him quite well. We were at university together.'

'Really? Did he ever ask you anything about me?'

'I can't answer that,' he said, apologetically. 'Very sorry.'

I turned my head and looked at Bensimon who was sitting behind his desk, his fingers steepled in front of his face.

'Because you can't remember?'

'No. Because he was my patient.'

'Patient?' I was astonished at this news. I sat up and swivelled myself around. 'What was wrong with him?'

'Obviously I can't answer that, either. Let's just say that Captain Munro had serious problems of a personal nature. I can't go any further than that.'

I sit in 3/12 Trevelyan House with a bottle of whisky and a cheese-and-pickle sandwich I bought from the pub on the corner of Surrey Street. I telephoned Blanche and told her what had happened and she was all sympathy and warm concern, inviting me to come round and stay with her. I said that day would come soon enough but I had to be on my own at the moment. There will be an inquest, of course – so we must wait before we can bury her – my mother, Annaliese. I want tears to flow but all I feel is this heaviness inside me – a leaden weight of resentment, this grinding level of anger that she should have felt she had no more choice than to do what she did. To take her jewels off and walk into the sea until the waters closed over her.

17. A Cup of Tea and a Medicinal Brandy

THE NEXT DAY PASSED slowly, very slowly, Lysander felt, as if time were responding to his own desultory moods. He kept to himself as much as possible, staying in Room 205 with the door closed and locked. At midday he sent Tremlett out to buy him some pastries from a luncheon-room in the Strand. He ran through the plans he had made for the evening again and again. He was trying to convince himself that this exercise would be significant, possibly revelatory. At the very least he would be wiser – one step closer, perhaps.

In the middle of the afternoon, Tremlett called him on the telephone.

'The White Palace Hotel on the line, sir.'

'I don't stay there any more.'

'They say your wife has been taken ill.'

'I'm not married, Tremlett – it's obviously a mistake.'

'They're very insistent. She had a fainting fit, it seems.'

'All right, put them on.'

He waited, hearing the clicks and buzzes as the connection was made. Then the manager came on the line.

'Mrs Rief is in a very, ah, agitated state.'

'There is no "Mrs Rief", as it happens,' Lysander said. Then he realized. 'I'll speak to her.'

He heard the receiver being held away and footsteps approaching.

'Hello, Hettie,' he said.

'You've moved,' she said accusingly, angrily. 'I couldn't think how else to find you.'

'I'll be there in ten minutes.'

He took a taxi to Pimlico and found her in the residents' lounge of The White Palace with a cup of tea and a medicinal brandy. He locked the door so they wouldn't be interrupted but Hettie took this as an invitation to intimacy and tried to kiss him. He pushed her away gently and she sulkily sat down again on the sofa.

'I've got three whole days,' she said. 'Jago thinks I'm on a sketching holiday on the Isle of Wight. I thought being on an island would convince him more.'

'I can't see you, Hettie,' he said. 'There's a flap on – I'm working day and night. That's why I sent you the telegram.'

She frowned and tucked her knees up underneath her. She pouted and tapped her forefinger on her jawbone – one, two, three – as if counting down, mentally. Then she pointed the finger at him.

'There's someone else,' she said, finally. 'I'm right, aren't I?'

'No . . . Yes.'

'You're a swine, Lysander. A bloody fucking swine.'

'Hettie. You went and got married. We have a child but you didn't even bother to tell me.'

'That's different.'

'Please explain how.'

'What have you done to me, Lysander?'

'Hang on a second. Can I remind you of events in Vienna in 1913? You had me in prison with your damned lies. How dare you?'

'I was helping you. Well, maybe not at first, but I was later.'

'What're you talking about?'

'Those men persuaded me to drop the rape charge so you could be set bail. Udo was furious, practically threw me out –'

'What men?'

'Those two at the embassy. The attachés – I forget their names.'

'Munro and Fyfe-Miller.'

'If you say so.'

Lysander began to think fast.

'You saw Munro and Fyfe-Miller?' he asked. 'While I was under arrest?'

'We had a few meetings. They told me what to do – to change the charge. And they gave me money when I asked for some. After you escaped they were very helpful – offered to take me to

Switzerland. But I decided to stay – because of Lothar.' She looked at him aggressively, as if he were somehow to blame for all the mess. 'They asked me lots of questions about you. Very curious. And I was very helpful, I can tell you that. Told them all sorts of interesting titbits about Mr Lysander Rief.'

Was she lying again, Lysander wondered. Was this pure bravura? He felt confusion beginning to overwhelm him once more. He reached over and finished off her brandy. First Munro turned out to have been Bensimon's patient and now there seemed to be some form of collusion between Munro, Fyfe-Miller and Hettie. He tried to see what the connections and consequences might have been but it was all too perplexing. What had really happened in Vienna in 1914? It made him very uneasy.

Hettie leapt up from the sofa and came over to him, sliding on to his lap, putting her arms round his neck and kissing him – little dabbing kisses on his face, pressing her breasts into his arm.

'I know what you like, Lysander. Think what fun we can have – three whole days. Let's buy lots to eat and drink and just stay in. We can take all our clothes off . . .' She reached for his groin.

'No, Hettie. Please.' He stood up, slipping easily out from under her – she was so small, so light. 'I'm engaged to be married. It's over. You should never have come. I explicitly told you not to come. You've only yourself to blame.'

'You're a bastard,' she said, tears in her eyes. 'A fucking mean bastard man.' She carried on swearing at him, the volume increasing, as he put on his greatcoat and picked up his cap. He left the room without looking round. He didn't mind the abuse but the last thing she screamed at him was, '– And you'll never see Lothar in your life!'

The New London Theatre of Varieties, just off Cambridge Circus, was indeed new to Lysander. He would never have acted there as it was mainly a variety and vaudeville hall, although one that specialized in 'ballets, French Plays and Society Pieces'. In the theatre guide he'd consulted – he wasn't interested in the programme but the facilities – he had read that 'the tourist will find that the audience forms part of the entertainment'. This was a code, he knew, for 'prostitutes frequent the lobby bars'. The New London was an obsolescent type of Victorian theatre where the public could drink at the theatre bars without having to pay for the show. It was originally a way of supplementing the night's takings but the system inevitably brought other trade with it. Lysander remembered some old actors of his acquaintance reminiscing fondly about the prices and the quality of the streetwalkers available – the higher up you went in the theatre – from the stalls to the bars at the dress circle, upper circle, amphitheatre – the cheaper the girls. A better class of gentlemen also came to these public theatre bars because it provided perfect camouflage – there was plenty of time to scrutinize and select while ostensibly doing something entirely innocent: going to the theatre – how very cultural and educative.

The show had begun by the time Lysander slipped into his seat. A 'ballet' of French maids and a hairdresser as far as he could tell.

'Sorry I'm late,' he said to Vandenbrook and turned slightly to gain a better angle on him. He was in a suit, his hair was oiled flat with a middle parting and he had combed down the uptilted ends of his moustache. He already looked entirely different from the usual person he presented to the world – weaker-looking and much less attractive.

'Got the spectacles?'

Vandenbrook fished in his pocket and put them on.

'Ideal. Keep wearing them.'

They were clear-lensed, plain glass with wire rims, borrowed from a theatrical props agency in Drury Lane. As the ballet continued Lysander ran through the plan once more, making sure Vandenbrook understood exactly what to do. There was no need to whisper or even lower his voice as the auditorium was loud with a sustained growl of conversation and the to-ing and fro-ing of people leaving their seats and going to the bars and drinks counters that ringed the stalls. Many of them, Lysander noticed, were uniformed soldiers and sailors. Almost everyone seemed to be smoking so he offered Vandenbrook a cigarette and they both lit up as the ballet ended and the comedy sketch began.

When the curtain came down the Master of Ceremonies reminded them that the top of the bill in the second half of the evening's entertainment was the 'celebrated West End actor' Mr Trelawny Melhuish, who would be reciting the soliloquies of Hamlet, Prince of Denmark. Lysander and Vandenbrook filed out into the aisles and headed for the stalls' lobby bar. To be or not to be, Lysander thought.

'We'll split up here,' he said, as they reached the curtained doorway that led to the lobby.

The stalls' lobby was a wide, curving, low-ceilinged corridor, dimly lit with flickering gas sconces and very crowded with people who had come in off the street and those who were now pouring out of the auditorium. Lysander edged his way towards the central bar opposite the stairs leading up from the entrance. Standing some way back, a silent trio, in civilian clothes as he'd specified in the telegrams he'd sent to them, were Munro, Fyfe-Miller and Massinger. He glanced back to make sure that Vandenbrook was nowhere near him but couldn't spot him in the throng. Good.

He approached the three men, circling round behind them. They all looked ill at ease, uncomfortable in this bibulous, flushed, shouting crowd. Even better, Lysander thought.

'Gentlemen,' he said, suddenly appearing in front of them. 'Thanks for coming.'

'What're we doing here, Rief? What kind of tomfoolery is this?' Massinger snarled at him.

'I had to make sure I wasn't followed,' he said. 'I don't trust anyone at the Directorate.'

'What's going on?' Munro said, his eyes flicking around the

faces of the crowd. 'What's your game, Rief? What was so damn urgent to bring us all here?'

'I've found Andromeda,' Lysander said, immediately gaining their full attention.

'Oh, yes?' Fyfe-Miller said with undue scepticism, Lysander thought. Over Fyfe-Miller's left shoulder Lysander could see Vandenbrook circling closer. The disguise was excellent, Lysander thought – Vandenbrook looked like a timid accounts clerk out on the town looking for sin.

'Yes,' Lysander said. He had to draw this out a little, give Vandenbrook as much time as possible. 'It's someone quite high up.'

'It's not Osborne-Way – don't waste our time.'

'It's his number two,' Lysander said. 'Mansfield Keogh.'

The three looked at each other. They clearly knew who Keogh was.

'Mansfield Keogh,' Massinger said. 'Good god almighty.'

'Yes, Keogh,' Lysander said, half aware of Vandenbrook moving around their group. 'Everything fits. The trips to France tally. Only he had all the information in the Glockner letters.'

'But why would he do it?' Munro said, sounding unconvinced.

'Why does anyone?' Lysander said, looking at all three of them pointedly. 'There are three reasons why someone betrays their country – revenge, money,' he paused. 'And blackmail.'

'Nonsense,' Massinger said. Munro and Fyfe-Miller kept quiet.

'Think about it,' Lysander said.

'How do any of those categories fit Keogh?' Fyfe-Miller said, frowning.

'His wife died recently, very young – maybe it's driven him a bit insane,' Lysander said. 'But I don't know, in the end. I was just gathering evidence, not looking for motives.'

'Well, we can ask him when we arrest him,' Munro said with a thin smile. 'Tomorrow – or maybe tonight.'

Everyone fell silent contemplating the reality of the situation.

'So – Keogh is Andromeda,' Massinger said, almost to himself.

'Well done, Rief,' Munro said. 'You took your time but you got there in the end. I'll be in touch. Keep going to work in the Annexe as usual.'

'Yes, good hunting, Rief,' Fyfe-Miller added, allowing himself a wide smile. 'We thought you'd be the man to winkle him out. Bravo.'

A bell began to clang, announcing the second portion of the evening's entertainment. The crowd began to drift back into the auditorium and for the first time Lysander became aware of the painted women standing around.

'I'll leave you chaps here,' he said with a smile. 'I'm going to watch the rest of the show. Best to go out one by one.' He turned and walked away, glad to see no sign of Vandenbrook.

'Evening, my lord,' one of the doxies said to him, smiling. 'Doin' anything after?'

He glanced back to see Massinger leaving. Fyfe-Miller and Munro were talking urgently, their heads close together. I'll give it twenty-four hours, Lysander thought, pleased with the way everything had run – something would happen.

Vandenbrook was in his seat already, smoking, waiting for the curtain to go up.

Lysander joined him and handed him a pint of lager beer. He had one for himself.

'Well done,' he said. 'Do you like this stuff? I developed quite a taste for it in Vienna.'

'Thanks.' He seemed a bit subdued and sipped at the froth at the top of the glass.

'Well?'

'I didn't recognize any of them. Except that fellow with the step-collar. He looked familiar somehow.'

'Massinger?'

'I think I may have seen him before. In my War Office days. Is he an army man?'

'Yes. So – conceivably he might know who you were.'

'Possibly – he seemed familiar.'

Lysander thought – it was hardly evidence. The orchestra in the pit began to play a military march and the curtain rose to reveal a chorus of girls in khaki corsets and bloomers carrying wooden rifles. Cheers, whoops and whistles went up from the audience. This was what they wanted to see – not Mr Trelawny Melhuish reciting soliloquies.

'So Massinger could be Andromeda,' Lysander said.

'Andromeda? What's that?'

'That's the codename we gave you. When the search began.'

'Oh, right.' Vandenbrook looked a little uncomfortable at the thought he had been identified by a code word, Lysander supposed. 'Why Andromeda?'

'It was my choice, actually. Taken from a German opera. *Andromeda und Perseus* by Gottlieb Toller.'

'Oh, yes. It's a bit saucy that one, isn't it?'

'Never saw it,' Lysander said, his eye suddenly caught by a tall, leggy dancer who reminded him of Blanche. He put a sixpence in the slot that freed the catch on the opera glasses fixed to the back of the seat in front of him and raised them to his eyes for a closer look. Might as well enjoy the show, he thought.

18. No Eureka Moment

LYSANDER COULDN'T SLEEP SO sometime between three and four in the morning he went through to his kitchen and made himself a draught of chloral hydrate. Bensimon's somnifacient didn't work at all and he was beginning to suspect it was a placebo. He put half a teaspoon of the crystalline powder in a glass of water, stirred it vigorously and drank it down. Not much left in the packet he saw – he was rather racing through it. Bad sign.

As he waited for the familiar effects of the drug to start, he ran over the events of his elaborately planned encounter at the New London Theatre of Varieties. In a way he was disappointed – there had been no Eureka moment, no detonation of understanding and clarity – but something had been said this night, something inadvertently given away that he hadn't quite grasped. Yet. Perhaps it would come to him. More and more he was convinced that Vienna held the key – those last months before the war began . . . He felt the chloral begin to work – the room swayed, he sensed his balance going. Time for bed and sleep at last. He walked carefully back through to his bedroom, a hand on the wall to steady himself. God, this stuff was strong – he flung himself on the bed feeling consciousness blissfully slipping away. Vienna. That was it. So it must be . . .

'You all right, sir?' Tremlett said. 'Look a bit under the weather.'

'I'm perfectly fine, thank you, Tremlett. Got a lot on my mind.'

'Going to have a bit more on your mind, I'm afraid, sir. Colonel wants to see you.'

Lysander smoked a quick cigarette, checked his uniform thoroughly so that Osborne-Way wouldn't have the satisfaction of claiming he was 'improperly dressed', and walked briskly down the passageway to the Director of Movements' office.

Osborne-Way's secretary could not meet his eyes as she showed him in. Lysander saluted and removed his cap, stood at ease. Osborne-Way sat behind his desk looking at him and did not offer a chair.

'Captain Keogh was arrested at his house this morning at six o'clock. He's being held at New Scotland Yard.'

Lysander said nothing.

'No answer, Rief?'

'You didn't ask me a question, sir. You made a statement. I assumed a question would be following.'

'People like you make me wonder why we're fighting this war, Rief. You make me sick to my stomach.'

'I'm sorry to hear that, sir.'

'How some actor-popinjay like you wound up as an officer is a disgrace to the British Army.'

'I'm just trying to do my bit, sir. Like you.' He pointed to his wounded-in-action bar on his sleeve. 'I've done my time in the front line and have the scars to prove it.' He enjoyed the fleeting look of discomfort that crossed Osborne-Way's face – the lifelong staff officer in his cushy billet with his all-expenses-paid weekends in Paris.

'Mansfield Keogh is one of the finest men I know. You're not fit to tie his bootlaces.'

'If you say so, sir.'

'What evidence have you got against him? What's your grubby little enquiry dug up?'

'I'm not at liberty to tell you, sir.'

'Well, I'm damned well ordering you to tell me! You filth! You scum of the earth!'

Lysander waited a second or two before replying – accentuating the drawl in his voice, ever so slightly.

'I'm afraid you'll have to talk to the Chief of the Imperial General Staff about that, Colonel.'

'Get out of here!'

Lysander put his cap back on, saluted and left.

Back in Room 205 he found a telegram waiting.

ANDROMEDA. SPANIARDS INN. 7 AM TOMORROW.

Not even twenty-four hours, Lysander thought, impressed. So, something had happened last night after all. He had just enough time to make sure everything was prepared.

19. Waiting for Sunrise

LYSANDER HAD THE TAXI drop him at the top of Heath Street, in Hampstead, by the pond and the flagstaff, deciding he'd rather approach the Spaniards Inn on foot. It was 5.30 in the morning and still dark night, as the French would say. He was wearing a black overcoat and scarf with a black Trilby. It was cold and his breath was condensing thickly in front of him as he began the half-mile walk from the flagstaff to the inn along Spaniards Road, along the top of the heath. He could see very little – the streetlamps were very widely spaced on Spaniards Road – but he knew that all London lay to his south and he could hear the noise of the wind in the great oaks of Caen Wood on his right hand side – the creak and rub of huge branches like the masts and cross trees of a sailing ship at sea – timber under strain. The wind was growing, fierce and gusty, and he jammed his hat more firmly on his head, telling himself as he marched along that the key element at the moment was calmness – stay calm at all costs, whatever happened. Everything was planned, everything was in place.

Soon he stood by the little toll-house where the road narrowed opposite the Spaniards Inn and he smoked a cigarette, waiting for sunrise. Sunrise and clarity, he thought – at last, at last. In the final minutes of darkness he felt more secure, oddly, his back against the wall looking across the road at an inn – there was a light now on in a dormer window – where Charles Dickens himself had enjoyed a drink or two. In his pocket he had a torch and a small hip flask with some rum and water in it. A little tribute to his soldiering life – the tot of rum before the morning stand-to in the trenches – a life that he was about to abandon for ever, he hoped.

He shone his torch at his watch – 5.55 – an hour to go. He sensed the faintest lightening – tree trunks in the thick wood behind him beginning to emerge and solidify in the thinning darkness and, looking upwards through the branches with their remaining autumn leaves, he thought he could make out the sky above, the faintest lemony-grey, the packed clouds bustling by on the stiff westerly breeze.

He took a nip of rum, enjoying its sweetness, its warm burn in his throat and chest. A horse and dray clip-clopped by, a coal merchant. Then a telegraph boy buzzing past on a motorbike. The day beginning. He hadn't even tried to sleep last night – no chloral – but instead had written up a long account of his investigation into the Andromeda affair, its history, his suppositions and his conclusion. It had kept him occupied and made sure his mind was alert even though he was fully aware that the document he was producing was a contingency – a contingency in case he didn't survive the next few hours.

He decided not to follow that line of thought – everything was geared to triumphant, vindicatory success – he had no intention of risking his life if he could help it. It was definitely lightening now. He stepped away from the toll-house and moved a few yards into the wood. The sun's rays would be spearing over Alexandra Palace through the hurrying clouds, slowly illuminating the villages of Hornsey and Highgate, Finchley and Barnet to the east. Now he could actually see the heave and sway of the branches above his head, feel the gusts of wind tugging capriciously at the ends of his scarf. The inn was revealed to him, opposite, its white stucco façade glowing eerily; lights were on in many of the windows and he could hear a clanging sound from the yard behind. He moved a little way further back into the trees. Whoever was coming should think that he or she had arrived early and first – he didn't want to be spotted.

He smoked another cigarette and sipped at his rum. He could read his watch now without the aid of his torch – twenty minutes to go. For a moment he had another attack of doubt – what if he was wrong? – and he ran through his deductions again, obsessively. It seemed entirely conclusive to him – his only regret being that he had not had the time or the opportunity to try his theory out on anyone. The rationale and the judgement had to stand on its own terms, its inherent credibility self-sufficient.

A motor taxi puttered up the hill from Highgate and continued on its way. There was a little more traffic on Spaniards Road – a man wheeling a barrow, a dog-cart with two boys driving – but it was ideally quiet. He had a sudden urge to urinate, quickly unbuttoned his fly and did so. Trench-life again, he thought – a tot of rum and a piss before you went over the top. Think of the big attacks – tens of thousands of soldiers suddenly emptying their bladders. He smiled at the image this conjured up and –

A taxi pulled into the yard beside the inn.

Inside he saw a man in a Homburg lean forward and pay the driver.

Christian Vandenbrook stepped out and the taxi drove away.

Lysander shouted furiously from the shelter of the trees.

'Vandenbrook! What the hell are you doing here? Get away!'

Vandenbrook hurried across the road. He was wearing a long tweed coat that almost reached his ankles.

'I sent you the telegram!' he shouted, peering into the wood, still not seeing where Lysander was. 'Rief? I know who Andromeda is! Where are you?' He saw Lysander and ran up to him, panting. 'It came to me after the theatre – I just had to confirm a few things before I told you.' He stepped behind a tree and looked down Spaniards Road where it sloped towards Highgate. 'Someone's following me, I'm sure. Let's get away from here.'

'All right, all right, calm down,' Lysander said and they headed down a beaten earth path that led deeper into Caen Wood. Vandenbrook seemed unusually tense and watchful. At one point he pulled Lysander off the pathway and they waited behind a tree. Nothing. No one.

'What's happening?' Lysander asked.

'I'm sure I was followed. There was a man outside my house this morning. I'm sure he got into a motor and followed my taxi.'

'Why would anyone follow you? – You're imagining things. So – tell me what you know.'

They were deep in the wood by now. In the grey, pearly dawn light Lysander saw that the trees around them – beech, ash and oak – were ancient and tall. Stands of holly grew at their feet and the undergrowth on either side of the pathway was dense. They could have been in virgin forest – it was hard to believe they were in a borough of north London. The wind was growing stronger and the trees above their heads whistled and groaned as the branches bent and yielded. Lysander gathered in the flying ends of his scarf and tucked them in his coat.

'D'you want a nip of this?' he held out his hip flask. 'It's rum.'

Vandenbrook took a couple of large gulps and handed it back.

'Tell me,' Lysander said. 'So, who's Andromeda?'

'It's not a he – it's a she. That's what was confusing you.'

'And? –'

'The person who's blackmailing me is a woman – a woman called Anna Faulkner. Don't be confused by the name. She's Austrian. The enemy.'

'She's dead. She killed herself.'

'I know but –' Vandenbrook stopped, looking suddenly shocked. 'How do you know this?'

'Because she is – she was – my mother.'

Vandenbrook stared at him and Lysander saw his expression change from excited near-panic to something colder, icier. All pretence gone. Two men in a wild wood at dawn with a gale blowing about their heads.

Vandenbrook reached into the pocket of his coat and drew out a revolver. He pointed it at Lysander's face.

'You're under arrest,' Vandenbrook said.

'Under arrest? Are you mad?'

'You and your mother – you were in it together – two Austrian spies. You were both blackmailing me.'

Lysander didn't mean to laugh but one burst out of him all the same.

'I have to hand it to you, Vandenbrook – you're exceptional.

You're the best actor I've ever seen. Better than any of us. Best ever. You missed your vocation.'

Vandenbrook allowed himself a small smile.

'Well, we're all actors, aren't we?' he said. 'Most of our waking lives, anyway. You, me, your mother, Munro and the others. Some are good, some are average. But nobody really knows what's real, what's true. Impossible to tell for sure.'

'Why did you do it, Vandenbrook? Money? Are you stony broke? Did you want to get back at your father-in-law? Do you hate him that much? Or was it just to feel important, significant?'

'You know why,' Vandenbrook said, evenly, unprovoked. 'Because I was being blackmailed – blackmailed by that bitch Andromeda –'

A fiercer gust of wind whipped Lysander's hat off and, an instant later, Vandenbrook's head seemed to explode in a pink mist of blood, his body thrown violently down to the ground by an invisible force.

Lysander closed his eyes, counted to three and opened them. Vandenbrook still lay there, the left half of his skull gone, matted hair, brains bulging, spilling, blood flowing thickly, like oil. Lysander picked up his hat, put it on and backed off so he couldn't see. He turned to find Hamo striding through the trees, shouldering his Martini-Henry.

'You all right?' Hamo asked.

'Sort of.'

'I would have plugged him earlier – soon as he drew his gun – but I was waiting for your signal. What took you so long?'

Lysander wasn't really concentrating. He was looking at Vandenbrook. From this angle all he could see was a small red hole under his right ear.

'Sorry, Hamo, what were you saying?'

'Why did you wait so long to take your hat off?'

'I was trying to squeeze some more information from him, I suppose. Get a few more answers.'

'Risky thing to do when a man is pointing a gun at your nose.

Strike first, Lysander, and hard. That's my motto. That's why I used a dum-dum. One-shot kill required, no messing about.'

Hamo went to check on the body and examine the effects of his expanding bullet. Lysander took a notebook from his pocket and tore a sheet from it.

'So this is the man responsible for your mother's death,' Hamo said, looking down on Vandenbrook.

'Yes. And he managed to kill her without so much as laying a finger on her. He was going to use her – and me – as his ticket to freedom.'

'Then may he rot in hell for several eternities,' Hamo said. 'A good morning's work, I say.'

Lysander scribbled a word on the sheet of paper and unclipped a safety pin from behind his lapel. He stooped and pinned the note to Vandenbrook's chest. It read, 'ANDROMEDA'.

'I assume you know what you're doing,' Hamo said.

'Oh, yes.'

Lysander prised the revolver from Vandenbrook's fingers and walked a few yards away before firing one shot into the ground. Then he fitted the gun back into Vandenbrook's hand, pushing the forefinger through the trigger guard.

'That little pop-gun couldn't do that damage,' Hamo said, almost sounding offended.

'They won't care. Andromeda killed himself – that's all they need and want. We won't hear another word about it. Where's your motor?'

'Round the corner on Hampstead Lane. I think he thought he was being followed – had the taxi take all sorts of turnings and doublings-back. Didn't want to risk him spotting me.'

Lysander put his arm around his uncle's shoulders and squeezed. He had tears in his eyes.

'That was absolutely the right thing to do, Hamo. I can't thank you enough.'

'I told you to call on me, my boy. Any time.'

'I know, now we have our secret.'

'Silent as the grave.'

They walked away from Vandenbrook's body, through the wood towards Hampstead Lane, as a weak sun managed to spear through a gap in the rushing clouds and, for a few seconds, the light was burnished, a pale gold.

20. Autobiographical Investigations

MY MOTHER'S GRAVE IS in the north corner of St Botolph's graveyard, Claverleigh's parish church. It is a bare and rather cold patch but away from the vast spreading yews that line the path to the porch and that make the place look dark and grim. I wanted some light to shine on her. Hugh Faulkner has planted two flowering cherries on either side of the headstone. I'll come again in the spring when they're in blossom and think about her in more tranquil times. Her headstone reads,

ANNA LADY FAULKNER

1864–1915

Widow of Crickmay 5th Baron Faulkner
1838–1915

Formerly wife of
Halifax Rief
1840–1899

Mother of
Lysander Rief

'For ever remembered, for ever loved'

So our complicated personal history is edited down to these stark facts and these few words and numbers.

I never went back to the Annexe – I kept nothing in Room 205 – and was glad to be rid of the place with its persistent, lingering odour of antisepsis. I did return to The White Palace Hotel in Pimlico to collect my unforwarded mail and provide the management with my new address. I had grown strangely fond of flat 3/12 Trevelyan House and I gave up the lease on Chandos Place when the news reached me of poor Greville Varley's death in Kut-al-Amara, Mesopotamia, from dysentery. Amongst my mail – mainly circulars and commercial solicitations (the bane of any serving officer's postal life) – was a letter from Hettie:

Lysander, darling,

Can you forgive me? I was so horrible to you because I was so upset. However, I should never have said the things I did (particularly about Lothar – photograph enclosed). I feel ashamed and I rely on your tolerant and understanding nature. I have decided to divorce Jago and go to the United States. I want to live in a peaceful, neutral country – I'm sick of this ghastly, endless war. A friend of mine runs an 'artists' colony' in New Mexico, wherever that may be, so I am going to join him and become a teacher.

I have to tell you that Jago is not taking this at all well and, perversely, thinks you are to blame. Apparently he has been going up to London and following you. When you saw him the night of the Zeppelin raid he panicked and confessed all to me.

I know we will always be friends and I wish you every bit of good luck for your forthcoming marriage (lucky girl!).

All my best love, Hettie (never more Vanora)

PS. If you could possibly find your way to send £50 to me care of the GPO in Liverpool I'd be undyingly grateful. I set sail for 'Americay' in two weeks.

LINES WRITTEN
UNDER THE INFLUENCE OF CHLORAL HYDRATE

The heat, that summer in Vienna, was immense.
It slammed down out of a white sky, heavy as glass.

I do not hope
I do not hope to see
I do not hope nor see

Why were those bands playing in the Prater?
No one told me what was going on.

She was *schön*.
She was *sympatisch*.
We couldn't be left alone
At the Hôtel du Sport et Riche.

I do not see hope
Hope does not see me

Blackblackblackblackwhiteblackblackblack

We turned on our backs in the flax
We strove in the shadows of the apple grove
We found bliss beneath the trellis of clematis
Roll me over, lay me down and do it again.

It's black, alack – I can't see a thing.

Tara-loo, Madame, tara-lee, tara-loo-di-do

I dream of a woman.

★   ★   ★

Blanche and I have set a date for our wedding in the spring – May 1916. Hamo is to be my best man. Blanche and I spend many nights together but I find I still need chloral hydrate to sleep. I visit Dr Bensimon in Highgate once a week and we talk through the story of the last two years. Parallelism is working, slowly – I'm beginning to live with a version of events in which the man with the moustache and the fair-haired boy scramble out of the sap before my bombs explode. They're both lightly wounded but both regain the German lines. The more I concentrate on this story and manufacture its precise details the more its plausibility beguiles me. Perhaps one night I'll sleep peacefully, unaided by my chemicals.

I wrote to Sergeant Foley at the Stoke Newington Hospital for the Blind but have received no reply to date. Perhaps it might be better if I don't learn any more facts about that night – it's been hard enough dislodging the ones that are haunting me – but I feel I need to see Foley and explain something of what was really going on.

I have an audition tomorrow – my old life returning. A revival of *Man and Superman* by George Bernard Shaw.

I sit here looking at Hettie's photograph of Lothar that she sent me. A studio portrait of a little glum boy – close to tears, it seems – dressed to all intents and purposes as a girl in some embroidered pseudo-peasant smock. Long, dark curly hair. Does he look anything like me? One minute I think – yes, he does. And the next I think – no, not at all. Is he really, truly mine, in fact? Hettie betrayed Udo Hoff with me – might she not have been betraying me with somebody else? Can I ever be certain?

And on this note I think back, as I often do, to that October dawn on Hampstead Heath as I was waiting for sunrise, waiting for Vandenbrook to arrive. I knew it would be him and I hoped that sunrise that day would bring understanding and clarity with it – or at least clearer vision. And I thought I had it as I pinned 'Andromeda' to Vandenbrook's coat. Everything solved, explained. But as the day wore on other questions nagged at me, troubled me and set me thinking again, until by dusk all was confusion once more. Maybe this is what life is like – we try to see clearly but what we see is never clear and is never going to be. The more we strive the murkier it becomes. All we are left with are approximations, nuances, multitudes of plausible explanations. Take your pick.

I feel, after what I have gone through, that I understand a little of our modern world now, as it exists today. And perhaps I've been offered a glimpse into its future. I was provided with the chance to see the mighty industrial technologies of the twentieth-century war machine both at its massive, bureaucratic source and at its narrow, vulnerable human target. And yet, for all the privileged insight and precious knowledge that I gleaned, I felt that the more I seemed to know, then the more clarity and certainty dimmed and faded away. As we advance into the future the paradox will become clearer – clear and black, blackly clear. The more we know the less we know. Funnily enough, I can live with that idea quite happily. If this is our modern world I feel a very modern man.

I met Munro at noon by the north-east lion at the foot of Nelson's Column in Trafalgar Square. It was a grey, cold day of intermittent rain and drizzle and we were both wearing rubberized trenchcoats, like a couple of tourists. A heavy shower had passed through ten minutes before and the paving stones were glossy and lacquered, the wet smoky façades of the surrounding buildings – the Royal College of Physicians, the National Gallery, St Martin's – almost a velvety black. The brief sun was trying vainly to break through the thick grey clouds, managing only to illumine some breeze-blown interstices, and this, coupled with the gloomy effect of the heavy purpley mass of more rain coming up the Thames estuary, cast a curious gold-leaden light on the scene, making the vistas down

Pall Mall, Whitehall and Northumberland Avenue seem lit by arc-lights, artificial and strange, as if the city blocks could be struck like stage scenery and re-assembled elsewhere. I felt uncomfortable and edgy, troubled by the weather and the curious light, almost as if I were in a theatre, acting.

MUNRO: Why are we meeting like this, Rief? All very melodramatic.

LYSANDER: Indulge me. I like public spaces at the moment.

MUNRO: We found 'Andromeda', of course, up on the heath, with your note on him. The police called us . . . Everything tidied up nicely. We're grateful, I must say.

LYSANDER: He was very clever, Vandenbrook. Very.

MUNRO: Not clever enough. You caught him and dealt with him. I read your deposition – very thorough.

LYSANDER: Good. He was never being blackmailed, you see. That was the first of his clever ideas. He had everything prepared in case he was ever found out. There was no ten-year old girl, no genuine statement, no pearls. It gave him an excuse – and it might have saved him the hangman if he hadn't shot himself.

MUNRO: Yes . . . How did you know it was him – in the end?

LYSANDER: I admit – I'd been completely convinced by his blackmail story. Then he gave himself away – just a little slip up. Even I didn't notice it when he said it – it was something I remembered a few hours later as I was trying to get to sleep.

MUNRO: You're going to tell me what it was, I'm sure.

LYSANDER: That night we all met at the theatre, Vandenbrook made a reference to the cover of *Andromeda und Perseus*.

MUNRO: Glockner's source-text –

LYSANDER: Exactly. I mentioned it – the opera – and he said he had heard it was a 'saucy' opera. How could he know? He'd never seen it. But he had seen the libretto with its provocative cover because he'd stolen it from my mother's office and used it as the master-text for the Glockner code.

MUNRO [thinking]: Yes . . . What was that meeting in the variety theatre all about?

LYSANDER: I wanted Vandenbrook to look you over – you, Fyfe-Miller and Massinger. See if he could identify you. I still believed he was being blackmailed at that stage.

MUNRO: Are you saying you suspected one of us?

LYSANDER: I'm afraid so. It seemed the obvious conclusion at the time. I was convinced it was one of you three – that one of you was the real Andromeda. Until he made his slip-up.

MUNRO: I don't understand –

LYSANDER: When I was in Vienna I knew this Austrian army officer who had been accused of stealing from the officers' mess. I'm sure now that he was guilty but there were eleven other suspects. So he hid behind a screen of other suspects and manipulated them very adroitly – just like Vandenbrook. And he got away with it. When there are many suspects the inclination is to suspect anyone and everybody – which means you probably never find the real suspect. It's a very clever ruse. But I had this strong feeling that the whole business was connected to Vienna in some way. You had been in Vienna, Fyfe-Miller as well – and so had Massinger, apparently.

MUNRO: Yes, Massinger came to Vienna. And you were in Vienna, also.

LYSANDER: So I was. And Hettie Bull. And Dr John Bensimon. The only person who hadn't been there was Vandenbrook. And that's what gave him away. He hadn't been there, yet he knew about *Andromeda und Perseus*. And, most importantly, what was on the cover of the Viennese libretto. Glockner's Dresden libretto had no 'saucy' cover. Just plain black lettering on white. A tiny, fatal, error. But I was the only person who knew that. The only one.

Munro looked thoughtful, stroking his neat moustache with his middle finger in his habitual gesture. I sensed that he was desperate to find something wrong with my reasoning, some flaw in the logic – almost as a matter of intellectual pride and self-esteem, as if he was annoyed by the case I had built and wanted to bring it down, somehow.

MUNRO: All of the Glockner letters were posted in London.

LYSANDER: Yes.

MUNRO: So you're saying Vandenbrook took them to a south-coast hotel. Left them there. Then had them picked up the next day by a railway porter and brought back to him in London. He then encoded them and sent them on to Geneva.

LYSANDER: It was part of his cover. He was unbelievably thorough. Everything was thought through. Everything had to fit his essential blackmail story – that there was another person controlling him. Another Andromeda, if you like. A more important one.

MUNRO: He certainly took pains.

LYSANDER: And they nearly paid off for him. By the way, how did you know the Glockner letters had London postmarks?

MUNRO: You told me.

LYSANDER: Did I? I don't remember.

MUNRO: Then it must have been Madame Duchesne.

LYSANDER: Must have been . . .

MUNRO: How can you be sure that Vandenbrook was Andromeda?

LYSANDER: How can you be sure about anything? It's my best guess. My most considered deduction. My most cogitated interpretation. Vandenbrook was very shrewd – and an exceptional actor, incidentally, far superior to me. I wish I had half his talent. And he had established an invisible layer of power above him that made him look like a victim, a dupe, a pawn. Don't look at me, I'm small fry, he was saying – the real control lies elsewhere. I believed it for a while but it was a total fabrication.

MUNRO: Then why did he try to deliver the last letter?

LYSANDER: That was the beginning of the ruse. He saw I had come into the Directorate and he knew exactly what I was looking for – and that I might very well narrow the suspects down to him – so he put his escape plan into operation. Of course he encoded the Glockner letters himself. He had the master-text. But he had to cover himself in case I found him out. And of course I might never have come upon the last letter, but he couldn't risk it.

MUNRO: Isn't that a bit too subtle? Over-subtle? Even for Vandenbrook?

LYSANDER: This is your world, Munro, not mine. I think 'too subtle' or 'over-subtle' are its defining features, don't you? The triple-bluff? The quadruple-bluff? The third-guess? The tenth-guess? Normal currency in my limited experience. Why don't you ask an expert like Madame Duchesne? Ask yourself, come to that.

Munro frowned. He looked like a man who was still not convinced by the argument.

LYSANDER: You don't look convinced.

MUNRO: Well, next summer's offensives will give us a final answer, I suppose, as to whether the leak is staunched or not.

LYSANDER: I suggest you go and spend a few days in the Directorate of Movements and its associated departments. It's all there. Mountains upon mountains of hard fact – so easy to read. It's too big, Munro. The war machine is too gigantic and gigantically obvious – you can't hide anything when it's on that massive scale and when you're as close as I was. Anyone could have been Andromeda – it just happened to be Vandenbrook.

Munro looked at me, quizzically, as if I were some fractious and rascally schoolboy who was forever disrupting his classroom.

LYSANDER: Think of our armies as cities. There's a British city, and a French city and a German city and a Russian city. And then there's the Austrian city, the Italian and the Turkish. They need everything a city needs – fuel, transportation, power supply, food, water, sanitation, administration, hospitals, a police force, law courts, undertakers and graveyards. And so on. Think how much these cities need on a daily basis, how much they consume, on an hourly basis. There's a population of millions in these cities and they have to be kept running at all costs.

MUNRO: I see what you mean. Yes . . .

LYSANDER: And then there's the final, unique ingredient.

MUNRO: What's that?

LYSANDER: Weaponry. Of every imaginable type. These cities are trying to destroy each other.

MUNRO: Yes . . . It does make you think . . .

He was silent for a while and kicked out a foot at a pigeon that was pecking too close to his brilliant shoes. The bird flapped away a few feet.

MUNRO: Why did you kill Vandenbrook?

LYSANDER: I didn't. He killed himself. When I confronted him with the evidence about the libretto. He drew a gun and shot himself. Search his house – you'll find the vital clue. The *Andromeda und Perseus* libretto is the key to all this.

MUNRO: We can't search his house. It wouldn't do. Grieving widow, little weeping girls who've lost their father. Distinguished officer who took his own life, injured in battle, suffering from the awful pressures and stress of modern warfare . . . No, no. And his father-in-law would have something to say about us sending men in and tearing the place apart.

LYSANDER: Then you'll have to take my word for it, won't you?

Silence. We looked at each other, giving nothing away.

MUNRO: I was sorry to hear about your mother.

LYSANDER: Yes. It's a real tragedy. She just couldn't cope, I suppose. But it was something she wanted to do. I respect that.

MUNRO: Of course . . . Of course . . . What about you, Rief? What do you want to do now?

LYSANDER: I want my honourable discharge. No more army for me. My war's finished.

MUNRO: I think we can arrange that. It's the least you deserve.

We shook hands, said a simple goodbye and walked away from each other, Munro heading back down Northumberland Avenue to Whitehall Court and me strolling up the Strand to Surrey Street

and 3/12 Trevelyan House. I didn't look back and I assume Munro
didn't, either. It was over.

21. Shadows

IT IS A DARK, foggy, drizzly night in London, near the end of 1915.
The fog, pearly and smoky, seems to curl and hang – as if from a
million snuffed candles – around the city blocks like something
almost growing and sinuously weedy, blanketing and vast, seeking
out doorways and stairways, alleyways and side streets, the levels of
the roofs quite invisible. The streetlamps drop a struggling moist
yellow cone of luminescence that seems to wane as soon as the
light hits the shining pavement in its small hazed circle, as if the
effort of piercing the engulfing murky darkness and falling there
were all it could manage.

You are standing shivering in the angle of two walls in Archer
Street, peering out, trying to discern the late-night world go by,
your attention half-caught by the small crowd of enthusiastic
theatre-goers waiting with their programmes for an autograph as
the cast of *Man and Superman* leaves the stage door after the show.
Exhalations of rapture, an impromptu smatter of applause.
Eventually the people drift away as the actors come through, sign,
chat briefly and leave.

The light is switched off but you see that the door opens one last
time and a man appears with a raincoat and a hat in his hand. He
looks up at the opaque night sky, checking on the dismal weather,
and you will probably recognize him as Mr Lysander Rief, who is
playing the part of John Tanner, the leading role in *Man and
Superman*, by Mr George Bernard Shaw. Lysander Rief looks tired
– he looks like a man who is not sleeping well. So why is he
quitting the theatre so discreetly, the very last to leave? He puts his

hat on and sets off and – vaguely curious – you decide to follow him, left into Wardour Street and then quickly right into Old Compton Street. You keep your distance as you watch him make his way home through the thickening condensations of the night. He pauses frequently to look around him and, as he goes, he takes an odd swerving course along the street, crossing and re-crossing the roadway, as if keen to avoid the bleary yellow circles cast by the streetlamps. You give up after a minute – you've better things to do – and you leave Mr Lysander Rief to make his erratic way home, wherever that may be, as best he can. Good luck to him – he's evidently a man who prefers the fringes and the edges of the city streets, its blurry peripheries – where it's hard to make things out clearly, hard to tell exactly what is what, and who is whom – Mr Lysander Rief looks like someone who is far more at ease occupying the cold security of the dark; a man happier with the dubious comfort of the shadows.

A NOTE ON THE TYPE

The text of this book is set in Bembo. This type was first used in 1495 by the Venetian printer Aldus Manutius for Cardinal Bembo's *De Aetna*, and was cut for Manutius by Francesco Griffo. It was one of the types used by Claude Garamond (1480–1561) as a model for his Romain de L'Université, and so it was the forerunner of what became standard European type for the following two centuries. Its modern form follows the original types and was designed for Monotype in 1929.

About the author

About the book

Insights,
Interviews
& More . . .

Read on

Meet William Boyd

WILLIAM BOYD has received worldwide acclaim for his novels. They include *A Good Man in Africa* (1981, winner of the Whitbread Award and the Somerset Maugham Prize), *An Ice-Cream War* (1982, shortlisted for the 1982 Booker Prize and winner of the John Llewellyn Rhys Prize), *Stars and Bars* (1984), *The New Confessions* (1987), *Brazzaville Beach* (1990, winner of the McVitie Prize and the James Tait Black Memorial Prize), *The Blue Afternoon* (1993, winner of the 1993 Sunday Express Book of the Year Award and the 1995 Los Angeles Times Book Award for Fiction), *Armadillo* (1998), *Any Human Heart* (2002, winner of the Prix Jean Monnet), and *Restless* (2006, winner of the Costa Book Award for Novel of the Year). His novels and stories have been published around the world and have been translated into more than thirty languages. He is also the author of a collection of screenplays; a memoir of his schooldays, *School Ties* (1985); and three collections of short stories: *On the Yankee Station* (1981), *The Destiny of Nathalie 'X'* (1995), and *Fascination* (2004). He also wrote the speculative memoir *Nat Tate: An American Artist 1928–1960*—the publication of which, in the spring of 1998, caused something of a stir on both sides of the Atlantic. A collection of his nonfiction writings from 1978 to 2004, titled *Bamboo*, was published in October 2005. His tenth novel, *Ordinary Thunderstorms*, was published in 2009.

His eleventh novel, *Waiting for Sunrise*, was published in 2012.

Born in Accra, Ghana, in 1952, Boyd grew up there and in Nigeria. He was educated at Gordonstoun School and attended the universities of Nice (Diploma of French Studies) and Glasgow (M.A.Hons in English and Philosophy) and Jesus College, Oxford, where he studied for a D.Phil in English Literature. He was also a lecturer in English Literature at St. Hilda's College, Oxford, from 1980 to 1983. He is a Fellow of the Royal Society of Literature, an Officier de l'Ordre des Arts et des Lettres, and an Honorary Fellow of Jesus College, Oxford. He has been presented with honorary Doctorates in Literature from the universities of St. Andrews, Stirling, Glasgow, and Dundee. In 2005 he was awarded the CBE.

His screenwriting credits include *Stars and Bars* (1987, dir. Pat O'Connor), *Mr Johnson* (1990, dir. Bruce Beresford), *Aunt Julia and the Scriptwriter* (1990, dir. Jon Amiel), *Chaplin* (1992, dir. Richard Attenborough), *A Good Man in Africa* (1993, dir. Bruce Beresford), *The Trench* (1999, which Boyd also directed), and *Man to Man* (2005, dir. Régis Wargnier). He adapted Evelyn Waugh's *Scoop* for television (1988) as well as Waugh's Sword of Honour trilogy (2001). His own three-part adaptation of his novel *Armadillo* was screened on BBC 1 in 2001 and on A&E in the U.S. in 2002. His film about Shakespeare and his sonnets, *A Waste of Shame*, was made in 2005 for BBC 4. His four-part adaptation of his novel *Any Human* ▶

Meet William Boyd *(continued)*

Heart was broadcast on Channel 4 in November 2010 and on *Masterpiece* in the U.S. in February 2011. It won the BAFTA in 2011 for Best Drama Serial. His two-part adaptation of his novel *Restless* is being filmed in 2012 for the BBC. He has written two original TV films about boarding-school life in England: *Good and Bad at Games* (1983) and *Dutch Girls* (1985).

In 2012 he was invited by the Estate of Ian Fleming to write a new James Bond novel. It will be published in 2013 (by Harper in the U.S.).

He is married and divides his time between London and southwest France. ◠

Boyd on Vienna

WHY DO CERTAIN CITIES haunt
the imagination? Not just the cities
themselves but the cities of a particular
historical period. In my own case I can
identify four such cities—Los Angeles
in the 1970s, Lisbon in the 1930s, Berlin
in the 1920s, and Vienna in the years
just before the First World War. Thus
captivated, I wrote fiction—short stories,
chapters of novels—set in all of these
cities long before I ever visited them.
This is the mark and measure, I suppose,
of their allure—it's vicarious; it works at
a great distance—but it must be some
conveyed sense of atmosphere, the spirit
of place, that prompts the fascination.
Perhaps the most telling factor is a
powerful feeling that you would have
liked to have lived there yourself.

One of the amazing aspects of
Vienna—or certainly the central city,
the Inner Stadt, bounded by the great
circling boulevard of the Ring—is how
easy it is to imagine living there, not
just in the early years of the twentieth
century but also in the nineteenth and
even the eighteenth century as well. It's
so beautifully preserved and maintained
that you can turn a corner and draw up
with a shock, imagining that Mozart or
Brahms could have seen the identical
view. But Vienna in its fading pomp, in
the last years of the Austro-Hungarian
Empire (1867–1918), is present before
you in almost every street scene or vista.
Freud's Vienna, Wittgenstein's Vienna,
Egon Schiele's Vienna. ▶

Boyd on Vienna *(continued)*

The Austro-Hungarian Empire was, as empires go, comparatively short-lived; it began in 1867 with the Ausgleich—the "Compromise" that saw the old Austrian and Hapsburg Empire transmogrified into a new Austria-Hungary, a strange hybrid empire with a dual monarchy and whose imperial life ended in 1918 with defeat in World War I. In fact, Austria-Hungary contained many other countries, ethnic groups, and eleven recognized languages. This curious amalgam of peoples included Germans, Hungarians, Czechs, Slovaks, Poles, Ukrainians, Slovenes, Croats, Serbs, Romanians, and Italians. For nearly its entire existence, its emperor was Franz Joseph I. He reigned for sixty-eight years, dying in 1916 at the age of eighty-six. The multigenerational length of his reign gave an illusion of permanence, of timeless durability, but as the old man grew ever more aged, the prospect of his death generated a collective sense of impending disaster. This paranoia— this growing fearfulness—resonates in the literature of the period, but there was a general feeling throughout the Empire that everything would change once the old gentleman passed away. His son and heir, Crown Prince Rudolf, committed suicide at Mayerling in 1889. Franz Joseph's nephew, Franz Ferdinand, became the archduke and the heir presumptive to the Empire. There was at least the notion that the dynasty would continue until, in June 1914,

66 There was a general feeling throughout the Empire that everything would change once the old gentleman passed away. 99

Franz Ferdinand and his wife, Sophie, made a state visit to Sarajevo.

Traces of that pre–First World War world do remain in Vienna. You can still go to the Café Landtmann where Freud enjoyed a kapuziner and a cigar. You can sit in the Café Sperl—my favorite—and imagine Egon Schiele wandering in with one of his models. You can eat Sacher Torte and drink schnapps in the Hotel Sacher and watch the patisserie chefs at work in Dehmel much as Joseph Roth and Robert Musil would have done. Somehow, Vienna has managed to preserve the authenticity of its old style of life in a way that most other European capitals haven't. It's true that Jean-Paul Sartre would still recognize the Café de Flore and Alberto Moravia the Câffè Greco, and Charles Dickens would feel at home in the Grapes by Limehouse Basin, but the relentless, homogenizing, modernizing hand of the twentieth and twenty-first centuries is making all cities of Western Europe come steadily to resemble each other. But for the moment, at least, parts of Vienna seem miraculously preserved.

Perhaps this is because the clock metaphorically stopped for Vienna when Archduke Franz Ferdinand was assassinated in Sarajevo in June 1914 and the First World War began a few weeks later. In those first fourteen years of the twentieth century, Vienna, more than anywhere else, was the fulminating, bewitching crucible where the modern world was invented. It doesn't seem ▶

> **"** Somehow, Vienna has managed to preserve the authenticity of its old style of life in a way that most other European capitals haven't. **"**

too fanciful to posit the idea of a form of modern Renaissance that took place in the city over the first decade or so of the twentieth century and that transformed our culture permanently. There have been artistic and social upheavals in other cities at various times—Paris, London, New York, and Berlin have all been the cynosure of cultural movements—but was there ever such a concentration of genius across the broad spectrum of thought and culture that could be found in Vienna and the Austro-Hungarian Empire during those early years of the twentieth century? If we start drawing up some lists of names, the idea appears more and more plausible. In literature: Rilke, Kafka, Roth, Musil, Zweig, and Schnitzler. Music: Mahler, Schoenberg, Webern, and Berg. Architecture: Otto Wagner and Adolf Loos. Painting: Klimt, Schiele, and Kokoschka. Philosophy: Wittgenstein and the origins of the Vienna Circle. Journalism: Karl Kraus. The brew is almost too rich. Then throw in Adolf Hitler and, of course, the sine qua non, Sigmund Freud.

However discredited Freud is today as a thinker and founder of psychoanalysis, there is no doubt that we are, like it or not, all Freudians now. What Freud did—to put it very simply—was to schematize the workings of our unconscious mind. However wrongheaded and unscientific his theories proved to be, they had the

> 66 However discredited Freud is today as a thinker and founder of psychoanalysis, there is no doubt that we are, like it or not, all Freudians now. 99

effect of creating one of those revolutions in human understanding and self-knowledge that ranks with, for example, Copernicus (we are living a small planet revolving around a small star—we are not the center of the universe) and Darwin (we are animals, part of the fauna of this small planet). Freud established that our conscious mind perhaps only accounted for fifty percent of our behaviour; the irrational, the unknown, the repressed, the neurotic, and the taboo became an irreducible part of the explanation of our human persona. A modern, complex, troubled sensibility was established for the new century— a century that very quickly was going to upset all certainties and all complacent confidence about human progress.

The assassination of Archduke Franz Ferdinand on June 28, 1914, was the single direct cause of the First World War. It's highly unusual to be able to point to this utterly random congruence of events, this arbitrary chain of sheer happenstance, and to see it as the tipping point, the moment the world changed for ever. Gavrilo Princip's squeeze of the trigger as he aimed at Franz Ferdinand was, so hindsight now tells us, like a shot from a starting pistol. It signaled the end of the Austro-Hungarian Empire—and the fact that nothing would ever be the same again. The modern world—our world—had begun. ⌒

> ❝ Gavrilo Princip's squeeze of the trigger as he aimed at Franz Ferdinand was, so hindsight now tells us, like a shot from a starting pistol. ❞

Author's Picks
Books That Inspired
Waiting for Sunrise

ONE OF THE BENIGN CONSEQUENCES of researching and writing a novel is that—for a while—you can become an expert, or at least a pseudo-expert, on certain subjects. For example, the writing of my eleven novels has familiarized me with topics such as primatology, the Philippine-American War of 1899 to 1902, loss adjusting, appendicitis, the Third Battle of Ypres, the River Thames' Marine Support Unit, Gödel's Incompleteness Theorem, the Spanish flu pandemic of 1918 and 1919, the Hoo Peninsula, Jean-Jacques Rousseau, cloud seeding, Lisbon . . . and so on.

Waiting for Sunrise is no exception. This is my third novel where the central character has to become a spy for a while, and so I have thoroughly studied the genre and developed distinct tastes for a certain type of superior spy novel. Early twentieth-century psychoanalysis, the supply of munitions and transport on the Western Front, the street layout of Vienna's Inner Stadt, Strindberg's *Miss Julie*, the end of the Austro-Hungarian Empire, Georgian architecture, ferry services from Geneva to Evian, and the Cinque Ports are among the arcana that I've informed myself about during the writing of the novel and are now a little less arcane.

For each novel I acquire a small library of books—usually secondhand and from the Internet—that I pile around me on my study floor both for reference and reassurance. I eventually ended up with about two hundred books for *Waiting for Sunrise*. Here is a small selection.

The Man Without Qualities
by Robert Musil

The great novel of Vienna before the First World War—Vienna's *Ulysses*, if you like. Musil (1880–1942) wrote the novel over a number of years between the two world wars. It's a curious book, alternating passages of utter tedium with beguiling and acute social observation, but what is particularly intriguing about it is its tone of voice—this is the mind-set of the Viennese intellectual at the beginning of the twentieth century.

The Radetsky March
by Joseph Roth

If Musil is the great novelist of the city, then Joseph Roth (1894–1939) is the great novelist of the Empire. Roth was born in the eastern province of Galicia (now part of Poland), and his many works of fiction are a loving recreation of the "Crown lands," as the further flung regions and principalities of the Dual Monarchy were known. Roth's masterwork, *The Radetzky March* (1932), barely features Vienna at all, in fact, but, like Musil, he wrote it with full benefit of hindsight. After the ▶

> [*The Man Without Qualities* is] the great novel of Vienna before the First World War— Vienna's *Ulysses*, if you like.

First World War, Europe would never be the same again and both Roth and Musil in their novels bear rueful witness to a vanished world.

The Vertigo Years
by Philipp Blom

A superb history of early twentieth-century modernist movements in Vienna covering all aspects of society and culture. The title refers to the underlying sense that things were going too fast.

The Secret Agent
by Joseph Conrad

Perhaps the first spy novel to be written by a leading novelist (published in 1908). It is told more from the point of view of a covert anarchist rather than a professional spy, but it is an attempt to understand the psychology of an undercover agent.

The Quest for "C": Sir Mansfield Cumming and the Founding of the British Secret Service
by Alan Judd

Sir Mansfield Cumming was the first head of the Secret Service, founded in 1909. Judd peels away the secrets and shows how MI5 and MI6 began to evolve during the First World War. It was somewhat crude and driven by trial and error as the first-ever professional secret service began to feel its way.

> 66 Europe would never be the same again and both Roth and Musil in their novels bear rueful witness to a vanished world. 99

Her Privates We
by Frederic Manning

If you want to know what it was really like to be a soldier in the trenches of the Western Front, then this is the novel. It is wholly honest and unflinching. This is how the ordinary soldier spoke, thought, and felt, all myths stripped away. The best novel to have come out of the war.

A Strange Eventful History
by Michael Holroyd

A fascinating biography of the Victorian-Edwardian theatrical superstars Ellen Terry and Henry Irving and their families. We not only understand what the theater was like then, but we also see modern dramaturgy emerge. A wonderfully insightful glimpse into a forgotten theatrical age.

The Spy Who Came In from the Cold
by John le Carré

A terse, dark, and chilling insight into the Cold War. Le Carré sets the standard here for the intellectual spy-novel. It's perhaps his finest, though his *Tinker, Tailor, Soldier, Spy* and *The Perfect Spy* run it close.

Good-Bye to All That
by Robert Graves

A flamboyant but enduring memoir of the First World War. Graves was a young officer and was badly wounded. He wrote with tremendous verve and brio—and with as much honesty as ▶

> **❝** If you want to know what it was really like to be a soldier in the trenches of the Western Front, then [*Her Privates We*] is the novel. **❞**

was possible at the time. Published in 1929.

Thunder at Twilight: Vienna 1913/1914 by Frederic Morton

A classic analysis of Viennese Life before the beginning of the First World War. Morton reveals the febrility and the tensions of the extraordinary number of writers, artists, musicians, and thinkers living in the city at the time. An expert analysis of the impending sense of doom that afflicted Austro-Hungarian culture—the sense that the old world was about to end forever. ∾

where Margot played she managed to remain that way. The "Little Princess," Kathi called her.

Once Anne, newly washed and dressed, was playing happily in a mud puddle when Kathi tried to remove her. Anne wanted Kathi to tell her a story first. Kathi said she didn't have time but Anne insisted it could be a *short* story.

Both girls delighted in hearing over and over again the tale, handed down from his mother to Otto, of the two Paulas. Good Paula and Bad Paula. Since they were invisible the only way to tell them apart was by their actions. Good Paula obeyed her parents, was nice to her sister, and finished everything on her plate. Bad Paula was, well, bad. She played with her food, annoyed insects and small animals, and was generally a trial. Predictably Margot clearly favored Good Paula, while Anne was torn between the two.

Their happy home was, however, being threatened by the world outside their door. Otto and Edith saw the danger increasing with each passing day.

They sat in stony silence through dinners in which their companions suggested that Hitler should be given a chance. Perhaps he could improve the dire economic conditions. Equally troubling were discussions in which people made light of the situation. He'll go away, he won't last. Just wait it out, they said.

The Franks did not think Hitler was going to fade away. His anti-Jewish views were becoming alarmingly popular.

For most of their lives, religion had mattered little. Now there was something sinister about being Jewish. Now, because they were Jewish, friends and neighbors had become people to be feared.

The country where they were born and raised — the country that they loved — was disintegrating all around them, transforming itself into something they didn't recognize and where they were not welcome.

The writing was on the wall, but most didn't see it. Otto and Edith Frank did.

They would have to go. To stay was simply too risky.

Edith was heartbroken. They would have to pack up everything they owned and go to a strange, new country. And where would they go?

Otto favored Amsterdam. He had traveled there frequently and had good business connections now. He liked the Dutch — they were a liberal and tolerant people who had remained neutral in the First World War.

Aachen, where Edith was born, was not far from Amsterdam. At least she and the girls could continue to visit her family.

In the summer of 1933, it was decided.

Thanks to some help from his relatives, Otto had lined up a job in Amsterdam. He would be working for Opekta, a Frankfurt-based company that manufactured pectin, the ingredient that made ground-up fruit turn to gel and, therefore, become jam or jelly. Otto would be establishing their Amsterdam branch.

Edith and the girls would stay with Edith's mother in Aachen while Otto went on ahead to Amsterdam, got settled in his new position, and found a nice place for them to live.

They would build a brand-new life there, far away from Hitler, Nazis, and their ideas of racial purity and racial hatred.

Margot was seven, Anne four.

Amsterdam, Holland

Thoughtfully and methodically, as with everything he did, Otto Frank assembled his staff: Johannes Kleiman, a bookkeeper whom Otto had known for a number of years; Victor Kugler, Otto's right-hand man who supervised the staff and ran the office when Otto was out; full-time typist Bep Voskuijl; and Hermine Santrouschitz.

Hermine was born in Vienna, Austria. When the First World War ended, thousands of children were malnourished because of the scarcity of food. In desperation some of the children were sent to countries that had enough food. After the child regained his health he would be returned home. Eleven-year-old Hermine was sent to Holland, and became so close and comfortable with her new family that she never returned to Vienna. Her foster parents adopted her and gave her a Dutch nickname, Miep.

When Miep was hired, Otto Frank took her to the company kitchen. He gave her a recipe and the ingredients necessary for making jam: pectin, fruit, sugar, etc. Then he left. Miep's cooking thus far had been limited to making coffee, but she succeeded, and in the coming weeks, as Otto brought different fruits requiring different proportions, Miep always turned out delicious jam.

Now that she had acquired firsthand knowledge of the proper way to make jam, she could communicate this to the housewives who were Opekta's customers.

Soon Miep was doing just about anything: answering telephone inquiries from the housewives, helping with the bookkeeping, and doing routine office work. Calm, confident, and dependable, she became Otto's executive secretary.

Progressive Otto put signs on trucks, created ads for newspapers, and made films to persuade housewives to make more jam.

Later when they decided to diversify the business he hired chain-smoking, fast-talking, joke-loving Hermann van Pels. He was an expert in spices, and his hypersensitive nose could distinguish and identify any herb. In the annex behind the front office and warehouse building Otto built his private office and a staff kitchen. He left the second and third floors of the annex unused.

They all worked well together. His employees appreciated the respectful and courteous way Otto treated them and repaid him with their best efforts and their loyalty. Otto worked longer hours in Amsterdam than he had in Frankfurt — most days he didn't come home until late. And his traveling forced him to be away for days at a time.

He found a third-floor apartment in a modern complex at 37 Merwedeplein, situated between wide, well-laid-out avenues in the same section of the city that Miep lived in. It was a perfect place to raise a family.

In December, Edith came with Margot and oversaw the delivery and unpacking of her fine, antique furniture. Anne stayed with her grandmother and uncles in Aachen. In February 1934, Anne was placed on the table in the new apartment in the middle of the other gifts as a special birthday present for her sister.

The Franks decided to send Anne to a Montessori school. The informally structured, ungraded school emphasized individual development and self-motivation rather than conformity and obedience. Pupils were not required to remain in their seats — they could walk around and even talk during class, which would suit the Franks' free-spirited younger daughter just fine.

Both girls could walk or ride their bikes to school.

Margot adjusted immediately to her new school and made friends easily. She read constantly and was consistently at the head of her class. (Although both parents respected the role of education they made it clear that good grades were not nearly as important as becoming a happy, healthy person.) Margot was turning out to be a studious (something emphasized by her eyeglasses), introspective, well-mannered girl more than willing to go unnoticed. Quite unlike her younger sister.

Anne liked her kindergarten where she immediately made friends with Hanneli "Lies" Goslar who, it turned out, lived right below the Franks. They met Suzanne "Sanne" Ledermann, who lived around the corner (but went to a different school), and the three became close friends. (Margot and Sanne's older sister, Barbara, became good friends also.) After a while the three of them were nearly inseparable, preferring to remain apart from the other, less sophisticated girls in the neighborhood.

The ongoing construction in the still-developing area provided them with the world's best playground thanks to the piles of sand and construction material. (There was a "real" playground located in the middle of the complex.)

They wrote with chalk on the sidewalks, played marbles, hopscotch, hide-and-seek, and tag. They rolled hoops, rode scooters, roller-skated, and in the winter skated on the ice. Anne, annoyed that she had to use her sister's old, out-of-fashion skates, pestered her parents until they bought her new ones, the kind with the blade already stitched to the shoe.

The girls did cartwheels and handstands, seeing how long they could remain on their hands, something Anne was not good at because of her trick shoulder (which also prevented her from going to gym class). They performed plays in school and in various living rooms, which Anne *was* good at, and collected and traded picture postcards of movie stars and royalty. The girls passed around little autograph books, which were all the rage, in which they wrote their own poetry and added their own drawings.

They called one another via secret whistles, but no matter how much Anne tried to practice and how hard everyone tried to help she just couldn't learn to whistle. Endlessly inventive, when calling for her friends, Anne sang through the mail slot.

Visiting Mr. Frank's office was another favorite activity. They played secretary, placing urgent phone calls, paging one another on the intercom, and doing some important typing.

Summers and holidays they frequently vacationed together. They named one hotel they stayed at the Tomato House because of the vegetarian-only menu. They went to an amusement park and enjoyed their first visit to a house of mirrors. Anne learned to swim, which she became quite good at, bicycled in the countryside, and took the standard houseboat tours of some of the many Dutch canals.

Anne loved babies and couldn't stop herself from sneaking a peek beneath the covers of a passing carriage. When Lies's baby sister Gabi was born, Anne loved to help take her for a stroll.

Lies and Anne were in the same class and sat next to each other most of the time. Anne, always a critical and demanding friend, thought Lies confided in her nervous and irritable mother too much and that she was a little too shy (but compared with Anne, anyone was).

Anne's invariably cheerful personality coupled with her mischievous mind made her endlessly fun to be with. Her irresistible and instinctual sense of humor bordered at times on the slapstick. She purposefully would move her trick shoulder in and out of its socket, a sure crowd pleaser.

As they grew up together the three girls spent more and more time reading fashion magazines, gossiping about their favorite film stars, and discussing boys.

Anne was style conscious before any of her friends. When going to the dressmakers on Merwedeplein she knew just where she wanted the hemline of her dress and how big the shoulder pads should be. Vain and critical about herself, as she was about everyone around her, Anne thought her best feature was her hair. And that fiddling with it all the time was the best way to make sure it was still there.

Both daughters had health problems that concerned their parents. Margot had stomachaches too frequently, and Anne was frail with a possible heart condition. She had a recurring fever and would have to stay in bed, resting for days at a time, something easily bored Anne truly hated. Her condition, however, seemed to improve as she grew.

Her mother was also concerned about things other than Anne's health. She appreciated Anne's talents as a comedian and was gratified and pleased by her close relationship with her grandmother and uncles. They were always greatly amused by her. Once, when she and her grandmother got on a crowded streetcar, five-year-old Anne asked aloud if anyone was going to offer their seat to this poor old lady.

But Edith wanted Anne to be more like Margot, to behave and listen when she was told to do something. Anne resented being compared with Margot, the model child, and it created some distance between them.

Edith disapproved of Anne's insistence on always being the center of attention. Anne was too talkative, forcing

Margot to take a backseat all of the time. She was rebellious, impertinent, stubborn, and headstrong in the extreme.

Edith agreed with Ruth Goslar: "God knows everything, but Anne knows everything better."

Edith believed Anne was spoiled by her permissive and indulgent father. His daughter's boldness made him laugh (at least most of the time), and her sparkling personality was the only thing that took his mind off his worries. The two of them had a special and strong attachment, coupled with an exclusive verbal and nonverbal communication. They would take long walks together and make up stories. When Anne would spin out of control, not an infrequent occurrence, only Pim could calm her, just as he did when she was an infant. Only now instead of songs and soothing touches he whispered reminders about self-control. Anne's invariably positive response was fueled by her intense drive to do anything to avoid displeasing her adored and devoted father.

She was truly a daddy's girl.

Edith and Anne clashed time and time again. From Anne's perspective her mother just wasn't the kind of woman she admired and, therefore, wasn't providing what Anne needed.

And Edith was having a difficult time of her own.

She resented being forced to leave Germany and was angry that she would never be able to return. She was perpetually homesick, enjoyed talking about the past, and had great difficulty adjusting to life in Holland. She did not make friends as easily as her sociable husband. He and the girls readily adapted to the customs of their new homeland. Margot and Anne soon considered themselves Dutch girls, no longer German. Unlike her daughters, who had effortlessly learned to read, write, and speak perfect Dutch, Edith gave up trying, even after a neighbor offered to help. Thereafter she spoke it badly and with a strong German accent. Both girls made fun of her, and Anne resented her mother speaking German. German was the language of Nazis.

A permanent bitterness was slowly settling over Edith.

She needed something to make her feel more secure and she turned to her religion. Margot joined her mother when she went to the synagogue and developed her own interest in Zionism. The Zionist philosophy of creating a homeland in Palestine for Jews from all over the world appealed to many young Jews. She also went to Hebrew school, something Anne, supported by her equally not religious father, refused to do.

Margot and Edith became closer as Anne drifted further and further away from her mother.

Otto and Edith's unpretentious elegance and genuine hospitality made their apartment the place to be. Margot's and Anne's friends loved to visit.

Despite her personal torments, Edith made sure that her home was just that, a home — with all the warmth that implies. She prepared excellent meals — stews and wursts — and delicious treats: strawberry tarts, rolls topped with cream cheese and chocolate bits, and cornflakes with grated apples and cream. She served cold lemonade and bottled milk when everyone else had their milk put into a can by the grocers and brought back to the house. Everyone loved the lazy Susan that sat in the middle of the large circular dining room table so you could spin it around and take whatever food you wanted.

Otto always had time for the kids. He tried (unsuccessfully) to teach Lies to ride her bike and successfully to feed her little sister — a famously difficult chore — chatting away amiably all the while.

The Franks' apartment became a social center for the adults in the area also. Miep and her fiancé, Jan, the van Pelses (Hermann, his wife, Auguste "Gusti," and their son, Peter, who was Margot's age), Friedrich "Fritz" Pfeffer, a dentist, the Ledermanns, and the Goslars.

Edith and Ruth Goslar often went to the synagogue together, and the two families frequently celebrated the Friday night Sabbath meal at the Goslars'. Edith welcomed the Goslars' religious observance while Otto and Anne respectfully (only sometimes in Anne's case) endured it. Margot soaked up the talk about Zionism and moving to Palestine, something the Goslars hoped to do one day.

The van Pelses, Ledermanns, Goslars, and Fritz Pfeffer had much in common. Like the Franks they had all fled Germany and feared the future. Otto pointed out during these dinner discussions that Holland had remained neutral during the First World War. He was sure they would continue with that policy. But privately he worried that the Germans would attack despite Holland's declared neutrality.

Increasingly they talked about the anti-Jewish laws that were being passed in Germany and the worsening situation there.

On the morning of November 8, 1938, they read about a seventeen-year-old German-born Jewish boy named Herschel Grynszpan. He had become enraged when he received a postcard from his distraught sister telling him that their parents, along with twelve thousand other Jews, had been forcibly taken from their homes in Germany and were being herded into "relocation camps" along the German-Polish border. Herschel was close to his family, and he decided that he would take revenge by killing a member of the German embassy in Paris (where he had fled to).

He left a note for his uncle:

My dear relatives, I couldn't do otherwise. God must forgive me. My heart bleeds when I think of our tragedy and that of the 12,000 Jews. I have to protest in a way that the whole world hears my protest, and this I intend to do.

I beg your forgiveness.

HERSCHEL

Boldly claiming he had important documents to deliver, he bluffed his way into the office of an attaché named Ernst vom Rath. Firing at point-blank range five times, he hit his victim twice. The wounds proved fatal, and on November 9, 1938, vom Rath died.

The act was followed immediately by anti-Jewish rioting throughout Germany. Thousands of Jewish-owned stores and businesses and hundreds of homes and synagogues were destroyed and set on fire. People fleeing the burning buildings were shot. Thirty thousand Jewish men were arrested and sent to "labor camps," and hundreds were humiliated and murdered in the streets. An untold number committed suicide.

At the time a portion of the German population thought that the riots were a spontaneous reaction to the news of the assassination. But that was just Nazi propaganda. In fact, Adolf Hitler, top Nazi officials, and the police had instigated and orchestrated *Kristallnacht*, the "Night of the Broken Glass," as it came to be called because of the shattered glass that littered the streets the morning after.

Herschel surrendered without a struggle and said:

"The Jewish race has a right to live, and I do not understand all the sufferings that the Germans are inflicting upon them. If you are a Jew you can obtain nothing, attempt nothing, and hope for nothing. You are hunted like an animal. Why this martyrdom?

It was not with hatred or vengeance that I acted, but because of love for my parents and for my people who were subjected unjustly to outrageous treatment. Nevertheless, this act was distasteful to me and I deeply regret it. However, I had no other means of demonstrating my

feelings. It was the constantly gnawing idea of the suf-
fering of my race which dominated me. For 28 years my
parents resided in Hanover. They had set up a modest
business which was destroyed overnight. They were
stripped of everything and expelled. It is not, after all, a
crime to be Jewish. I am not a dog. I have the right to
live. My people have a right to live on this earth."

His trial was eventually called off, and although it is assumed Germans killed him there is no evidence. His fate remains unknown to this day.

In September 1939, the German army invaded Poland, revealing that the policy of appeasement that England and France had followed was a failure. They had allowed Germany to re-arm and mobilize militarily and invade foreign territories and countries (Austria and Czechoslovakia), all clear violations of the Treaty of Versailles. Hitler's continued military aggression, now into Poland, forced the two countries to declare war on Germany.

Occupation

In the early morning hours of May 10, 1940, the German army attacked neutral Holland with no warning. They attacked Belgium, Luxembourg, and France that same day. Queen Wilhelmina came on the radio, which everyone was desperately listening to, and promised that Holland would not give up without a fight. She advised the population to remain calm. Three days later the queen was forced to flee to the relative safety of England. She continued to broadcast from London, assuring her country that the government would never compromise with Hitler and never give up.

There were conflicting reports in the early stages of the invasion. Telephone service was interrupted and people panicked, rushing to stores to stock up on food and running crazily in the streets trying to find out what was actually happening.

Some Jewish residents headed for the harbor, trying to board boats for England. Few got out.

German planes bombed Rotterdam, destroying the central part of the city, and dropped leaflets on Amsterdam warning that they would be next. On May 14, 1940, four days after the invasion began, the Dutch government surrendered and Holland was neutral no more.

German soldiers marched in the streets of Amsterdam.

The Franks, along with 130,000 other Jews in Holland, were trapped.

Within weeks local Dutch Nazi groups were insisting that Jewish-owned shops identify themselves. By the end of the year there were signs in coffeehouses, cafes, and restaurants saying that Jews were not welcome.

Beginning in 1941 and lasting for the next two years, a long list of anti-Jewish restrictions was put into effect.

≡ All Jews in Holland had to register with the authorities. Their identification books had a large J stamped on them.

≡ All businesses owned by Jews were to be reported. Jewish doctors and dentists were no longer allowed to treat Christians. Many placed ads in newspapers and magazines soliciting business from Jews to make up for the loss of their Christian patients.

≡ Restrictions were placed on the amount of money, jewelry, and precious objects Jews could own. Wedding rings, pocket watches, and four pieces of silverware per person were allowed.

≡ Parks, tennis courts, swimming pools, beaches, zoos, theaters, movie houses, museums, and libraries were off-limits.

≡ Owning radios, riding in cars, using public transportation, and owning a bicycle were forbidden. Even walking was restricted. There was no traveling without a permit, certain streets were designated as Jewish streets, and there was a 6:00 P.M. to 8:00 A.M. curfew.

≡ Shopping was confined to the hours of 3:00 P.M. to 5:00 P.M. and only in Jewish-owned stores.

≡ Jewish children were no longer allowed to attend school with Christian children — they would have to go to their own schools.

Faced with the overwhelming military power of the Germans, the majority of Jews and Christians cooperated. They feared that if they didn't things would get worse. And they hoped that if they did they could live through it.

Brave speeches by the Dutch government in exile and by England's combative and courageous Prime Minister Winston Churchill were intended to keep up morale. And there were reasons for hope. Hitler's plans for a quick conquest of Russia were stalled in the face of fierce resistance and the punishing Russian winter. After being attacked at Pearl Harbor on December 7, 1941, by Japan (Germany's ally), the United States had entered the war. Surely an invasion of Europe would come any day now. Surely the war would be over soon.

But day after day, week after week, Holland's Jewish population was being identified, isolated, and persecuted.

"Enjoy what there is" was one of Edith's favorite expressions. Now the Frank family struggled to do just that: to maintain a semblance of normal life in the increasingly anti-Jewish atmosphere of occupied Holland.

Margot continued with her Hebrew classes and joined a Zionist youth organization. There she talked with her friends about the anti-Jewish laws that were being passed.

They also debated their faith in God and the pride or shame they felt because they were Jewish.

Otto Frank, tenaciously clinging to his belief that Germany was the home of Goethe and Schiller and not Hitler and Goebbels, hired a journalist to give Margot and her friends lessons in German literature.

Somehow Margot managed to concentrate on her schoolwork and continued to earn excellent grades. She tried not to show how worried she was but her stomach problem betrayed her inner turmoil.

In April 1940, Anne and Margot continued writing to their two American pen-pal sisters, ten-year-old Juanita and fourteen-year-old Betty Wagner. (Otto translated Anne's and Margot's letters into English.)

Dear Juanita,

I did receive your letter and want to answer you as quick as possible. Margot and myself are the only children in our house. Our grandma is living with us. My father has an office and mother is busy at home. I live not far from school and I am sitting in the fifth class. We have no hour-classes we may do what we prefer, of course we must get to a certain goal. Your mother will certainly know this system, it is called Montessori. We have little work at home.

On the map I looked and again found the name Burlington. I did ask a girl friend of mine if she would like to communicate with one of your friends. She wants to do it with a girl about my age not with a boy.

I shall write her address underneath. Did you yourself write the letter I received from you, or did your mother do it? I include a post-card from Amsterdam and shall continue to do that collecting picture-cards I have already about 800. A child I used to be at school with went to New-York and she did write a letter to our class some time ago. In case you and Betty get a photo do send a copy as I am curious to know how you look. My birthday is the 12th of June. Kindly let me know yours. Perhaps one of your friends wil [sic] write first to my girl friend, for she also cannot write English but her father or mother will translate the letter.

Hoping to hear from you I remain
your Dutch friend
Annelies Marie Frank

Anne enclosed a letter from Margot for Betty:

Dear Betty Ann,

I have only received your letter about a week ago and had no time to answer right away. It is Sunday today, so I can take the time to write. During the week I am very busy as I have to work for school at home every day.

Our school begins at 9 A.M. till noon then I go home by my bicycle (if the weather is bad I go by bus and stay at school) and return for class beginning at half past one; we then have clas [sic] until three o'clock. Wednesday and Sunday afternoons we are free and use our time to play tennis and row. In the winter we play hockey or go skating if it is could [sic] enough. This year it was unusually cold and all the canals were frozen; today is the first really spring day, the sun shining bright and warm. Generally we have lots of rain.

In the summer we have a two months holiday, then a fortnight at Christmas and so on Easter; Whitsuntide only four days.

We often listen to the radio, as times are very exciting, having a frontier with Germany and being a small country we never feel safe. In our class most of the children communicate with one or the other so I do not know children who would want to take up correspondence. I have two cousins, boy living at Basel, Switserland [sic]. *For American ideas this is not far but for us it is. We have to travel through Germany which we cannot do or through Belgium and France and in that we cannot either. It is war and no visas are given.*

We live in a five room flat attached to the only sky-scraper of the city being twelve storeys [sic] *high! Amsterdam has about 800,000 inhabitants. We are near the sea shore but we miss hills and woods. Everything being flat and a great part of the country lying below sea level, therefore the name Netherland.*

Father is going to business in the morning and returns about 6 P.M.; Mother is busy at home. My grand-mother is living with us and we rented one room to a lady.

Now I think I have told you quite a lot and am expecting your answer.

With kindest regards
your friend
MARGOT BETTI FRANK

P.S. Many thanks for Juanita's letter as Anne is writing to her I need to write myself.

MARGOT

33

Anne had been sad to leave her Montessori school and the teachers were equally sad to see her go. But she enjoyed her new Jewish school. She and Lies were still together, but Sanne went to a different Jewish school. The two girls walked to school each morning and, although not initially in the same class, contrived to end up together.

Anne made another good friend in her new school, Jacqueline van Maarsen, who was called Jackie. They met the first day of school when Anne pedaled her bicycle next to Jackie and suggested that they ride home together. Within days they agreed on being best friends.

Jackie also had previously attended a Montessori school, (not Anne's), and Anne liked her for lots of reasons. She collected picture postcards of movie stars and also liked the Joop ter Heul series of books that was about a girl just like them. They read sections aloud and acted out scenes for each other. In addition, Jackie was quite knowledgeable about boys and other things, thanks to her informative older sister. Anne tried to talk to Margot (whose fully developed figure she was jealous of) and her mother about sex, but both were reluctant to discuss it with her. Her father pretended to discuss it but basically dodged the issue.

Jackie didn't leave with Anne for school in the morning because Jackie was invariably late. However, she accompanied

Anne when Anne went to be tutored in math and waited outside for her until she was done.

Reserved Jackie appreciated Anne's assertiveness, honesty, and sense of humor. Once when Anne came for a sleepover she brought, along with her cosmetic case filled with hair curlers, an empty suitcase. She just didn't feel like she was truly traveling unless she had a suitcase with her. Another time, when they were having dinner Anne abruptly announced that she had to go bathe her cat, Moortje. When someone pointed out that cats really didn't like to be bathed, Anne, clearly considering the remark preposterous, said that she had bathed her a number of times and Moortje never once uttered a word of protest.

And they talked about the Germans, about what had happened to their lives, and about how scared they were. Jackie told Anne about how embarrassed she was when she wasn't allowed in the pool along with the rest of her swim club. And about her cousin David who had, they recently learned, died in one of those so-called labor camps.

Unlike Jackie, who enjoyed being alone, Anne needed to have someone around. And even though she had three very good friends and an ever wider circle of acquaintances, she worried that she didn't have that one true best friend, that one special person she could talk to about her innermost feelings.

Anne read a lot — Greek and Roman mythology and genealogy were her favorite areas of study. In school she did well in subjects she liked, but in others like math (which she had to repeat in sixth grade), she struggled to get good grades and to pay attention in class.

Her math teacher, despite his good sense of humor, was annoyed with Anne's social activities during class. He made her write two essays, hoping to break her of the habit of talking while he was lecturing. One was titled "A Chatterbox." Anne's essay contended that talking was a feminine characteristic and something she had inherited from her mother, and therefore she could do little about.

Her math teacher appreciated Anne's irresistible sense of humor and genuine writing talent but not that she continued to talk just as she had done before. The third time he assigned a five-hundred-word essay titled "Quack, Quack, Quack, Said Mistress Chatterbox."

With characteristic flair, Anne turned the punishment into an opportunity to be creative and, equally important, to be in the limelight. She wrote a charming poem (with help from her poetic friend Sanne) about a mother and father duck and their baby ducks — who chattered too much. Her math teacher read the poem out loud, adding his own comments, not only to Anne's class but to others.

Of course he was not aware that behind his back Anne referred to teachers in general as "the biggest freaks on earth."

After school, Anne and her friends did their homework in the Franks' sitting room; Lies couldn't work at home because of her insistent little sister. They also played Monopoly in the living room and made sandwiches in the kitchen while feeding Moortje.

Anne enjoyed being popular and the center of attention, something her upbeat personality entitled her to. She drew people to her like a magnet; they wanted to be with her and around her. She and her friends formed a Ping-Pong club, since one of them had a table at home and Ping-Pong was one of the few activities not yet banned by the Nazis. After meetings they went to the Cafe Delphi or the Oasis, an ice cream parlor whose owners were Jewish. They had twelve-cent strawberry ice cream that they ate outside on the sidewalk while they watched the boys go by.

Boys interested Anne much more than homework. With her piercing, probing, gray-green cat eyes and intensely-serious-one-minute, hopelessly-playful-the-next openly flirtatious personality, Anne was popular with boys, especially older boys.

She was younger than her first two boyfriends, Peter Schiff and Hello Silverberg. Hello's grandfather disliked the

37

boy's given name, Helmuth, and had mercifully bestowed Hello upon him. Hello and Anne were introduced by his cousin. Hello had a girlfriend at the time but once he met Anne, the other faded. Hello's friends and his grandmother (whom he lived with) considered Anne much too young for worldly sixteen-year-old Hello. Hello thought Anne's friends were childish, and Anne told him she agreed. He was attracted by her unique personality and insatiably curious mind — an attraction that was only emphasized by her alleged youth. He accompanied her to school at times and they went on walks together, talking about everything under the sun.

Otto and Edith liked Hello: He was good-looking and well-behaved. Margot agreed, the two of them having in common the Zionist meetings they attended. And Hello fully appreciated the Franks' gracious hospitality and genuine interest in him.

Anne wanted her thirteenth birthday to be extra special. Something to take her mind off the ever-encroaching darkness of the outside world.

Being deprived of going to the movies was a particular hardship for Anne, who loved movies and closely followed the careers and private lives of her favorite film stars. She could easily rattle off who was in what film and what year, throwing in the reviews as well. She even fantasized about someday being a film star herself.

The Franks regularly rented movies and a projector and had the girls and their friends over, Otto on projector and Edith on refreshments.

That was the plan for Anne's birthday party. Anne and Jackie created official-looking invitations with the precise time, row and seat number, and warning that this was strictly invitation only.

Then they gave them out to everyone: friends, neighbors, classmates, and Margot's friends. This year, for the first time, everyone was Jewish. Some of Anne's former friends in the neighborhood were now wearing the uniform of the Dutch Nazi Youth Movement.

After dinner and a delicious dessert (one of Edith's strawberry tarts) the shades were pulled down and a film about a dog who rescues a lighthouse keeper was shown.

Anne received lots of gifts — almost to compensate for the grim reality outside — a blue blouse, Variety (the latest Monopoly-like board game), books, two brooches, and carnations from Hello.

But for Anne the highlight of her birthday was the diary she had wanted. Anne had decided with certainty that she wanted to be a writer, preferably a famous one. She had seen the diary in Blankevoorts, her favorite bookstore. It was really one of the autograph books she, Lies, and Sanne had been writing poetry in for years. The one she wanted was square with a checkered cloth cover and an oval clasp with a strap so she could lock it. She was going to write in it with her favorite fountain pen, the one her grandmother had given her.

Pim got the diary for her, as she knew he would. That was all that really mattered.

Otto made the adjustments necessary to continue his business. Because of another new regulation, he changed the name and legal ownership so that it was free of Jews, on paper at least. In reality he continued to run it as he always had.

The company had moved into its new headquarters at 263 Prinsengracht, right along the canal. It was a four-story building with double doors opening from the street into the warehouse. There were offices on the second floor and storage on the third and fourth. After a while they had expanded to the annex behind the front building. The two buildings were connected by a corridor.

Always plagued by an inner nervousness, Otto struggled mightily not to show the strain of walking the two miles back and forth to the office every day, of worrying about the business, of worrying about the fate of his family.

He and Edith tried to protect their children from what was happening in the world around them but it was impossible. They knew that Mr. Ledermann had already burned all the books he owned that were written by Jewish and other now-forbidden authors, fearing that possessing them might bring even more trouble. And there was nothing they could do to prevent the girls from hearing German military vehicles rumbling in the streets below their windows or the unnerving sound of night bombers as the British planes flew over Holland on their way to attacking German cities.

Otto assured Margot and Anne that Mr. Goslar's views were wrong — Germany would not win the war. America would not allow that to happen, Otto explained. And they believed him.

And they believed Edith was right as well when she told them to "enjoy what there is." They tried to look at things as positively as they could. Walking was good for your health. They didn't have to go to movie theaters to see films; they could watch at home. If they couldn't go to concert halls to hear music, they could go to Sanne's house and hear her parents play. Not being able to swim or play tennis in the summer or skate in the winter wasn't the worst thing in the world, was it?

In late April 1942, all Jews were required to wear a six-pointed Star of David made of yellow fabric with *Jood* (Jew) in black letters mocking Hebrew writing. The star could be obtained at distribution stations throughout Amsterdam and had to be paid for with ration stamps.

The star had to be sewn on — merely fastening it with a pin was a punishable offense — and placed breast high on the left side of an outer garment. It was to be worn at all times when outside (even on the balcony or backyard of your home).

One part of Amsterdam became known as Hollywood, another the Milky Way, because of so many stars seen there.

Many Dutch Christians also wore the star and yellow flowers to show their support. They considered this a shameful chapter in their country's long liberal history. After they were beaten by the increasingly brutal German soldiers and Dutch Nazis, their show of solidarity evaporated.

Some were not so sympathetic. They were glad to see the hated Jews finally getting what was coming to them.

Teachers in the Jewish schools did their best to convince their beleaguered students that they should look upon the stars as a badge of honor and not a sign of shame.

Little children seeing their older brothers and sisters wearing the star complained that they also wanted to wear one.

The star visibly marked the Jews of Holland.

As always, there were lies, rumors, misinformation, and self-delusion. They were just being taken to a labor camp. The Germans needed their labor because the war was taking so many of their men. Since they were needed to perform this important labor, surely they would be treated properly. Life in the labor camps wasn't so bad, some said. The work was hard, but there was at least enough food. The circular the Germans issued minimalized the threat. They said bring books, writing materials, postcards to write home, so how bad could it be?

But why had no one returned from these so-called labor camps, others asked. And what of the rumors that they were murdered there?

When the roundups first began there were warnings. People were able to sneak out to a friend's for a few nights if they knew they were on the list. Now that they had so obediently registered — just a formality, they were told — the notices for the call-ups were being sent via registered mail to their homes. Now the Jewish stars they were required to wear made them that much easier to identify. Now there was no place to hide.

Some looked to the Amsterdam Jewish Council for guidance. The Council claimed to be working with the Germans, helping them to communicate with the Jewish community. They were, they said, attempting to make the best of things. They urged compliance, not resistance, as the only wise path to take.

But some said the Jewish Council was looking out for themselves and their well-connected friends and they cared nothing for the rest of the Jewish population. They were collaborating with the Germans and saving their own skins, that's all.

No one was quite sure what the truth was and no one quite knew what to do.

One thing was certain: The roundups were tearing families apart, literally.

The teenagers who were being called up were old enough and smart enough to think for themselves. Some wanted to go, telling their distraught parents that they were strong, that working in a labor camp was something they could handle. By going they hoped to spare their parents further hardship.

But sometimes it was just the opposite. The child did not want to go but the parents insisted, afraid that if the child didn't go, the entire family would be jeopardized.

Some families chose another alternative. Whole families took an overdose of sleeping pills, sliced their wrists open, or closed the windows and turned on the gas.

The Franks had hoped they had put all this behind them nine years ago when they left Frankfurt. Now they knew that it had followed them.

Like thousands of other families they agonized over their limited choices.

Edith wanted to leave. But if they left Holland where would they go? Was Switzerland safer than Holland? Should they go to Palestine? Who knew what was there? Peru? Argentina? What about America?

They knew that the forbidding and complex American immigration laws were nearly impossible to overcome. The quota system wouldn't let them in unless they had an American sponsor — someone who would guarantee that they wouldn't arrive destitute and have to be supported by the government. And even if by some small miracle they did get visas, how would they live once they got there? How would Otto make a living? How would his family survive?

Some parents were sending their children out of the country without them. Even sending siblings to separate places, as a further precaution in a world gone insane.

Otto and Edith discussed sending the girls to live with relatives in England but couldn't do it. The family must not be separated, this much they agreed on.

They would remain in Holland. That was the best choice. That was their best chance. Otto was certain, even if Edith was not. Like so many other Jews trapped in occupied Holland they would go into hiding. But time was running out. If they didn't go soon it might be too late.

Otto knew just where they could go. He had been thinking about it and working on it for months. It was an audacious and, therefore, risky plan. But it was the only one that would allow him to continue to earn money and keep the family together. Soon everything would be ready. By July 16 they could go into hiding.

Sunday, July 5, 1942, was a sunny summer day. Anne was on the back terrace reading and soaking up the sun while her sister and mother were inside. Otto had gone out and was expected back around five.

At three o'clock the postman arrived with a registered letter. It was from the Central Office for Jewish Immigration and was notification that Margot was to report so she could be taken to a labor camp. The order said she should bring a blanket, food, towels, sheets, toilet articles, a plate, cup, spoon, winter shoes, socks, two pairs of underpants, overalls, and a suitcase or backpack with her name, birth date, and "Holland" marked on it.

When Otto returned and Edith showed him the notice he knew immediately that they couldn't wait until July 16. He had told Margot and Anne that they might have to go into hiding, it was just sooner than expected. His calm explanation did little to reduce his daughters' fears.

Otto wanted to go into hiding with Hermann van Pels and his family. But Edith wanted to be with the Goslars. Otto pointed out that Gabi was too small, and to make matters even more complicated, Ruth Goslar was pregnant. They couldn't consider going into hiding with a small child and an infant.

But that wasn't the only reason Otto chose the van Pels family. One of Otto's main concerns was seeing to it that the business kept running, kept making much-needed money for him and his family. Hermann van Pels was essential to that plan, and he would no doubt want his family to join Otto's in hiding. There was really no choice.

Now time was up. They would have to go — even if the preparations were not quite complete. Everyone who worked for Otto in the office — Kleiman, Kugler, Bep, and Miep — knew what to do. The trust and good will that had developed between Otto Frank and his employees over the past nearly ten years was about to be put to the ultimate test. He would be relying on them to save his life and the lives of his family.

And they too would be risking a great deal. Anyone caught helping Jews in hiding would be sent to prison, or worse. Otto had already spoken to each of them, and each had agreed without hesitation to do whatever was required.

For weeks they had helped carry in supplies, a little at a time: canned goods, dried vegetables, clothes, bedding, sheets, towels, cooking utensils, eating implements, dishes, and rugs. Furniture from the residences of the Franks and van Pelses had been "sent out to be upholstered" (so the children wouldn't suspect anything) but was really moved on weekends, at night.

Miep had been preparing for the difficult task of buying the food each day. A task made even harder by rationing and by buying for so many people — and not just people — Jews in hiding. She would have to be sure not to shop at the same stores so that no one became suspicious. Hermann van Pels had taken her with him numerous times to a butcher he knew well. He wanted the butcher to recognize Miep so he would give her extra rations for them when they were in hiding. Although Miep wondered why he would go to a butcher near the office rather than where he lived, she said nothing.

Jan and Miep (who were married by now) came over at eleven o'clock that Sunday evening. They put on layers of

Otto's and Edith's clothing and stuffed as much as they dared under their raincoats and into their pockets. After they unburdened themselves they came back for another load.

Anne wanted to know where they were going to hide, but her father would not tell her, even now.

Mr. Goldschmidt, who rented the large apartment upstairs from the Franks, decided this was a good time for a visit. His presence forced them to act as if nothing out of the ordinary was happening, an added strain on an already eerie evening.

As frightened as Anne was, she was so emotionally drained that she went right to sleep. At 5:30 A.M. Monday morning, her mother woke her up.

At 6:00, as agreed, Miep returned to take Margot. Her satchel was filled with schoolbooks and she was wearing four layers of clothing, but not her yellow star.

Miep had brought her bike over the night before. Margot had not turned hers in (as Jews had been required to do) because her parents thought it might be useful in an emergency.

Margot usually rode fast but that morning she pedaled at an even, unhurried pace, hoping to give the impression that Miep and she were just two Dutch working girls on their way to their jobs, as usual, on a Monday.

Margot had no idea where Miep was taking her.

Meanwhile Otto, Edith, and Anne readied themselves to leave. Otto left a purposely misleading note for Mr. Goldschmidt, one that would lead him to think they had departed for Switzerland. And it asked that a neighbor take care of Moortje, the cat.

They left the breakfast dishes uncleared, the beds unmade, and clothes scattered all over. All to further give the impression of a sudden, hurried leave-taking.

They too wore layers of clothing as well as hats and scarves. Anne carried her stuffed schoolbag, having packed her precious diary first, then hair curlers, a comb, schoolbooks, and some letters. As they walked through the steaming summer rain, Otto told Anne where they were going.

It was 7:30 A.M.

Cars drove by without stopping, knowing it was too dangerous to offer Jews a ride.

By then Miep had already brought Margot to the hiding place: 263 Prinsengracht. They would be hiding in the empty annex of their father's office building. The rear-building annex was connected to the front one by a narrow corridor and a staircase. It could not be seen from the street. They would be living on the second and third floors and in the attic space.

Although terrified and nearly in shock from enduring the past twenty-four hours, Margot showed no emotion. Soaked by the rain, Miep and she put their bicycles in the storeroom.

Miep led Margot up the stairs, past her father's office, up the stairway to the landing that led to the hiding place. Leaving Margot there, Miep returned to her desk.

Upstairs, alone, in the annex hiding place, sixteen-year-old Margot waited for her parents and her thirteen-year-old sister to join her.

PART TWO

HIDING

The Diary of Margot Frank

≡ A RE-CREATION ≡

JULY 6, 1942–JULY 31, 1944

MONDAY, JULY 6, 1942

I wish I could stop crying but I can't. It was all I could do to control myself on the way over here.

I'm so frightened.

The seconds pass by like hours and the walls feel as if they are closing in on me. I hope Daddy, Mommy, and Anne come soon.

WEDNESDAY, JULY 8, 1942

Daddy and Anne have been working for the past two days. Laying out the rolled-up rugs; moving furniture around; unpacking cartons; putting away pots, pans, and dishes; taking the clothes that are piled high on the beds and sorting them; sewing together material to make crude curtains for the windows and tacking them up. They've even scrubbed the kitchen floor.

Two busy little bees, chatting away as if there is nothing out of the ordinary going on here. As if we're on vacation and about to have the time of our lives.

It is all I can do just to lie here quietly, trying to gather my strength. Like Mommy I have been unable to eat anything.

THURSDAY, JULY 9, 1942

Since the occupation there hasn't been a day when I didn't feel the overwhelming burden of having to cope. Actually, it is quite remarkable how many compromises you can make; how much you can adjust to and still say you are enjoying your life.

This is even worse than when we had to leave Frankfurt. I don't remember being this frightened then. Perhaps I was too young to fully realize all that was happening. Now, unlike then, we are not going to something — to another country where we hoped to live in peace. Now we are running from something. We are "undergrounders," as the Dutch say. Like common criminals we are in hiding. As if we did something we ought to be ashamed of. As if being Jewish were a crime.

I do my best not to break under the strain. Daddy has enough on his mind. But just thinking about it makes me shudder.

I keep hoping this is some grotesque nightmare from which I will soon awake. I feel crushed by the weight of it all. We will never overcome the hardships that have been so unjustly heaped on us. Why do people hate us because we are Jewish? Even Daddy cannot adequately explain it to me, and as much as I read, I still can't fathom where all the hatred comes from.

FRIDAY, JULY 10, 1942

Anne was ecstatic that Daddy thought to bring her picture postcard collection of film stars. She has the energy of a thousand people and has wasted no time pasting them up. Her collection is so vast they now cover one entire wall of our small room. It does make it decidedly less dreary.

Daddy and Mommy are right next door. Mommy is trying her best but she takes everything too much to heart. She burned the pea soup rather badly, which I think is making her feel even worse.

SATURDAY, JULY 11, 1942

Not only did I break the vacuum cleaner but something "blew" when I pulled out the plug cord from the socket, and now we have no light.

I have a bad cold. Cycling here in the rain didn't help matters, I'm sure. In addition the building is quite damp. No matter how much codeine Mommy gives me it doesn't go away. I am forbidden to cough for fear of someone hearing.

SUNDAY, JULY 12, 1942

Tomorrow the van Pels family will arrive. We will have to accommodate living in these confined quarters with a whole other family. I can't even imagine what it's going to be like.

Daddy likes Mr. van Pels and enjoys his jokes. Mrs. van Pels is humorous in her own way. I don't know where their son, Peter, gets his shyness from, certainly not his parents.

TUESDAY, JULY 14, 1942

The van Pels family arrived yesterday.

Mrs. van Pels shamelessly carted along her chamber pot that she had concealed in a hatbox. She displayed it proudly for all to see before placing it safely under her bed. Mr. van Pels brought his folding tea table and Peter his cat — which I don't quite understand because we were not allowed to bring ours.

Mr. van Pels told us what happened after we left our apartment last week. Mr. Goldschmidt read the note Daddy "accidentally" left and reacted just as he hoped: Mr. Goldschmidt thinks we have gone off to Switzerland. Some of the neighbors said they saw all of us cycling away in the early morning hours and another said we had been taken away by a military van in the middle of the night.

Mr. van Pels told Anne about Lies and Jackie coming to call and how shocked and saddened they were to find that she and her family had vanished. They wanted to have something to remember her by so they took her swimming medals, even though they knew the Germans forbid anyone from removing anything from a house in which Jews have lived. It appears anything we leave behind they want for themselves.

SUNDAY, JULY 19, 1942

Miep and her new husband came to celebrate their first anniversary with us. Mrs. van Pels prepared a delicious meal and created a rather humorous menu as a keepsake. Anne named the restaurant "The Annex" and invented witty names for each course. One was named after the street the

Gieses live on and another after their butcher. They stayed the night, which was quite an exciting event for us.

THURSDAY, JULY 23, 1942

As I said it is astonishing the things you can adjust to and still maintain your equilibrium.

I wake at seven o'clock, the latest, and wait patiently in line to use our one bathroom. Everyone *must* finish their morning ritual before eight-thirty, when the warehouse workers arrive and the office is open for business.

After eight-thirty we have to keep our voices low, almost a whisper, and walk around in slippers or stocking feet. This is so that none of the warehouse workers downstairs or businesspeople who happen to come by the office will know we are here. No running water and no using the bathroom (we have to use jelly jars in the meantime).

During the midday break, when the warehouse workers are out having lunch, we can move around a little more freely, turn on the faucet, and use the toilet. That's when Miep, Bep, Mr. Kugler, and Mr. Kleiman come for a visit. Mr. Kugler and Mr. Kleiman bring Daddy much needed information about the business so he can continue to make important decisions. Mr. Kleiman brings bread (he knows someone who owns lots of bakery stores) and books, a rather appropriate combination. Every Monday Mr. Kugler brings Anne her precious *Cinema and Theater* magazine. Bep brings the milk and Miep gets the shopping list for the day, while Anne pesters her for news, any news, about friends, neighbors, anything, and everything.

At five-thirty, when the workday is over, someone comes up and gives us the all clear. Then we can walk around, flush the toilet, luxuries like that. We eat every meal upstairs in what is the van Pelses' bedroom by night, but our communal kitchen-living room by day.

Most evenings we go downstairs and listen to the BBC news from London on the radio in Daddy's office. At nine we move all the chairs out of the way, pull out the beds (Anne's is so short that she has to use a chair to extend it), and distribute the sheets and blankets, thereby converting our living quarters into sleeping quarters.

TUESDAY, JULY 28, 1942

It is nearly impossible to find someplace quiet during the day. Someplace where I don't have to listen to anyone's complaining or arguing. I read and do my schoolwork and shut out the rest as best I can.

FRIDAY, AUGUST 7, 1942

Mommy and I light the Sabbath candles.

TUESDAY, AUGUST 18, 1942

I wish Mr. van Pels would stop badgering me about my appetite, or lack of. Frankly I can't imagine why anyone would have one, considering.

The other night we had meat and eels and Mr. van Pels asked me why I didn't put some meat on my bread. Then Anne took some cheese and Mr. van Pels said that she couldn't have it because cheese was only for those who ate their meat, or some such thing. Then, of course, Anne and Mr. van Pels were off and running at the mouth. Anne loves to argue with adults.

SUNDAY, AUGUST 23, 1942

Mommy and Anne got into an argument about, of all things, barley soup. Anne complained that it was too hot, and Mommy said that Anne never eats anything that was too hot. Then Mommy insisted that Anne eat the meat that was in the soup, and Anne refused. Then Mr. van Pels said something — I don't even remember what it was (I try not to listen to half of what goes on at dinner). I was trying to cut the fat off my meat and Anne got mad because no one was saying anything about that, my cutting the fat away, and she went on about how everyone always picks on her.

I wanted to scream.

TUESDAY, AUGUST 25, 1942

Bep's father built a bookcase in front of the door that reveals the stairway that leads up to where we're hiding. It has concealed hinges so it can be swung open and will be filled with old-looking file folders from the office to further obscure the entrance.

WEDNESDAY, AUGUST 26, 1942

Anne has worked herself into a state because Peter and I are allowed to read books that she isn't, due to her age. She thinks Daddy and Mommy treat her like a baby and don't realize that she's not a child anymore. I must say she has a point. On the other hand, Anne doesn't like to be told no to anything, no matter what it is.

THURSDAY, AUGUST 27, 1942

More Frank-van Pels arguments over inconsequential issues such as who's using whose bed linen and dinner plates. Anne broke one of Mrs. van Pels's soup bowls, which led to accusations (somewhat valid) that Anne is not careful or considerate.

Daddy does his best to remain above the fray, quietly reading his beloved Dickens.

Friday, September 4, 1942

Anne is knitting a sweater and working on Daddy's family tree. I spent most of the afternoon peeling potatoes and scrubbing pots and pans with Mommy.

There is no more butter.

Monday, September 14, 1942

Bep told us that one of Anne's friends was deported with her family. Usually our visitors try not to tell us too much bad news from the outside world. And the newspapers they bring are heavily censored by the Germans. Still, we are able to piece it together and we can guess how bad it is.

Wednesday, September 16, 1942

Mrs. van Pels is constantly on Anne about her endless chattering. Although she has a point, that's simply the way Anne is and nothing on earth is going to make her change.

THURSDAY, SEPTEMBER 17, 1942

Mr. Pfeffer may be coming into hiding with us. I have met him once or twice when he came to the house and he seems quite pleasant, if somewhat standoffish. Miep says he's very intelligent and a good dentist.

SUNDAY, SEPTEMBER 20, 1942

Anne is working on her French irregular verbs while I tend to my studies. I want to make sure I keep up because I don't want to have any difficulties when I return to school.

MONDAY, SEPTEMBER 21, 1942

I am being driven to distraction by that awful Westerkerk clock that Anne is so fond of. The church is just down the street and it sounds off every fifteen minutes, mercilessly reminding me that I am trapped here and not at home, where I long to be.

TUESDAY, SEPTEMBER 22, 1942

Anne and I are helping Daddy to improve his Dutch, which is quite a chore. Peter is having difficulties with his English lessons.

SUNDAY, SEPTEMBER 27, 1942

More arguing, this time over the proper way to address employees. During the course of the discussion Anne told Mommy that she shouldn't say "servants," rather she should say "household help." If that wasn't bad enough Anne had to add that "after the war" Mommy will have to adjust to changes like that.

Anne says "after the war" with annoying frequency and Mommy is, to put it mildly, not as optimistic as Anne is and so it has become a constant irritant. Mommy questions whether or not there is going to be an "after the war" soon or that we will approve of its composition.

I find it all deeply disturbing.

TUESDAY, SEPTEMBER 29, 1942

Although it was quite difficult under the circumstances everyone tried to make Mrs. van Pels's birthday a special occasion. We prepared a nice meal: tongue, cauliflower, potatoes, and apple tarts for dessert.

Anne put a fur on Daddy's head, which was funny, but then Mr. van Pels snatched my glasses from off my nose and he put the fur on, which was even funnier.

All the people in the office gave her something, as did our family. Her husband presented her with red carnations.

I dearly hope I don't have to celebrate my birthday here.

WEDNESDAY, SEPTEMBER 30, 1942

More bickering about petty things such as dish towels and vegetables — who is and isn't cleaning them, and who is and isn't eating theirs.

Mrs. van Pels, it appears, has decided that Anne's eating habits are her concern. When Anne responds unkindly to her endless needling, Mrs. van Pels accuses her of being spoiled. Daddy and Mommy usually don't respond, rightly considering that kind of thing beneath them. Daddy did, however, point out to Mrs. van Pels that Anne has learned to tolerate her long speeches without interrupting, which he considers a sign of maturity. Daddy was using humor to make a point.

As if this whole discussion wasn't lowly enough, it sank even further with unsolicited descriptions of the various intestinal problems caused by eating vegetables, the details of which I would rather not record here.

SATURDAY, OCTOBER 3, 1942

Mommy and Anne are fighting again and this time Mommy started to cry. It doesn't help matters at all that Anne is so outspoken about preferring Daddy to Mommy. Anne must learn that, although she may feel strongly about something, some things are best left unspoken. Actually, it's my considered opinion that most things are best left unspoken.

SUNDAY, OCTOBER 4, 1942

Anne and I had a nice bath. We have to use the soap sparingly, of course, and there isn't actually a *bathtub*, just a washtub that's barely big enough. I enjoyed the soothing hot water and even more the feeling of finally being clean.

Each of us here prefers to take our baths in different places. Daddy in his office; Mommy and Peter in the kitchen; and Mr. van Pels in his room. As far as I can tell Mrs. van Pels has chosen not to bathe thus far. One has to wonder what the future holds as far as that's concerned.

Anne and I take our bath downstairs in the front office. We don't like to bother hauling the water up the stairs (we have only cold water on our two floors), and besides, we like to be in the office on the weekends, when no one is there.

While one of us bathes, the other can (carefully) peek out from behind the curtains at the people visiting friends and going places. Anne enjoys looking out more than I do. I find it frustrating because it makes me think about my own friends, Barbara and Jettke, and what they're doing now.

MONDAY, OCTOBER 5, 1942

Bep brought Anne and I new skirts from Bijenkorf's, which was so thoughtful of her. The material is a bit on the rough side, which is typical of the wartime goods we have learned to accept.

Bep also set up a correspondence course in shorthand for the three of us that I am looking forward to.

TUESDAY, OCTOBER 6, 1942

Yesterday Anne and I were reading together and she talked about how anxious she is to start her period. I think my sister is too eager to rush through her youth, even though it's only just begun.

THURSDAY, OCTOBER 8, 1942

More unfortunate news from the world outside. They are searching houses without warning and picking up people in the middle of the night — a job made easier for the Nazis because of the yellow stars all the Jews must wear. Jews don't dare go out without it. One man was taken away recently just because he took the J off his identity card. Thousands have been seized and taken away in the recent roundups.

SATURDAY, OCTOBER 10, 1942

Miep and Mr. Gies came to dinner and to spend the night. (Anne and I slept in Daddy and Mommy's room so the Gieses could have ours.) They are so brave. Miep pretends it's just the most normal thing in the world but we all know that the two of them, along with Mr. Kugler, Mr. Kleiman, and Bep, are risking their lives for us every day.

After the delicious dinner we prepared (topped off by spiced gingerbread, biscuits, and coffee), the men went down to listen to the radio. I don't like listening to the radio anymore. The Germans have conquered half the world: Holland, Belgium, Norway, Denmark, Greece, France — will England soon succumb? There are barely believable reports about the Germans killing Jewish people in large numbers using machine guns and poison gas.

Here, in Holland, Nazis are taking hostages and every time a German soldier or official is shot or there is an act of sabotage, a number of the hostages are executed in retaliation. No one knows for certain even if there really have been acts of sabotage or if it's just an excuse to murder them in cold blood.

Miep told us about Westerbork, which is the labor camp eighty miles north of Amsterdam where they are taking all the Jews they round up. She said they don't have adequate food, water, or bathroom facilities there.

I can't remember the last time I slept through the night.

TUESDAY, OCTOBER 13, 1942

Peter and Anne dressed up the other night. Anne wore Peter's suit and Peter one of his mother's dresses. It gave everyone a much needed laugh. Peter is, I think, a bit odd.

WEDNESDAY, OCTOBER 14, 1942

Mommy and Anne are getting along a little better, which is a relief. Truthfully I don't think we can afford

these petty squabbles. Our life is oppressive enough
without them.

I for one refuse to participate.

THURSDAY, OCTOBER 15, 1942

I was working on my shorthand when Daddy and Anne
asked me to help them with one of Anne's math problems.
It had them both stumped. Honestly I didn't think it was
that difficult and was surprised at Daddy.

SATURDAY, OCTOBER 17, 1942

We weighed ourselves this morning and Anne is
thrilled that she has gained so much weight — seventeen
pounds. She does look healthy, considering. She asked
if I wanted to help her with the office work she's doing
and I declined, which I think annoyed her.

SUNDAY, OCTOBER 18, 1942

Anne's finger hurts terribly so she is unable to do any
ironing.

She was able, however, to put up some more photo-
graphs from her film star collection. She put them up
with corners, so that they can be safely taken down

"after the war." I do not know how she summons up the courage to think so positively all the time.

MONDAY, OCTOBER 19, 1942

Mr. van Pels has decided he doesn't want to sit next to me at dinner anymore because my eating habits, which are too discriminating for his tastes, are spoiling his appetite. I haven't seen any diminishment in his appetite. I'm surprised he can eat at all, given the fact that he never takes his cigarette out of his mouth. I think the severe cigarette rationing is the real source of his current irritable mood.

It's quite all right with me, the new seating arrangement, because now I sit next to Mommy, which I much prefer.

TUESDAY, OCTOBER 20, 1942

We had quite a scare this morning. No one told us that someone would be coming to fill the fire extinguishers in the building. Thus, without warning, we heard quite a commotion right outside the door that leads to the stairway — the one hidden by the bookcase. Bep, who was visiting with us at the time, was therefore trapped.

We couldn't very well let her go down the stairs while he was there. We all listened quietly, waiting for him to stop. At one point it sounded as if he was knocking on the bookcase, which petrified all of us. Finally we heard Mr. Kleiman calling from the other side and knew it was safe.

As it turns out the hooks that allow the bookcase to be swung open had jammed, and no one could come up and warn us he was coming.

Our lives consist of hours of dread punctuated by bursts of pure panic.

WEDNESDAY, OCTOBER 21, 1942

Mrs. van Pels and Anne have discovered something new to argue about: Mrs. van Pels's rather obvious flirtation with Daddy. (Subtlety is not her strong suit.) She strokes his hair and reveals more of her leg than is appropriate or aesthetically pleasing.

Daddy, of course, pays no attention to Mrs. van Pels, a minor factor that doesn't slow her down one bit.

THURSDAY, OCTOBER 22, 1942

For the past few nights Anne and I have lain in bed together and talked about all sorts of things. I'm not nearly as comfortable talking about some of these topics as Anne is, but my sister is not familiar with the concept of embarrassment. Brazen is her middle name.

Usually Anne just babbles on about her most favorite topic, herself, which is fine with me. She's almost always entertaining and diverting, if not profound. I don't particularly like talking about myself anyway. But this time Anne seemed genuinely interested in hearing what I thought.

She wanted to know what my plans for the future were. I think she talks about the future — "after the war" — so much because it keeps her from getting depressed.

I think she misinterpreted my hesitancy in responding as secretiveness. Anne thinks everyone is like her and knows precisely what they are going to do for the entire rest of their lives. Of course the fact that she frequently changes her mind — one day she wants to be a famous writer, the next a famous Hollywood movie queen (famous being the constant) — doesn't truly register.

I must admit I did enjoy talking to her about my plans to become a midwife and my dreams of someday settling in Palestine.

I asked her if I could read her diary, and much to my surprise, she agreed. Anne is very guarded about her diary. Even before we went into hiding she was like that. At school or at home, she would hide what she was writing from presumably prying eyes with her hands. Here, if anyone comes near while she is writing, she slams it shut. She is much more conscientious about her diary than I am about mine. She works on it in our room and Daddy and Mommy's — never upstairs.

She wanted to know if I thought she was pretty. I told her she was and that she has particularly nice eyes, but that didn't seem to satisfy her.

FRIDAY, OCTOBER 23, 1942

Daddy began reading A Tale of Two Cities aloud. Now, too, it seems like the best of times and the worst of times. The best because of my family and friends and the life we had built in Amsterdam. The worst because of the Nazis who have ruined it all.

THURSDAY, OCTOBER 29, 1942

Anne and I both had colds last week, and now Daddy is sick. He has a rash and a high fever. Mommy is hoping that the fever will sweat it out of him. Of course, we don't dare call a doctor.

"Only his daughter had the power of charming this black brooding from his mind. She was the golden thread that united him to a Past beyond his misery, and to a Present beyond his misery: and the sound of her voice, the light of her face, the touch of her hand, had a strong, beneficial influence with him almost always. Not absolutely always, for she could recall some occasions on which her power had failed; but they were few and slight, and she believed them over."

— DICKENS

MONDAY, NOVEMBER 9, 1942

I was immersed in a book — reading is the only thing that takes my mind off my dismal surroundings. I put it down and went upstairs to get something to eat. When I returned Anne had picked up my book and was looking at the drawings in it.

Anne is easily bored due in large part to her microscopically short attention span — especially if she hasn't taken her valerian. She is always ferreting around for something to relieve her boredom, so she stumbled upon my book. The fact that I was reading it was of no concern to her.

Anne, who, with good reason, seems even moodier and more sensitive since we came here, apparently felt that the tone of voice I used to ask for it back was offensive or inappropriate in some way. She ignored me and continued to peruse the drawings at her leisure.

Mommy admonished Anne for her childish behavior and told her to return the book to me. Then, to make matters worse, Daddy came in and said something critical, also. Anne, predictably offended, flounced out of the room in dramatic fashion, leaving us to wallow in the gloomy wake she left behind.

She probably returned to her diary and wrote about how Daddy and Mommy favor me. (If this were true, why don't I feel that way?) And how they consider me the pretty one and the smart one. And how angry she is at them for always asking her to act more as I do. I wish she would stop complaining about that. And I wish she would stop teasing me about being a "model child" — I don't strive to be a model child, it's just the way I am.

WEDNESDAY, NOVEMBER 11, 1942

British and American troops have landed in Africa. This most welcome news, combined with the Russians' valiant stand at Stalingrad, has filled our hearts with hope.

Prime Minister Churchill said: "This is not the end. It is not even the beginning of the end. But it is, perhaps, the end of the beginning."

I think he is saying that it is going to take longer than we think. But the problem is, I don't know how much longer we have.

FRIDAY, NOVEMBER 13, 1942

It seems that Mr. Pfeffer is going to join us in hiding. He wants to wait a week because the Christian dentist he secretly works with still owes him some money and he wants to collect it. There was a long discussion about this and it was decided he has to be here by a week from tomorrow or that's that.

The plan, if he does come, is for him to go to the post office and wait there. Mr. Kleiman will then come by, bump into him, and lead him here — Mr. Pfeffer following a few discreet feet behind.

He is going to sleep in our room and I will move in with Daddy and Mommy. Having Mr. Pfeffer join us is going to put an additional burden on all of us, especially Anne, who has to share a room with him. But Daddy is right, the situation in Holland is worsening each day and we all must sacrifice so one more person can be saved.

As Dickens so eloquently puts it: "The common wretches were left to get out of their difficulties as they could."

MONDAY, NOVEMBER 16, 1942

Peter spends most of the day in his room with his cat, presumably sleeping. I must admit that he is handy at fixing things — he put up padding where we all hit our heads when we go downstairs. Also he seems to do his chores reliably, lugging the sacks of beans up from downstairs, getting the potatoes from the attic, chopping wood, and checking that everything's locked up downstairs at night.

The rest of the time he complains about one illness or the other, both real and imagined, and even wears a scarf to protect his neck from chills.

THURSDAY, NOVEMBER 19, 1942

Mr. Pfeffer was quite stunned to see us, thinking, as Daddy had planned, that we had all gone off to safety in Switzerland.

We were gathered upstairs around the dining room table, waiting with coffee and cognac. At first he thought that something must have gone wrong with our plans. He was duly impressed by our audacious hiding place.

Mr. Pfeffer said that he has been so frightened recently that he has been staying with various acquaintances at night rather than returning to his apartment.

His stories about the situation in Holland sounded so bad that now I think that maybe Anne is right. Maybe we are lucky to be here. (As always, whenever anyone tells us about what is happening, Mommy and Mrs. van Pels cannot hold back the tears. I do but it's not easy.)

So many kids my age have been taken away that the graduating classes at the Jewish schools have been reduced to a frightening degree. At one graduation ceremony a senior appealed to her teachers and parents in the audience for guidance. What should she do if she received a call-up notice as I had? No one had any answers for her. At another graduation a boy was taken directly from the ceremony and put into hiding by his nearly panicked parents.

The Jewish Council makes the situation even worse with their "exemptions," which means you won't be on the list for the call-ups. Naturally they are coveted by everyone. But people suspect the Jewish Council is corrupt. They give the "exemptions" to their friends, relatives, and those who can pay for them.

German military vehicles go from street to street in search of Jews. People sit in darkened rooms night after night, their bags packed, shaking with fear, wondering if it will be the last night they will sleep in their own beds. If tonight will be the night they are dragged away to some God-forsaken place. They sit and listen intently for the sound of vehicles stopping in front of their apartment, of doorbells ringing, of steps running up the stairs.

They dread waking in the morning and seeing who in the neighborhood is left. They watch helplessly as the moving vans remove the furniture from the homes of those taken away during the night. Furniture to be sent back to Germany for use by German citizens. Christian German citizens.

There are stories of mothers cradling babies in their arms and jumping off the backs of the trucks, running crazily from apartment building to apartment building, desperately looking for Jewish names on the mailboxes, hoping that whoever answers will be kind enough and brave enough to let them in.

People are being dragged out of old-age homes and there are rumors — hideous, bizarre, unbelievable rumors — that Jewish children, younger than me, are being murdered by poison gas.

Mr. Pfeffer has so many questions and he never asks only once. What is the procedure and schedule for the bathroom? What are the rules about noise? He appears to be in shock, and who can blame him?

FRIDAY, NOVEMBER 20, 1942

Mommy lights Sabbath candles while Mr. Pfeffer leads us in prayer.

SATURDAY, NOVEMBER 28, 1942

We have exceeded our electricity ration and will have to be more careful in the future. Now it is too dark to read after four-thirty.

Another stone added to our already heavy load.

FRIDAY, DECEMBER 4, 1942

Mr. Pfeffer and Anne don't seem to be getting along well at all. I don't know who is at fault but Anne is right about one thing: He does have a tendency to make tediously long, sanctimonious speeches.

MONDAY, DECEMBER 7, 1942

We celebrated Chanuka and Saint Nicholas's Day jointly as they fell so very close together this year. We lit candles and gave one another presents: flowers, chocolate, cigarettes (guess who), more chocolates, and sewing boxes.

THURSDAY, DECEMBER 10, 1942

Mr. van Pels is making sausages and some of them have to dry out so they are hung all around the dining room, which adds a note of pathetic humor to our otherwise humorless environment.

FRIDAY, DECEMBER 11, 1942

Mrs. van Pels was Mr. Pfeffer's first patient here and quite an impatient (and noisy) one she was. He had to use cologne instead of the proper disinfectant and vaseline instead of wax.

SATURDAY, DECEMBER 12, 1942

Peeling potatoes while Mommy irons.
Bratwurst and sauerkraut for dinner.

SUNDAY, DECEMBER 13, 1942

Yesterday we had a nice warm bath downstairs in the front office. Anne and I talked about the street urchins — as she so accurately calls them — who roam around the neighborhood. Like characters out of one of Daddy's Dickens stories, they don't have the proper clothing and are so hungry they eat scraps of food off the street. Some, the bolder ones I would imagine (though maybe they are just the hungrier, more desperate ones), stop people walking by and beg for food.

TUESDAY, DECEMBER 22, 1942

Mr. Pfeffer and my sister are certainly having their difficulties. He objects to Anne's talking so much and is constantly shushing her. He might as well object to the ocean having waves. He gets up early to do his arm-flapping exercises (as Anne describes them) and wakes her up, even on Sunday mornings. She says he is driving her absolutely mad.

TUESDAY, JANUARY 5, 1943

Anne had another fight with Mrs. van Pels. I don't know why Anne just doesn't ignore her. As Mommy so succinctly puts it, Mrs. van Pels is just too stupid to argue with.

WEDNESDAY, JANUARY 6, 1943

I have a constant headache that I am unable to rid myself of.

WEDNESDAY, JANUARY 13, 1943

Every night British bombers fly directly overhead on their way to destroying German cities. Although our spirits are lifted by this, sleeping through the night is becoming an impossibility. The piercing sound of the air-raid sirens begins just as soon as the planes cross the coastline. This is invariably followed by machine-gun and antiaircraft fire. Sometimes there are even midair battles between British and German planes — they are so near we can actually hear the engines' drone.

We are all worried that one of the bombs might fall near us and start a fire. This old wooden building would go up in a minute and then we would have to run out into the street. We have bags packed just in case, but everyone hopes it won't come to that.

Most nights Anne is so frightened that she comes in and gets into bed with Daddy or lies down on the floor next to him, wrapped up cocoonlike in her blankets (sometimes she's so frightened she won't go to the bathroom until she hears that he is going). She says she feels safe and protected being near him. If only that were true. If only being near Daddy could truly protect us from all of this.

The other night Anne wanted to light a candle because the utter darkness in here makes all of this just that much worse. Daddy wouldn't allow it because it is too risky — what if someone saw there was a light on? But Mommy came to Anne's defense, lighting the candle herself and telling Daddy Anne was not, like him, a veteran soldier.

MONDAY, JANUARY 18, 1943
Daddy is endlessly inventive. He has created a file card system whereby we make note of all the books we read. The information includes title, author, publisher, date read, etc., etc. We treat each book we get as a precious commodity to be passed from person to person. We discuss them endlessly to pass the time, but I would much rather

read a book than talk about it. Currently I am reading Goethe's *The Sorrows of Young Werther*, which I find most enjoyable, although slow going.

WEDNESDAY, FEBRUARY 3, 1943

Mr. van Pels is *still* complaining about my eating habits. This despite no one, including his wife, paying any attention to him. He thinks I'm trying to maintain my figure. He doesn't see how ludicrous it is: as if having an appetite, living the way we do, is normal and not having one is abnormal. I simply try to eat healthy things like fruits and vegetables, not that I tell him that. Indeed it isn't any of his business, so I simply don't respond to him.

Fortunately Mommy couldn't stand his diatribe one more second and snapped at him, putting an instant end to it. Mrs. van Pels turned beet red when Mommy intervened, although I'm not sure if it was because she was embarrassed by her husband or angry at Mommy.

THURSDAY, FEBRUARY 11, 1943

In my estimation all the petty quarrels that are always taking place between one resident or the other (present company excluded) are the result of living in such close proximity. There is absolutely no privacy here — something you take for granted until you have it taken away from you.

TUESDAY, FEBRUARY 16, 1943

The most disappointing birthday of my life and the less said about it the better.

MONDAY, FEBRUARY 22, 1943

Mr. and Mrs. van Pels are the opposite of Daddy and Mommy. Daddy and Mommy are so civilized and discreet when they disagree. But the van Pelses don't care what they say to each other or who hears it.

WEDNESDAY, FEBRUARY 24, 1943

That clock is driving me crazy.

THURSDAY, FEBRUARY 25, 1943

The van Pelses have been arguing in the most frightful fashion, screaming wretched things at each other, stamping their feet (not during business hours, of course); neither one listening to a word the other is saying (not that either one is saying anything worthwhile).

Sometimes Daddy and Mommy listen intently to the

argument, trying to judge whether or not it is becoming so bad that they will have to intervene.

After the storm has blown over they have these lovey-dovey reconciliations, complete with cute nicknames. (Kerli is his for her and Putti is hers for him.) It's absolutely nauseating. If you ask me it's no mystery why Peter is as forlorn and lost as he is.

FRIDAY, MARCH 5, 1943
Reading Heine:

How love and faith and humor
Had disappeared from the earth,
How the price of coffee had risen,
And how little a mark was worth.

Gone are the childish pretendings,
And everything else rolls past,
Money and world and eras,
And faith and love and trust.

TUESDAY, MARCH 9, 1943
When Anne feels blue she sometimes takes to wandering from room to room, like a ghost in that ghastly

90

nightdress she insists on wearing. Other times she just sleeps most of the day.

I think Anne's exuberant personality helps her hide from her fears — fears about what will become of us. Her bravery is formidable but is being sorely tested here.

That's one of the differences between us — I don't pretend not to be scared.

MONDAY, MARCH 15, 1943

Shadow kisses, shadow bliss,
Shadow life, forever gay!
Do you think, dear foolishness,
Everything is here to stay?

What we lovingly possessed,
Fades away like reverie;
Hearts grow heedless in the breast,
Eyes forget to see.

— Heine

TUESDAY, MARCH 23, 1943

I had a handsome homeland long ago.
The oak there grew so tall,

Meek violets curtsied low.
I dreamed it all.

In German I was kissed, in German heard
(Hard to believe how sweet they seemed)
The words "I love you" then!
It was all dreamed.

— Heine

FRIDAY, MARCH 26, 1943

Last night Peter heard someone fiddling with the warehouse door and came and whispered something about it to Daddy. The two of them went downstairs to investigate while I tried to calm down Anne, who was as usual a nervous wreck and white as a sheet (which is not to say I wasn't; I just control it).

As it turned out there was indeed someone down there. We all scurried upstairs and sat quietly for hours, waiting it out, hoping for the best. Mr. van Pels had a bad cold and his coughing was making us all nervous. We gave him some codeine that fortunately worked at once. It was quite a while before Daddy came up and reported it was all right.

The shortage of food and the severity of general

92

rationing has resulted in a sharp increase in the number of burglaries in the area. We are tormented by the ever present possibility that someone might break in — looking for something to steal and sell on the black market. They then might hear us and call the police. So many people are eager to collect the reward for turning in Jews in hiding.

We must be more careful. Even something you wouldn't normally think twice about — like leaving the chairs where they are downstairs after listening to the wireless. Even just leaving the wireless tuned to the BBC could mean the end for us if someone breaks in and discovers it.

SATURDAY, MARCH 27, 1943

We have rats, of all things. As if there aren't enough rats around outside, we have to have them inside as well. When Peter went to get some old newspapers he put his hand on the trapdoor leading up to the attic and a rat bit his hand, actually drawing blood.

Peter is going to have his cat sleep there, which will hopefully have an effect.

SUNDAY, MARCH 28, 1943

We listened to Hans Rauter give a speech on the radio. He is the head of the Nazi police. He said that all Jews have to be out of Germany and any of the countries currently occupied by July 1.

It's hard to believe that all this is really happening. That people are actually able to convince themselves that there is someone who is the cause of all their trouble. That all they have to do is rid themselves of these people — these Jewish people — and all their worries and woes will vanish into thin air. As if life could be that simple.

THURSDAY, APRIL 1, 1943

There was an important business meeting downstairs and Daddy was very concerned about how it would turn out. He is frustrated that he is unable to run the business the way he has in the past. He wanted me to help him lie on the floor and listen. The meeting went on all morning and into the afternoon, by which time poor Daddy could hardly straighten up. Anne took his place but fell asleep. Fortunately I was able to report fully to Daddy all that he had missed.

FRIDAY, APRIL 2, 1943

Anne is so mean to Mommy sometimes. Usually Daddy goes to her at night but this time Mommy went because

Daddy was busy. She offered to say her prayers with Anne but she declined Mommy's gracious offer.

Mommy was crying when she returned to our room. "Love cannot be forced," she said, looking sad and stricken. She has dark rings under her eyes from lack of sleep and worries all the time. She sees no end to our plight and believes that the outlook is bleak.

Daddy tries to get her to think more positively, to take heart that the Allies are coming to save us, and to have more faith in the future, but I think Mommy resents his constant prodding.

She likes to talk to Miep, which I think helps. Even though Miep is incredibly busy when she comes up in the mornings she always takes time to listen to Mommy's worries, which helps relieve her burdens.

FRIDAY, APRIL 16, 1943

Anne thinks she is the only girl in the world who has ever suffered from being misunderstood; who has ever thought about her parents, friendship, loneliness, or the difficulties of finding someone to love for the rest of your life.

WEDNESDAY, APRIL 21, 1943

Listening to, or rather, should I say, sitting through, the dinner table conversation tonight I thought about how much I missed listening to Mr. Goslar talk about Palestine. I so long to talk again with my Zionist friends about our plans for settling there and building a better world.

MONDAY, MAY 3, 1943

All our clothes are the worse for wear. Daddy's trousers are frayed and his tie is dirty — I've never seen him look like this. Anne's shoes don't fit, she can't button some of her shirts, and her vests no longer fit around her not-so-skinny body. My bras are too small.

TUESDAY, MAY 11, 1943

Mr. van Pels thinks we might have to remain here until the end of the year, which is more than I can bear thinking about right now.

Sometimes I think Mommy is right and the war will go on and on and we will all grow old here.

TUESDAY, JUNE 1, 1943

The food situation here is dire. For two weeks we have had boiled lettuce and tasteless potatoes. We have to rely on canned foods: vegetables, fish, fruit, etc., etc. Daddy was so wise to think of stocking up on these items months before we went into hiding.

SATURDAY, JUNE 12, 1943

Anne's fourteenth birthday.

WEDNESDAY, JUNE 16, 1943

Nerves are on edge and tempers short. I remain aloof from all these petty arguments but am still saddened by them.

SUNDAY, JUNE 20, 1943

Anne says sharing a room with Mr. Pfeffer is horrible. He is completely out of sorts if he doesn't get his afternoon nap; continues to wake her early, even on Sunday mornings, because he insists on doing his exercises then; and spends an incredible amount of time in the bathroom. When she tries to go to sleep he tosses and turns fitfully and sounds like he is constantly gasping for breath. Besides that he snores terribly.

I can't judge these things because I haven't witnessed them firsthand. She's right, however, about his table manners, which are wanting, to say the least. He serves himself first and foremost (and the most) and seems totally unconcerned about how much is left for the rest of us.

WEDNESDAY, JUNE 23, 1943

Mr. Kleiman has obtained ration cards on the black market for us. Now we can get much needed items like clothes, medicine, etc., etc.

MONDAY, JULY 5, 1943

We have been here a year.

SUNDAY, JULY 11, 1943

Anne is having trouble with her eyes and might need glasses. Being trapped in here makes that somewhat complicated, to say the least. Mommy has been considering having her go with someone to the oculist. Naturally Anne was petrified by the idea. In the end it was decided that we simply can't risk it.

TUESDAY, JULY 13, 1943

The British have landed in Sicily, and Daddy says he has high hopes for a quick finish. We can't listen on the big radio downstairs anymore because it had to be turned in to the authorities. We have a little one up here that we can listen to, though.

Anne and Mr. Pfeffer have been arguing for days about the little table in their room. Anne likes to spend as much time as she can there. Sometimes she writes in Daddy's room and sometimes downstairs. But she can't write at the dining room table upstairs. There's simply too much commotion there and too many people with too much time on their hands.

It's really admirable how diligent she is about her diary. Although I find writing in mine comforting and illuminating I can't be bothered to record something each day and at such length as Anne does. Especially in view of how little actually happens here, at least as far as I'm concerned. But for my sister it's all one long, melodramatic movie, and each squabble and every quarrel is grist for her busy little mill.

Holding her fountain pen in that odd little grip she invented after she sprained her thumb, she spends countless hours agonizing over every word, updating every entry, constantly revising and rewriting. It's almost as if she truly expects that someday millions of people will be reading her diary. As if she really believes that someday she is going to become a world-famous writer. Well, at least it keeps her mind occupied.

Currently Anne is allowed to use the table from 2:30 to 4:00, which is when Mr. Pfeffer takes his afternoon nap. But she would like to use it more. Much to her credit she has tried to talk to Mr. Pfeffer, but he won't even condescend to discuss it with her. He claims he needs the desk for his own work that he considers infinitely more important than Anne's "childish scribblings."

Daddy defended Anne's writing, explaining that although it might seem trifling to Mr. Pfeffer it wasn't to Anne. Ever the diplomat, Daddy was able to work out a compromise. Anne will work at the table until five o'clock two afternoons and on weekends.

She and Mr. Pfeffer are not presently speaking.

FRIDAY, JULY 16, 1943

There was another burglary downstairs. They broke into the warehouse door with a crowbar or some such thing. They took some money from the cashboxes and our precious ration coupons.

MONDAY, JULY 19, 1943

Helping Bep with her office work (keeping the checking accounts up-to-date; filing correspondence; writing up invoices; maintaining the salesbook, etc., etc.), although tedious, makes me at least feel useful. Also, in some small way, I feel I am repaying her for her kindness.

They are all such angels: Mr. Kugler, Mr. Kleiman, Miep, and Bep. Bep is in and out and up and down all day getting small things for us. Day after day Miep comes and gets the shopping list. She then has to wait on line for hours and be sure to shop at various stores so no one will be able to tell she is shopping for eight in hiding. Somehow she manages to do everything competently and cheerfully. As if that wasn't enough she brings us books from the library on Saturdays, which I truly look forward to. I can survive without much food or water but I need to read.

FRIDAY, JULY 23, 1943

I told Anne I was thinking of signing up for a calligraphy course that is being offered by the same company that sent us the shorthand course. This managed, somehow, to become yet another argument between her and

Mommy. Anne wants to take the course but Mommy won't allow it because of Anne's worsening eyesight. She does spend a lot of time reading Greek and Roman mythology, doing family trees, and reading in general and, of course, writing in her diary every chance she gets. Mommy is afraid that taking the calligraphy course will be just too much for her.

SATURDAY, JULY 24, 1943

Anne took a survey about what was the first thing everyone was going to do "after the war." I agreed with Mr. van Pels about the long hot bath; Mrs. van Pels longs for some good pastries; Peter a movie; Mr. Pfeffer to see his wife; Daddy only wants to visit Bep's father; and Mommy wants a really good cup of coffee. Anne couldn't be pinned down to one thing. I think she just wants to be home, as we all do.

MONDAY, JULY 26, 1943

Air-raid sirens, shooting, and bombs falling all day long. It was so bad the house was shaking. The smoke from the nearby fires was so thick you could smell it and it turned the air gray. This continued through dinnertime, and we could hear the dreadful droning of the engines as the planes flew right above us.

TUESDAY, AUGUST 3, 1943

The van Pelses have been arguing all week. Mrs. van Pels cries every time she hears an air-raid siren.

TUESDAY, AUGUST 10, 1943

That awful clock has been silenced. The Germans need to melt down the bells for the war effort.

WEDNESDAY, AUGUST 11, 1943

The weather has been bad lately so there are no British bombers flying overhead and hence no air-raid sirens. Of course, this is a mixed blessing. The peace and quiet at night is welcome but the most important thing is that the war come to an end at the soonest possible date.

WEDNESDAY, SEPTEMBER 1, 1943

Sometimes at night, after the workers have all gone home and there is no one downstairs, the telephone rings. It rings and rings, and, of course, since there is no one down there, it goes unanswered. And sometimes the doorbell is rung as well. We never know who it is. It could be some of the kids in the neighborhood who seem to roam around at all hours or it could be the police.

Each night here is eerie in its own way.

THURSDAY, SEPTEMBER 9, 1943

Italy has surrendered to the Allies. We just heard the news on the radio. Maybe Daddy is right and this horrible war will be over soon.

THURSDAY, SEPTEMBER 16, 1943

Things are deteriorating here by the minute. There are so many individual quarrels and resentments spoken and unspoken that hardly anyone speaks at dinner.

Daddy has gotten tired of constantly negotiating truces between the always warring parties (present company excluded).

Anne's right, we have all forgotten how to laugh, but what is there to laugh about?

MONDAY, SEPTEMBER 20, 1943

Daddy measured our growth this morning. Anne is getting quite tall.

WEDNESDAY, SEPTEMBER 22, 1943

On top of our endless list of worries we can now add one more. Mr. van Maaren, who works in the warehouse, is acting suspiciously, according to Mr. Kugler and Miep. Although he appears to be a good worker he's always snooping around and asking questions about things that shouldn't concern him. Mr. Kugler found him one day scraping the blue tinting off the windows that overlook the entrance to our annex. Mr. Kugler had put it there for the express purpose of obscuring the view. When Mr. van Maaren is around our friends in the office are on their guard and especially cautious about coming up here for fear he will follow them.

No one trusts him but they are afraid to just dismiss him because he might then call the police.

FRIDAY, OCTOBER 29, 1943

Mr. and Mrs. van Pels are arguing over money again. The situation has been quite serious ever since Mr. van Pels lost his wallet and all the money in it one night when he was downstairs in the warehouse. Of course, now we all have to wonder who the thief is and does he know about us. They can't find a buyer for Peter's bicycle or for Mr. van Pels's suit, so Mrs. van Pels's clothes — her fur coats, dresses, shoes, hats, etc. — are the only alternative.

Mr. van Pels finally persuaded his reluctant wife to sell her precious rabbit-skin coat to a furrier that Mr. Kleiman knows. Mr. Kleiman got them a good price for it, but now they are arguing about what to do with the money. Mrs. van Pels wants to save the money until "after the war" when she can, once again, buy nice clothes for her wardrobe. Mr. van Pels insists they need it now for household expenses — meaning, I think, cigarettes.

After much histrionics (yelling, screaming, foot stomping, and weeping constant tears), Mr. van Pels prevailed.

SATURDAY, OCTOBER 30, 1943

Anne doesn't look well and we are all worried about her. She has always been frail and susceptible to any number of recurring illnesses. Mommy is constantly feeling her forehead to see if she has a fever and inquiring about her bowel movements. Mommy is also concerned that she is taking her valerian every day. Of course living here is certainly not good for anyone's health, mental or physical, least of all my sister's.

THURSDAY, NOVEMBER 4, 1943

Daddy insisted that I sign up for a Latin course with him. Honestly I'm not up to doing much of anything lately, but I have to admit that working on the Latin with Daddy helps pass the time.

MONDAY, NOVEMBER 15, 1943

Anne is upset because her favorite fountain pen — the one Grandmother gave her when she was nine and the only one she uses to write in her diary — was accidentally destroyed.

She must have left it on the table when she was writing in her diary. Daddy and I needed the table to do our Latin and so Anne occupied herself rubbing the mold off the beans so they could be cooked and eaten without making us sick. She seemed quite annoyed when Daddy and I arrived and must have left the pen on the table because the pen was cooked in the fire with the beans. Daddy found the clip of the pen, which was all that remained, in the stove.

SUNDAY, NOVEMBER 21, 1943

Mr. Pfeffer continues to complain to anyone who will listen that no one here likes him. (He does have a valid point.) He and Mr. van Pels are not currently speaking to each other, although no one knows precisely why. Of course the fact that Mr. Pfeffer refers to Mrs. van Pels as a not-too-intelligent female bovine and that Mrs. van Pels returns the favor by referring to his "finicky" nature might have something to do with it.

FRIDAY, NOVEMBER 26, 1943

My corrected Latin lessons came back and my correspondence teacher (who, of course, doesn't know my real name — she thinks I'm Bep Voskuijl) said that I was doing quite nicely.

SUNDAY, NOVEMBER 28, 1943

Anne was deeply troubled by a dream she had two nights ago. It was about Lies. Anne saw her in one of those horrible camps we have been hearing about. She looked pale and tired and was dressed in rags. She was hurt that Anne had left her to this cruel fate while she was safe, here, in our hiding place.

The dream disturbed Anne greatly. She talked, jumping from one topic to the next, about right and wrong and life and death. She said that sometimes she was so scared she just wanted to scream out loud. She says that she is losing what little faith she had in God.

I didn't really know what to say to her. Anne and I hardly talk these days, something I feel badly about. I wish I could bridge the distance that seems to be growing between us. I feel it is my responsibility since I am the older sister but it is difficult to talk to Anne sometimes.

Unlike my sister I try not to dwell on things like God. Of course maybe the reason I don't like to think about it is I don't want to admit that my faith is so precarious that under pressure — living as we all do now with the evil that surrounds us — I will abandon hope.

I'm not sure how I feel.

I just try to get from day to day without falling into the abyss.

WEDNESDAY, DECEMBER 1, 1943

There is only one solution to all of this: We Jews need our own homeland. A place of refuge that is ours, where we don't have to worry about fitting in or about being approved of. A place where we will no longer be the minority, tolerated when times are good and persecuted when a handy scapegoat is needed.

We will never be safe and secure until we are the majority and can dictate our own destiny.

We can no longer hope to be assimilated into the population at large, no matter what country we are born in: Germany, Britain, France, or America. It is not only Germany where hatred for Jews resides.

Daddy, I know, would never agree with me about this. His German heritage is too dear to him. But look at what has happened. He was wounded in the First World War fighting for his country; became an honest, hardworking businessman; raised a family and taught his children to know and appreciate all that is fine and good in German culture. He and Mommy have always considered themselves Germans first and foremost. Now, in an instant, they have become outcasts. Driven from their homes, forced to pack up all their possessions and flee. Only to be hounded wherever they go.

How right and prophetic Herzl was. Right that "We are a people. One people." And prophetic that, indeed, the time has come.

I only wonder if it is too late, not only for me, but for all of us.

WEDNESDAY, DECEMBER 15, 1943

I had a dream about Palestine.

It was just as I imagined it would be. Everyone was my

age and we were all working together untiringly and unselfishly. We were all pioneers in uncharted territory. Living communally, sharing everything. A whole different way of looking at life.

All my people, Jewish people. Every one of us utterly devoted to the higher cause of building a Jewish state.

I want to believe that Palestine is not just a utopian dream but a vision that can be realized.

WEDNESDAY, DECEMBER 22, 1943

Anne has a bad cold. She has to stifle the noise of her coughing by crawling under the blankets. Mommy plies her with one remedy after another: grape sugar, cod liver oil, calcium, milk and honey, hot and cold compresses, gargling, hot water bottles, etc., etc.; ad infinitum, ad nauseam.

SUNDAY, DECEMBER 26, 1943

We are closing out the year with yet more petty arguments and bickering. Recent topics of contention are which pots and pans to use and when, how to peel potatoes, and whether or not meat should have any fat on it.

Sometimes I think we should have gone into hiding with the Goslars. At least their babies were real babies. Grown-up babies is what we have here.

TUESDAY, DECEMBER 28, 1943

Miep made a Christmas cake with "Peace 1944" on it.
We can only hope.

WEDNESDAY, JANUARY 5, 1944

Anne seems so distant and distracted.

She asked me about the oddest thing. She wanted to
know if I remembered the time Mommy and I took her
for her dentist appointment and she rode her bicycle.
After the dentist we two decided to go shopping but
Mommy wouldn't let Anne go because of the bicycle,
which Mommy wanted her to take right home.

She wanted to know if I remembered laughing at her,
along with Mommy, despite her sobbing. She told me that
when our backs were turned she stuck her tongue out at us.

I remembered it vaguely, but Anne remembered it
with the utmost clarity, as if it happened yesterday.

TUESDAY, JANUARY 11, 1944

We have too much time on our hands. Too much time
to ponder, dwell, and obsess about our circumstances and
idiosyncrasies. We suffer without the daily distractions
we took for granted: school, work, friends, sports, social
activities, holidays — the common comings and goings of

112

the ordinary day. All the things that keep you active and occupied and prevent you from becoming insular and introspective in the extreme. All the things that keep you sane.

WEDNESDAY, JANUARY 12, 1944

Anne is, I think, developing quite a little crush on Peter van Pels. Frankly I don't think he can hold a candle to Hello but he is, shall we say, "eligible." Lately Anne has been helping him with his crossword puzzles, which appear truly to puzzle him.

THURSDAY, JANUARY 13, 1944

Anne's latest obsession is ballet, which she has been practicing practically every night. She's even made her own dance outfit — at least I think that's what it is. It formerly functioned as one of Mommy's slips. Her attempt to convert her gym shoes to ballet shoes was not quite as successful.

Last night she placed a cushion on the floor and held the heel of her foot while extending her leg — quite a feat.

SUNDAY, JANUARY 16, 1944

Mommy's birthday. The office staff presented her with a mocha cake made from hard-to-get prewar ingredients.

She fully enjoyed it — both the sentiment behind it and the cake itself.

Her birthday wish is to never see the van Pelses again for the rest of her life. They certainly are a trial.

FRIDAY, JANUARY 21, 1944

Mr. Gies and Mr. Kleiman talked about the heroic efforts of the Dutch underground. How they forge ID cards, get ration coupons, and steal registration cards from the files the Germans compiled so that the person no longer officially exists and, therefore, won't be taken away.

They risk their lives daily, telling one another as little as possible about their activities so that if they are caught they will not, indeed cannot, betray one another. They seek out priests who sometimes are willing to provide the names of good Christian families who offer to shelter Jewish children.

Then they try to find Jewish parents willing to place, for safety's sake, their precious children with these Christian families. They told how extraordinarily difficult it was for them, watching as the parents agonized over their decision, weighing one impossible choice against another. Should they put their children into the arms of strangers, no matter how well-meaning they were? Will this ensure that their children will survive? Does this mean that they will never see them again?

They told how difficult it was for them to watch the families cry as they turned their children over. Most, however, refused, believing as we did that the family had to remain together.

And the pain doesn't even end there. Once placed, the child might not be a good fit with the foster family or might accidentally betray himself. The neighbors might become suspicious. There are people all over Holland now eager to report Jewish children to the authorities and collect the reward. And so the children might have to be moved again and again.

There were times when they resorted to simply snatching children off the backs of German military trucks during a roundup.

One story was truly heartbreaking. A member of the underground was trying to persuade the parents of a young boy to let him take the child into hiding with a Christian family. The parents wanted to think about it overnight. When the underground worker returned the next day the entire family had been taken away.

MONDAY, JANUARY 24, 1944

Our dinner table conversation is less than stimulating. Most times we talk about how wonderful the meal is, a conversation which varies in length and intensity in inverse proportion to the actual quality of the meal.

Then all the adults (except for Daddy) tell unfunny jokes and boring stories that we've all heard so many times before that we can't wait till they end.

One wonders if Mr. Pfeffer really thinks any of us are interested in hearing how he learned to swim at the precocious (this is, I think, the point of this otherwise pointless story) age of four or the details of his wife's carefully chosen, expensive, and extensive wardrobe.

TUESDAY, JANUARY 25, 1944

The silly conversation we (Anne, Peter, and I) had a couple of days ago about the unknown gender of Peter's cat still brings a smile to my face. Anne and Peter are some combination: He's incredibly naive and my sister's fearless to a fault.

Lately sex seems to be her favorite topic, and I don't even want to speculate about what she and Peter are doing when they are together. They excused themselves so that they could have a closer examination and determine, with medical certainty, the cat's gender.

I stayed behind and finished peeling the potatoes.

SATURDAY, FEBRUARY 5, 1944

There are reports in the newspapers of a possible British invasion of Holland. This is, of course, the most welcome news. However (there always seems to be a however these days), there are grave complications to consider if and when it comes.

For one thing, British bombs might strike us and we might perish from a direct hit or from the fire caused by one that falls nearby.

Secondly, the Germans have said that they will do everything in their power to repel a British invasion, but if forced to withdraw, they will take the entire population with them. As absurd as that sounds, if we have learned anything in the past ten years it is that the Germans are capable of the most horrendous acts.

And there's more.

There are reports that the Germans will flood the entire country if the British invade. There are even maps showing which parts of Holland will then be underwater.

What would we do if the water from the canal right outside our door started to rise? Would the building collapse, since it's already wobbly and leans to one side even now? Would we have to abandon the building?

Anne thought the macabre turn the conversation then took was quite humorous: for example, Peter doesn't know how to swim; Mrs. van Pels doesn't have her bathing suit; should we get a small boat, etc., etc. Good material for her diary, I should think.

For me I find no humor in the situation.

TUESDAY, FEBRUARY 8, 1944

We have sunk so low that now a mere pin can cause an argument.

Two nights ago I was pulling the cover over me and a pin Mommy had left in a patch she had sewn stuck me. Daddy said something about Mommy's being too careless, which, although true lately, was all Anne needed. When Mommy came in Anne was quite mean to her, nearly accusing her of purposely leaving the pin in the patch, which was a foolish thing to say — Mommy would never do anything like that.

Mommy, visibly irritated, accused Anne of being sloppy herself, although some of the examples Mommy was pointing to were my things, which I admitted to but which did little good as the two of them are just constantly at each other's throats.

WEDNESDAY, FEBRUARY 9, 1944

Anne seems lost and listless lately, wandering once again from room to room, unable to concentrate on anything for more than a minute and never reading more than a paragraph at a time. She looks as if she's been crying again.

MONDAY, FEBRUARY 14, 1944

We were listening to music on the small wireless and Mr. Pfeffer was feebly fiddling with the dials in a futile attempt to improve the already quite satisfactory quality of the reception.

Understandably Peter lost patience with the whole thing and asked Mr. Pfeffer if it were possible that he might stop playing with the dials anytime soon.

I've never seen Peter look that angry, not even when his parents are picking on him (although he is more feisty lately than when we first came here, but then again all of us are). Mr. Pfeffer replied, in his typical condescending way, that he was trying to get it "just so." When Mr. van Pels joined in the fray on his son's side Mr. Pfeffer was forced to retreat and lick his wounds.

Mr. Pfeffer later told Mommy that Peter had apologized to him and he had graciously accepted. But, as it turns out, Peter did no such thing, and he and Mr. Pfeffer are not currently speaking.

WEDNESDAY, FEBRUARY 16, 1944

Another dismal birthday.

I'm eighteen.

TUESDAY, FEBRUARY 22, 1944

I think Anne's flirtation with Peter van Pels is escalating and becoming mutual. They both pretend not to be looking at each other throughout dinner, which is mildly amusing. And they spend a great deal of time in either his room or the attic. Anne says she likes to feel the sun and breathe the fresh air from the open window, look out at the chestnut tree and the blue sky with the seagulls floating by. She said it makes her happy, if only for the moment.

Frankly I don't think it's making Mommy too happy.

WEDNESDAY, FEBRUARY 23, 1944

The longer we remain in hiding, the more I think I will simply grow old here.

SATURDAY, FEBRUARY 26, 1944

Anne read part of one of her stories, the one she calls "Eva's Dream." It was quite good, although fragmented.

WEDNESDAY, MARCH 1, 1944

There has been another burglary downstairs.

Mr. van Pels discovered that the door leading to Mr. Kugler's office was open and the main office was in disarray, as if someone was looking for something. The projector and some important papers are missing.

Since the lock wasn't broken, everyone suspects an inside job, meaning Mr. van Maaren.

The burglar must have been startled by Mr. van Pels's entry and then ran. But this means that the burglar knows that someone was in the building, besides him, after hours. Hopefully it was just a common thief. If not, if it was Mr. van Maaren or someone else who now suspects our presence, then our lives are truly in danger.

We have little choice but to wait and hope.

Fear is our constant companion.

More arguments as everyone seems terribly irritable.

While we were cleaning up the kitchen (I hope some-day not to have to wash another dish or scrub another pan), Bep admitted that she was not very hopeful about the future. Mommy, who was trying to make her be pos-itive, said she should think about all the people who had it worse than she did.

Anne immediately jumped on Mommy, criticizing what she said to Bep. Mommy told Anne she should keep her thoughts to herself, something I'm sure Anne will never do.

Then Daddy got annoyed, which of course sent Anne completely over the edge.

I tried to calm her down, with little success. Anne per-sonifies the scientific dictum that bodies at rest tend to stay at rest and bodies in motion tend to stay in motion, especially her lips. Being quiet is not a natural state for her.

I don't think she realizes how impertinent she can be sometimes. I don't think that Mommy favors me, it's just that Mommy is so exasperated by her sometimes. And she thinks that Mommy doesn't want her to have her own opinions, but that isn't the case. Mommy just wants Anne to keep them to herself sometimes, especially around other people. Of course, now that we are around other people nearly all the time this is even more difficult for Anne than it was before. I think the situation is harder on her than any of us. We're so confined here that every encounter is a potential spark, every spark a potential flare-up, and every flare-up a potential conflagration.

SUNDAY, MARCH 12, 1944

Yesterday Anne seemed quite depressed and slept until four in the afternoon. We were all, naturally, very concerned, especially Mommy. I know Anne found all her questions annoying. Mommy is constantly inquiring after Anne's condition, sometimes on an hourly basis. The slightest untoward behavior by Anne gives rise to oceans of questions and concerns.

Anne put her off with her ubiquitous headache excuse. Anne told me once that sleeping is the only way she can sometimes escape the overwhelming sense of sadness that surrounds us here, so I suspect that was the reason.

TUESDAY, MARCH 14, 1944

The people from whom we get our ration coupons have been arrested. This is very bad news. We are nearly out of butter and margarine, which means porridge instead of fried potatoes. Mommy spoke yesterday about how dearly she would like a slice of nice, fresh rye bread.

Tonight we had kale that smelled so bad that my most dramatic sister ate with a perfumed handkerchief pressed to her delicate nostrils.

Truthfully I have no appetite.

MONDAY, MARCH 20, 1944

My sister is concerned that, because of her relationship with Peter (which is now in full flower), I will feel left out. Although I think it was thoughtful of her to consider my feelings I assured her that I wasn't in the least bit jealous. Honestly I can't imagine where she would get an idea like that. I haven't said two words to Peter since I've known him. Of course I didn't say anything about my true view of Peter. About what a dullard I thought he was. Nor did I say anything about his invitation to join them — an invitation I declined. I tried to tell her tact-fully that Peter was not someone I would ever consider having a relationship with.

I mentioned in the kindest way that Peter was more suited intellectually to her. I thought that was the best way to put it. Aside from his numerous shortcomings Peter and

I do not agree about religion. He once told me he would rather have been born a Christian and was going to become one "after the war." I could never care for someone like that.

I found her suggestion that I should look upon Peter as a brother incomprehensible. I offered, so as not to hurt her feelings, that I might possibly develop feelings for Peter someday.

I suggested that she might be misinterpreting my behavior as jealousy and admitted that in my heart of hearts I did hope someday to find someone of my own. I told her that the type of person I would choose for myself would have to be my intellectual equal and someone who would know me instinctually. Until then I was content to remain the odd one out. Given our present situation this is not about to change.

I assured her there was no reason on earth for her to feel any prick of conscience on my account because she spends so much time with Peter and she shouldn't for a moment think she was depriving me of anything.

I urged her to enjoy herself as much as possible, having found someone she wished to spend her time with.

THURSDAY, MARCH 23, 1944

A plane crashed into a school near here yesterday. Fortunately the children were not in it at the time, otherwise the damage would have been even greater. As it was, three people were killed and many more injured in the resulting fire. The Germans shot at the airmen as they parachuted to earth.

SATURDAY, MARCH 25, 1944

Anne is going nearly every night now to Peter's room. Mr. and Mrs. van Pels don't seem to mind much, but I think Daddy and Mommy are quite concerned.

MONDAY, MARCH 27, 1944

Mr. van Pels and Mr. Pfeffer tease Anne about spending so much time in Peter's room. "Anne's second home" they call it. I don't know which astounds me more, their immaturity or their insensitivity. My sister has to share a room with a man who is forty years older than she is. A man who, in my opinion, spends half his life writing letters to his wife and having Miep risk her life delivering them. Miep tells Mrs. Pfeffer that she doesn't know where he is and I think Mrs. Pfeffer is smart enough not to inquire further. Such are the times we live in.

TUESDAY, MARCH 28, 1944

The political debate continues and intensifies as the adults listen to the radio continually. Is the war going well? When will the British invade? Where are the Americans? Of course, what no one says out loud is will we be able to last.

WEDNESDAY, MARCH 29, 1944

Mrs. van Pels asked Anne if she could trust the two of them alone in Peter's room. Mommy has told Anne that she doesn't like the way Peter looks at her (Anne, that is) and she has to stop going up to his room so frequently.

It remains to be seen what Anne will do.

My sister is most willful.

THURSDAY, MARCH 30, 1944

Anne is very excited. Last night on the BBC, Mr. Bolkestein, who is the Minister of Education, Art and Science for the Dutch government in exile, made an announcement. They will be asking for those who have been writing letters and keeping diaries to send them to the government at the end of the war so they can document the civilian aspect of the war. So that future generations will know what we have had to endure.

Anne and I will both, of course, comply, but Anne sees this as a great creative opportunity and not, as I do, merely a civic duty.

She's contemplating rewriting everything she's written thus far, quite an undertaking if I understand her correctly. She's thinking of turning her diary into a novel of some sort called *The Secret Annex*.

MONDAY, APRIL 3, 1944

The food situation deteriorates daily. We can no longer hope to eat a variety of foods and have to be satisfied with whatever we can get. This means that sometimes we eat the same food day after day, for days at a time. Endive, spinach, kohlrabi, cucumbers, tomatoes, sauerkraut, kidney beans, and always potatoes.

WEDNESDAY, APRIL 5, 1944

Miep, Bep, and our other daily visitors try to hide as much as they can from us but each day they contribute different pieces of the puzzle that, when put together, is a Holland I don't recognize.

A Holland where people are cold due to lack of coal; wait in food lines for hours on end; can't leave their cars, even for a moment, because they will be stolen; worry that their homes will be broken into by roving bands of kids looking for something, anything, to sell on the black market; walk around in shabby clothes and worn-out shoes. (Even if you had enough money to take your shoes to the repair shop, it could take as long as four months and by then someone will have stolen them.)

FRIDAY, APRIL 7, 1944

Played Monopoly.

TUESDAY, APRIL 11, 1944

Last Sunday evening Mr. Pfeffer discovered that Peter and Anne had used the cushion he uses at night for a pillow to sit on up in the attic and Peter's cat was with them. He fears fleas — a valid fear, but not nearly worth the hysterical fit he threw.

After the tempest in a teapot subsided a real one arose.

At nine-thirty that same night Peter came downstairs, knocked, and asked if Daddy could help him with his English. As Anne pointed out, it was a preposterously transparent excuse. They then got the other two men and went down to investigate while we waited upstairs. We heard nothing for about fifteen minutes then a loud bang.

The men came up and told us to go upstairs to the

van Pelses' room, turn out the lights, and remain absolutely silent because they were expecting the police to come. Without any further explanation they returned downstairs.

A few minutes later they came back up and told us what had transpired. Peter had seen a large plank of wood missing from the warehouse door and, believing that someone was in the process of breaking in, came to get Daddy. When the other two joined them and they went downstairs they did indeed hear something. Mr. van Pels instinctively cried out, "Police," which caused the thieves to leave the building.

A couple walked by and shone their flashlight in. It was assumed they would call to report the break-in. Fearing the arrival of the police at any moment, we had to be quiet, which meant, among other things, not using the toilet (we had to resort to using Peter's wastepaper basket). To make matters worse it was Easter Sunday and the offices wouldn't be open until Tuesday so we would have to remain quiet for days.

Although everyone had to whisper, that didn't prevent them from panicking. Mrs. van Pels wanted to destroy the radio, and Mr. Pfeffer suggested Anne and I burn our diaries. As always I paid no attention to him, and Anne, who nearly had a fit, said that if her diary were to perish then so would she.

Fortunately the conversation went on to other fears, real and imagined. We were all terrified that we were about to be discovered. I trembled at the thought. What would I do? What would I say? What would they do to us?

The police did indeed come and came as close as the other side of the bookcase that hides the entrance to our hiding place. It was my worst moment. Fortunately they came no farther and left.

Finally Daddy used the office phone to call Mr. Kugler, who in turn told Miep, who came Monday morning and gave us the all clear. I didn't fully realize the awful state we were in until I saw the look on Miep's face when Anne ran up to her, sobbing, and threw her arms around her.

SATURDAY, APRIL 15, 1944

A number of changes have been made in the wake of the horrible scare last weekend.

For one thing a carpenter is coming to reinforce the warehouse doors. But also we are going to have to be even more careful. No sitting downstairs in the offices at night. Peter has to make his nightly rounds earlier. No using the toilet after nine-thirty.

MONDAY, APRIL 17, 1944

Peter didn't unlock the front door in the morning (it is locked from the inside at night), so no one could get in to work. He said he forgot. Mr. Kugler had to go in through a window and was quite disturbed at Peter's forgetfulness.

TUESDAY, APRIL 18, 1944

Gave my most grateful sister part of my chemistry exercise book to use for her diary keeping.

FRIDAY, APRIL 21, 1944

Everyone is even more on edge than usual. Mr. van Pels grows more irritable by the day without his cigarettes. Mr. Pfeffer never stops telling everyone what he thinks (he's an outcast, no one likes him, etc., etc.). Even Daddy looks like he's about to have a temper tantrum.

This is due, in large part, to the recent break-in. But also, I think, because of the incredible length of time we have been here. Almost two years, something none of us would have imagined when we began, not even Daddy. The strain is showing. Everyone gets on everyone's nerves more quickly and more frequently.

TUESDAY, APRIL 25, 1944

Daddy is sounding more optimistic about the course of the war than I've heard him in a while. He expects something big to happen within a month. Mr. van Pels disagrees. He says the invasion will never come.

I don't know what to believe.

WEDNESDAY, APRIL 26, 1944

Mr. Pfeffer refuses to obey the new, tighter security measures. He continues to go downstairs at night and sit in the office. He got into a heated argument with Daddy and Mr. van Pels, and both are barely speaking to him.

Mommy and Mrs. van Pels are insisting that he stop giving Miep letters to deliver to his wife. They rightly feel that it is too dangerous to allow it to continue.

THURSDAY, APRIL 27, 1944

We all have bad colds compliments of my sister. Mrs. van Pels complains about the lack of lozenges and tortures us with her horrendous nose-blowing.

TUESDAY, MAY 9, 1944

Daddy and Anne had a long talk about Peter. Daddy said he was disturbed to hear that she was more than

133

friends with him and that he did not approve of anything more intimate than friendship. He said that it was her responsibility to keep the relationship at a distance because boys can be counted on for only one thing, or words to that effect.

He told Anne that he liked Peter but that Peter did not have a strong character and she had to be the strong one. He suggested that she go to Peter's room less frequently.

Anne asked my advice, which I gave her. After that she wrote Daddy a letter, and from the sound of it, she didn't listen to a word I said, which didn't really surprise me.

The letter upset Daddy and he scolded Anne, saying that he and Mommy have always given her all their love, always stood behind her, and they were distressed to read her letter and hear that she seems to feel no responsibility for them.

Anne is now deeply upset and regrets, I think, writing the letter.

THURSDAY, MAY 11, 1944

Mrs. van Pels was cutting Peter's hair, as usual (Peter wears swimming trunks and sneakers for the occasion).

They got into an argument about the scissors, and Mrs. van Pels hit Peter, which is also not unusual. What was, though, was that Peter hit her back and then grabbed her arm and dragged her across the floor as she protested frantically and to no avail. He let go finally when they reached the base of the stairs leading up to the attic. I must admit that Mrs. van Pels's saving grace is that she can laugh at herself, which she proceeded to do, breaking the tension.

She blames the whole thing on our "modern society" that, she claims, teaches children to be rebellious and disrespectful to their parents.

FRIDAY, MAY 12, 1944

Daddy's birthday.

Presents: a decorative box, books, a bottle of beer, and a jar of yogurt, a tie, a pot of syrup, roses, carnations, and spiced gingerbread, which he shared with one and all.

I wrote him a birthday poem, as is our tradition.

THURSDAY, MAY 18, 1944

Listened to Mozart.

SATURDAY, MAY 20, 1944

Anne lost her temper again last night. One of the notebooks that she uses to keep her diary and short stories got soaked when a flower vase got knocked over.

She was near tears before she gave anyone a chance to speak and before she saw that there was no real damage as the wet papers were easily dried up.

Her reaction was so extreme and melodramatic that Daddy, Mommy, and I burst out laughing.

THURSDAY, MAY 25, 1944

The police broke into the home of the man we get our vegetables from and discovered the two Jewish people he was giving shelter to. He was, of course, immediately arrested. Besides our obvious concern for him, we now have to eat even less than we were. Since food has been scarce even before, this will take some doing. We will have to forgo breakfast and have porridge for lunch.

Each day we hear more stories about our fellow Jews being found in hiding and taken away.

Where does all this hatred for the Jews come from? As much as we discuss it here and as much as I read, I can't really understand it. Can all of this venom spring from the idea that "we" killed Jesus Christ? I find that difficult to believe. I think people just need someone to blame all their troubles on.

SATURDAY, MAY 27, 1944

All we talk about lately is the invasion — when will it come, where will it be? Some of us are hopeful, some not so hopeful. I'm afraid I, along with Mommy, fall into the latter category. Daddy and Anne are, of course, optimists. We listen to the radio night after night, hoping for news. Hoping for deliverance.

WEDNESDAY, MAY 31, 1944

It is unbearably hot in here and impossible to find any relief anywhere in the house. The windows have to remain closed all day, making it absolutely oppressive. Listening to Mrs. van Pels's threatening suicide on a daily basis, complaining about her shoes, and lacking clothing suitable for the summer makes being here that much more difficult to bear.

FRIDAY, JUNE 2, 1944

Anne says she longs for an end to this, no matter what it might be, even if it's bad. She thinks it would have been better, in the long run, if we hadn't gone into hiding.

137

That way we wouldn't have endangered Miep, Bep, and the others. She says that if we were all dead now the anxiety and torment would be over.

I wish she wouldn't say things like that. She doesn't know what she's saying half the time.

I just want it to be over. I want to go back to the life I had before all this started. Before the Nazis ruined my life.

MONDAY, JUNE 5, 1944

I must give Mr. Pfeffer credit, he is most consistent. No matter what is happening he finds something and someone to argue with. His most recent petty squabble involved Daddy and Mommy. The subject: how much butter he is entitled to.

TUESDAY, JUNE 6, 1944

D-day.

The Allies have at long last landed on French soil.

Hundreds of amphibious crafts are landing thousands of troops on the beaches; Allied planes are bombing the coast of France and dropping parachutists.

Prime Minister Churchill and General Eisenhower gave speeches on the radio. The American general, who is the commander of all Allied forces, said that this is the year of victory.

We all hope and pray that this is the real thing.

FRIDAY, JUNE 9, 1944

The Allies are progressing, despite the continued bad weather conditions. British and American troops have engaged the Germans. The radio broadcasts interviews with returning wounded soldiers.

It has been reported that Prime Minister Churchill wanted to land with the troops on D-day but was talked out of it by General Eisenhower.

We all (with the ridiculous exception of Mrs. van Pels) have the greatest admiration for Mr. Churchill, who, along with President Roosevelt, is doing everything he can to save us.

We must hold on, for the end of our time of trial is nearing.

MONDAY, JUNE 12, 1944

Anne's fifteenth birthday. She received art books, underwear, belts, a handkerchief, and assorted edible treats. I gave her a plated bracelet.

We ought to get an award for how well we have made do here.

WEDNESDAY, JUNE 14, 1944

The Allies are fighting the Germans, pushing them back, liberating French villages as they go.

SATURDAY, JUNE 24, 1944

The invasion continues.

The Russians are relentless and courageous.

We all have our fingers crossed.

TUESDAY, JUNE 27, 1944

Anne has become, I think, obsessed with the subject of sex. She said she thinks it's awful that everyone (and by this she means Daddy, Mommy, and me) always speaks about it in hushed tones and makes it sound so mysterious.

She complains that every time she tries to talk to one of us about it we put her off or, in Mommy's case, tell her to be sure not to talk to boys about it.

She thinks it would be better if parents in general and hers in particular would be more direct about it. She thinks all this stuff about "purity" and "the sanctity of marriage" is all just so much talk and has no place in her world. Her views are quite daring, but not without merit.

SATURDAY, JULY 8, 1944

Strawberries.

Someone Daddy knows from business got them for us. There are so many of them. We clean off the sand and make jam. We have strawberries with everything: porridge, milk, bread.

FRIDAY, JULY 21, 1944

A German general, along with other officers, has attempted to assassinate Adolf Hitler. Unfortunately the plot failed. Reports say that Hitler escaped with only some cuts and burns. The general was shot.

The attempt itself is, however, significant in its own right. If members of the German military see Hitler's madness for what it is, then the German population must also surely see. And surely they are growing tired of this senseless war. They will have only themselves to blame for all that befalls them from here on in.

SATURDAY, JULY 29, 1944

My sister and Peter no longer moon over each other during dinner, and Anne doesn't go up to his room nearly as much as she used to.

Anne says that their differences are coming between them. She also cites his penchant for swearing and talking about trivial matters.

Anne loses interest once she has captured her prey. She enjoys the hunt more than anything else.

MONDAY, JULY 31, 1944

Maybe I will be able to return to school by September.

PART THREE

DYING

Discovery

On the morning of Friday, August 4, 1944, a call came in to Gestapo headquarters. The caller said there were Jews hiding at 263 Prinsengracht. The department chief immediately dispatched SS Obersharführer Karl Josef Silberbauer to the address.

It was already a warm summer's day. The brilliant sun glinted through the trees that lined the canal, and its rays danced off the water reflecting onto the ceiling of the Opekta offices.

As she did every morning, Miep Gies first went up the stairs to get the shopping list for the day. She and Anne had talked; Anne as always had a thousand questions. Miep couldn't stay — she had to begin her work — but promised to return for a long talk later in the afternoon when she came back with the groceries.

Silberbauer and several Dutch police arrived in a car and parked outside. The doors of the warehouse were open and they entered the building and confronted Victor Kugler. Silberbauer said that he knew Jews were hiding in the building and demanded to be shown the office storerooms.

Kugler, seeing that he had no choice, led them down the hallway toward the front part of the building. Silberbauer ordered Kugler to open the bookcase. Kugler protested that it was only a bookcase but they both knew that Silberbauer knew better. The heavy bookcase, half-filled with worn-out gray file folders, was then yanked open, revealing the narrow stairway.

Kugler, a revolver in his back, led them up the stairs to the hiding place.

It was 10:30 A.M.

Otto Frank was giving Peter an English lesson in the small space just below the attic. Peter was having trouble spelling *double*, which had only one *b,* Otto pointed out.

Otto was startled when he heard someone coming up the stairs. Everyone knew to be quiet at that hour of the morning. Something was very wrong.

Suddenly the door opened and a man with a gun was telling them to raise their hands. They were searched for weapons and taken to the van Pelses' room where the van Pelses and Fritz Pfeffer were being guarded.

Then they were all ordered downstairs.

In the Franks' room Edith and her two daughters were standing with their hands over their heads. Edith looked distant, almost absent, Anne remained composed, and Margot cried silently.

Silberbauer wanted to know where they kept their money and other valuables. Otto pointed to the cupboard where the cash box was. Silberbauer, spying Otto's leather briefcase, turned it upside down, and shook the contents out. Anne didn't look as her diary, notebooks, and papers cascaded to the floor.

Silberbauer stuffed the now-empty briefcase with the Franks' money and jewelry and ordered a transport for his prisoners. He told everyone to return to their room and get ready to leave. They all had small bags packed in case of fire or other emergency.

Silberbauer noticed an army footlocker with Otto Frank's name and rank stenciled on it. Otto explained that he was a reserve officer in the German army during World War I. Silberbauer instinctively stiffened, nearly coming to attention. He was disturbed to find that Otto had been a German officer, and one who outranked him. Why hadn't he stepped forward before he went into hiding? They would have taken that into consideration. Given him privileged treatment.

. He asked Otto how long they had been in hiding. Two years, Otto replied to a disbelieving Silberbauer. To prove it Otto took Anne and put her up against the doorjamb where they had periodically measured her growth. It showed how much taller she had gotten since the last time they drew a line.

Downstairs in the office, Miep Gies, shaken by that morning's events, sat helplessly in her chair, listening. She heard heavy boots on the stairs and then Anne's lighter, almost inaudible footsteps. She thought how Anne had taught herself over the two years in hiding to walk so quietly she could hardly be heard.

It was one o'clock.

Outside Kleiman, Kugler, the Franks, the van Pelses, and Pfeffer were placed in the back of a windowless police transport and driven the five minutes to Gestapo headquarters.

They were all locked in a room where other people were already waiting on the long benches. Sitting next to Kleiman, Otto apologized for involving him. Kleiman dismissed his apologies, saying he did what he had to do.

Then he and Kugler were transferred.

Silberbauer interrogated his prisoners briefly and they were returned to their cells, men separate from women.

Westerbork

On August 8, 1944, the Franks, van Pelses, and Fritz Pfeffer were taken eighty miles north of Amsterdam to Westerbork, a sixty-acre camp created in 1939 by the Dutch government. It was a place where German Jews, fleeing their increasingly anti-Semitic homeland and hoping to find refuge in the nearby Netherlands, could be received.

In 1942, the Germans took over the camp. Inmates were now Dutch Jews forcibly taken from their homes. There were watchtowers and a high barbed-wire fence around the perimeter. Within that was a self-sufficient city containing a large, modern kitchen, a laundry, a post office, a hospital (with 1,800 beds, 120 physicians, and a staff of 1,000), schools (all children between the ages of six and fourteen were required to attend), a tailor, a locksmith, hairdressers, a book binder, and opticians. Activities included sports such as gymnastics, boxing, a choir, ballet, a camp orchestra, and a cabaret show put on by the prisoners that was renowned throughout Holland for its talented performers and hard-to-get opening-night tickets. All this was calculated to keep the prison population calm and distracted, therefore minimizing disturbances and resistance.

The Franks and the others were subjected to the tedious and humiliating registration process. They answered questions, filled out forms, waited on endless lines, completed more forms, and answered more questions.

"What I saw was a family . . . a very worried father and a nervous mother and two children. . . . They had sports clothes on and backpacks with them . . . and the four of them stayed together constantly."

JANNY BRANDES-BRILLESLIJPER

"Mr. Frank was a pleasant-looking man, courteous and cultured. He stood before me tall and erect. He answered my routine questions quietly. . . . None of the Franks showed any signs of despair over their plight. Their composure, as they grouped around my typing desk in the receiving room, was one of quiet dignity. However bitter and fearful the emotions that welled in him, Mr. Frank

Because they were arrested while in hiding, all eight were assigned to the Punishment Block. Unlike other prisoners they could not wear their own clothes. They were given blue prison overalls with red patches (identifying them as criminals) and wooden clogs that didn't fit. They were also given less food and more difficult work.

The day began at 5:00 A.M.

They took apart batteries with a small chisel and extracted the manganese and carbon rods that could then be recycled to aid the now-faltering German war machine. It was dirty, unhealthy work that resulted in constant coughing.

Otto tried to get better work for Anne, but was unable to.

"Otto Frank came up to me with Anne and asked if Anne could help me. Anne was very nice and also asked me if she could help me . . . he came to me with Anne — not with his wife and not with Margot. I think that Anne was the apple of his eye."

RACHEL VAN AMERONGEN-FRANKFOORDER

151

Anne welcomed the chance to talk to people and be out in the fresh air after two years indoors.

"In Westerbork Anne was lovely, so radiant. . . . She was very pallid at first, but there was something so intensely attractive about her frailty and her expressive face. . . .

Perhaps it's not the right expression to say that Anne's eyes were radiant. But they had a glow. . . . And her movements, her looks, had such a lilt to them that I often asked myself: Can she possibly be happy?"

MRS. DE WIEK*

"Edith Frank, Anne's mother, seemed numbed by the experience. She could have been a mute. Anne's sister, Margot, spoke little and Otto Frank was quiet too, but his was a reassuring quietness that helped Anne and all of us. He lived in the men's barracks, but once when Anne was sick he came over to visit her every evening and would stand beside her bed for hours, telling her stories."

MRS. DE WIEK

*A pseudonym

152

Those who were forced to exist at Westerbork did their best to keep their spirits up. They talked about the Soviet Union's Red Army advancing toward Germany; how the Germans were going to lose the war; and how it would be when it was over. Soon they could return to the life they had known. As long as they remained in Westerbork, in Holland, they would be all right.

By 1944, there were rumors — some felt more than rumors. There were concentration camps where Jewish people were being systematically murdered by Adolf Hitler's German government. Westerbork was now a "transit camp" — a "transit camp" to eastern Germany and Poland, where the concentration camps were. One hundred thousand people had been processed through the camp in the two years before the Franks' arrival. There were quotas to be filled, quotas for the trains bound for "the east." *East,* a word that once meant so little, merely a direction, was now a destination justifiably dreaded. Every Monday evening the names of those to be transferred the next morning were read out.

"In Westerbork one lived for two days, Tuesday and Wednesday. On Thursday you start to tremble. On Friday you were told that you were to leave on Tuesday. On

Saturday you tried to get out of it. On Sunday you were told you can't get out of it. On Monday you packed . . . as much as you can. . . . On Tuesday morning, six o'clock sharp, the cattle cars left for an unknown destination . . ."

JACK POLAK

The Nazis determined how many and when, but the Jewish administration within the camp determined who.

"When we heard that we were on the list, we tried everything we could do to change things, but it was no good. The people who compiled the list were mainly Jews, I think, and they did what they could to protect their friends and relatives. But for the rest, well, we just had to go."

EVA SCHLOSS

"On 2 September we were told that a thousand persons would leave in the morning. . . . During the night we packed a few things we had been allowed to keep. Someone had a little ink, and with that we marked our names on the blankets we were to take with us and we made the children repeat again and again the address where we were going to meet after the war, in case we got

154

Early in the morning of September 3, 1944, the prisoners began filing out of the barracks toward the trains, which came right into the center of the camp. The commandant, his dog, and the guards enjoyed watching what had become a weekly event.

Carrying their bundled-up belongings suspended by straps from their shoulders, as allowed, the prisoners walked in threes, as instructed.

They did not know for certain where they were going, but the rumors were terrifying.

There were 498 women, 442 men, and 79 children. Four of the men were Otto Frank, Hermann and Peter van Pels, and Fritz Pfeffer. Four of the women were Edith, Margot, and Anne Frank, and Auguste van Pels.

The train left Westerbork at 11:00 A.M. It was the ninety-third and last transport to leave Westerbork for "the east."

For Auschwitz.

All eight were in the same car. There was straw on the floor, a small bucket of water, and an empty one for elimination. There was little light and the only air came from a few holes in the roof. There was barely enough room to stand and the heat and awful smells were overwhelming.

"When the train stopped for the first time, we were already in Germany. Some bread and a pail of beet marmalade were tossed in.... We did not know where we were, since the train had not stopped at a station, but at a siding, and we could not ask because SS guards were patrolling up and down outside the train.

We stopped many times in the open country, some-where or other, and once the train suddenly started backing, so that someone cried, 'Look! We're going back to Holland!'

But we did not go to Holland. We went back and forth but deeper and deeper into Germany.... Now and then when the train stopped, the SS men came to the door and held out their caps, and we were supposed to put our money and valuables into the caps. Some of us actually had a few things left, sewed into our clothes, for instance, and there were some who took out what they had, flung it into the SS caps, and then the train went on. That was how it went, night and day, and night again."

MRS. DE WIEK

Anne watched through the cracks in the floor as the rails whizzed by and climbed up the bars so she could peer out of the small window.

"Mrs. Frank had smuggled out a pair of overalls, and she sat by the light of the candle, ripping off the red patch. She must have thought that without the red patch, they wouldn't be able to see that we were convict prisoners . . . for her it was important and she got some satisfaction from doing it.

Many people, among them the Frank girls, leaned against their mother or father; everyone was dead tired."

LENIE DE JONG-VAN NAARDEN

Auschwitz-Birkenau

Before March 1941, Adolf Hitler's goal had been the forced emigration of all Jews from Germany and recently conquered territories. Now that changed. The newly planned objective of the German government was the total physical annihilation of the eleven million Jewish people living in Europe.

In 1933, the German government began building a network of concentration camps. Some of these camps were for internment, some for forced labor, some in anticipation of deportation, and some, beginning in 1942, for the extermination of their inhabitants. Auschwitz-Birkenau was by far the largest and most lethal of these secretly constructed camps. The Nazis intended to keep their existence unknown to the population in the area, German citizens in general, and the world at large.

The site had been chosen because of its isolated location, which would help in that regard. In addition, there was access to rivers and rail transportation — transportation that could bring the people who were to be killed. Auschwitz's barracks, satellite camps, factories, and killing facilities eventually covered over twenty-five square miles. (For reasons of efficiency the SS — the branch of the German military responsible for implementing these plans — had turned from mass shooting to murder by poison gas.)

On the night of September 5, 1944, the transport carrying the eight from the secret annex reached its destination.

". . . the train suddenly came to a stop. The doors . . . were slid violently open, and the first we saw of Auschwitz were the glaring searchlights fixed on the train."

MRS. DE WIEK

"We were taken, with our baggage, to a large area that was lit up by extraordinarily strong lights — so strong that I had the feeling that they were moons. I thought, We're on another planet . . . and here there are three moons."

BLOEME EVERS-EMDEN

Trains were purposefully scheduled to arrive at night, adding to the feeling of confusion, helplessness, and disorientation. The night air was pierced by the fearsome sounds of barking dogs and loudspeakers crackling instructions: Anyone too weak to walk should board the nearby trucks with the red crosses painted on them. Kapos, head prisoners who helped the Nazis maintain order and discipline, hovered all around. Shaven-headed, strange-looking men in their striped uniforms whispered furtively, "Don't go into the trucks," to the uncomprehending and disbelieving new arrivals.

"A detachment of SS men with guns, whips, and clubs in their hands attacked us, separating the men from their wives, parents from their children, the old from the young. Those who resisted . . . were beaten, kicked, and dragged away. In a few minutes we were standing in separate groups, almost unconscious with pain, fear, exhaustion, and the unbearable shock of losing our loved ones."

DR. GISELLA PERL

Otto Frank, frantically struggling to make visual contact with his family, saw only his daughter Margot and the look of terror in her eyes.

160

"Now, with a handful of SS officers, the camp physician took over the direction of this infernal game. With a flick of his hand he sent some of us to the left, some to the right. It took some time before I understood what this meant. Of every trainload of prisoners, ten to twelve thousand at a time, he selected about three thousand inmates for his camp. The others, those who went 'left,' were . . . carted away."

DR. GISELLA PERL

Those judged able to work as slave labor for the Third Reich were spared. Those who weren't — anyone who was sick, disabled, over fifty, under fifteen (89 percent of the Jewish children in Europe were murdered in the death camps), pregnant, or a mother who refused to be separated from her children — were taken directly to the gas chambers.

Some were able to act transcendently:

"I came to Auschwitz August 22, 1944. I came with my mother, my brother, my father, my aunt and uncle, and my cousin. A neighbor of ours was with us. . . . He had a four-year-old child with him; he had lost his wife in the ghetto.

We got off the trains in Auschwitz and they separated the men right away. The women and children were on one side and the men on the other. When we got off the train and they separated the men, this little girl, the neighbor's child, was left alone. My mother (she was a saint) walked over to him and she said, 'Don't worry, I will take care of the child.' She took this child by the hand and she kept her, wouldn't let go of her. The child was alone and my mother wouldn't let the child stand alone.

Everything happened very rapidly. . . . My aunt was with her little boy in the front and my mother with this little girl by the hand and my brother, and I was the last one. My aunt and her little boy he motioned to the left, and when he asked my mother if this was her child and she nodded yes, he sent her to the left. My brother, being only twelve at the time, he sent to the left, and me he motioned to the right.

I realized my mother was on the other side and I wanted to run to my mother, I wanted to be with her. A Jewish woman who worked there caught me in the middle and said . . . 'Don't you dare move from here!' Because she knew that if I was on the other side I would go to the gas chamber. And she wouldn't let me move. . . .

This was the last time I saw my mother. She went

with that neighbor's child. So when we talk about heroes, mind you, this was a hero: a woman who would not let a four-year-old child go by herself."

Esther Geizhals-Zucker

Those sent "left" were told to undress and keep their clothes and shoes tied together. They were handed soap and the children were given toys. All to create the illusion that nothing bad was about to happen.

"... these men and women were ... forced ... to the 'Shower Room.' Above the entry door was the word 'Shower.' One could even see the shower heads on the ceiling which were cemented in but never had water flowing through them.

These poor innocents were crammed together, pressed against each other. Then panic broke out, for at last they realized the fate in store for them. But blows with rifle butts and revolver shots soon restored order and finally they all entered the death chamber.

One of the guards climbed up onto the roof, put his mask, gloves, and protective clothing on, and pulled a sealed tin up to him that was attached by a wire. The tin contained Zyklon-B which had previously been used to fumigate lice-infested buildings. He fed the green crystals into the duct on the roof.

The doors were shut and, ten minutes later, the temperature was high enough to facilitate the condensation of hydrogen cyanide . . . the so-called Zyklon-B . . . used by the German barbarians.

. . . One could hear the fearful screams, but a few moments later there was complete silence. Twenty to twenty-five minutes later, the doors and windows were opened to ventilate the rooms."

ANDRÉ LETTICH

Hair, gold teeth, and wedding rings were salvaged, as well as clothes that were sent back for German citizens to wear. The soap and toys were collected for use with the next group.

One out of every ten persons arriving at Auschwitz was put to death on the first day.

In the thirty-two months that Auschwitz was in full operation as an extermination camp it is estimated that 1.1 million people, the overwhelming majority of them Jewish, were killed.

Of the 1,019 people who arrived on the September 5 transport from Westerbork, 549 were murdered immediately.

The Franks, van Pelses, and Fritz Pfeffer, sent "right," survived that first day.

Those who survived this first selection process had to watch as the smoke rose up from the chimneys of the crematoria.

> "... not far from us I could see a tall structure spewing out bright flames.... This, I thought, was one of the strangest German symbols I had ever seen. None of us had any inkling of the awful truth."
>
> ANONYMOUS AUSCHWITZ INMATE

Otto, Hermann, Peter, and Fritz Pfeffer were taken to the main slave labor camp. Edith and her two daughters and probably Mrs. van Pels were taken to Birkenau, a unit of Auschwitz. All had numbers tattooed on their left forearms (something done only at Auschwitz-Birkenau).

> "... we were herded into a ... room ... smeared with disinfectant [and] ... received our prison clothing. I cannot think of any name that would fit the bizarre rags that were handed out for underwear. We asked ourselves what this 'under-clothing' was supposed to be. It was not

white nor any other color, but worn-out pieces of coarse
dusting-cloth."

Olga Lengyel

Their hair was rudely cut short and they were forced to strip so they could be searched and checked for lice.

". . . we were taken to rooms where we had to undress. That was an enormous shock for me. I was eighteen, shy, and had been brought up chastely, according to the prevailing morality. It goes without saying that I was embarrassed and ashamed. I remember an audible crack in my head, from being totally naked before the eyes of men. And then the thought came like a flash that, from then on, other norms and values would be in effect, that I would have to adjust to that, and that an entirely new life was beginning, or death was waiting."

Bloeme Evers-Emden

The secret-annex eight, among the thousands of other new arrivals at Auschwitz-Birkenau, struggled to adjust as well as they could as quickly as they could to their new, horrific surroundings and the degrading and dehumanizing daily routine.

"*Each camp consisted of endless rows of blocks — dirty, rat-infested wooden barracks — housing about twelve-hundred persons each. Along the inner walls of the barracks, there were three rows of wooden shelves, one above the other, and these shelves were our bedrooms, living-rooms, dining-rooms and studies, all in one. They were divided by vertical planks at regular intervals. Each of these cage-like contraptions served as sleeping-room for thirty to thirty-six persons.*"

DR. GISELLA PERL

"*Seven or eight women had to go in each one. We called it 'lined up like spoons.' Everyone had to turn around at the same time. You couldn't lie in the positions you wanted.*

The first night, a woman went outside the barracks; she was shot. That woman, horribly wounded, spent the whole night lying there, groaning. We didn't know what we should do — go out there or not — but the others shouted, 'No, no, you have to stay in bed; that's not allowed.' That woman lay there, dying, in a gruesome way. Then I knew, Yes, they really shoot people here. Early in the morning she was dead, lying in front of the barracks, and we saw that. From then on, I knew for sure that they would shoot people from the towers."

RONNIE GOLDSTEIN–VAN CLEEF

"Life in Auschwitz began at four o'clock in the morning when we had to crawl forth from our holes to stand for roll call in the narrow street separating one block from another. We stood in rows of five, at arm's length from one another, soundless and motionless for four, five, or six hours at a time, in any kind of weather, all year round. . . . The number had to be complete, even the dying and the dead had to be brought out to stand at attention. If anyone did not appear, she was tracked down and thrown into the flames, alive. The same punishment was meted out to those who collapsed, fainted, or cried out with pain when hit by a whip. Often, for God knows what reason, the SS decided to punish us, and after roll call all one-hundred-and-fifty thousand of us had to kneel down in the snow or mud, to stay there on our bruised, bleeding knees for another hour or two. How often did I see women fall out of the ranks in a dead faint, without being able to succor them, to bring them even the most primitive of comforts: a glass of water."

DR. GISELLA PERL

Some were so thirsty they drank water that was clearly marked poison.

After roll call, the 39,000 women, divided into work details, marched off as the camp orchestra played. Some were assigned to squeeze toothpaste out of toothpaste tubes looking for diamonds that new arrivals might have hidden. Most worked outside, winter and summer, twelve-hour days with no rest.

Hunger was a constant, painful companion. Food consisted of an indescribable brown liquid, dry black bread that had been made partly with sawdust, thin turnip soup, and sometimes a slice of sausage or piece of cheese. There were no utensils, and if you lost your bowl you went without. Some talked about their hunger obsessively; others believed that not talking about it was the only way to survive.

There was only one latrine for the entire women's camp, resulting in endless, long lines. Most had dysentery, adding to their embarrassment and discomfort.

The ill did not seek medical treatment and tried not to show weakness. They stuffed old newspapers in their clothes so that they didn't look as malnourished as they were and tried to make their cheeks look less pale. Anything to avoid being "selected," camp jargon meaning "chosen to go to the gas chambers."

". . . after only one week of prison, the instinct for cleanliness disappeared in me. . . . Why should I wash? Would I be better off than I am? Would I please someone more? Would I live a day, an hour longer? I would probably live a shorter time, because to wash is an effort, a waste of energy and warmth."

PRIMO LEVI

". . . we were standing outside and I saw a wagon the first day and [said] . . . 'What's he thrown on there? Dead bodies, oh my God!' I could hardly look. The next couple of days later I saw it. [and said] 'Oh, there's that wagon again that picks up the dead bodies.' And the next time I didn't even pay any attention to that wagon. So your brain starts functioning differently, because if you don't — you didn't do it on purpose — then you couldn't go on living."

ROSE DE LIEMA

Otto, Hermann, and Fritz Pfeffer were assigned to ditch-digging and Peter to the camp post office where the SS guards and non-Jewish prisoners received their mail. Peter's assignment enabled him to get extra rations, which he shared with his father and the other two men.

In early October 1944, Hermann van Pels injured his thumb while digging a trench and unwisely requested barracks duty. There was a "selection" among those barracks workers and Hermann van Pels was "selected" to be murdered in the gas chambers of Auschwitz. (Fritz Pfeffer had been transferred to another camp and died there on December 20, 1944.)

The average life expectancy of someone who lived past the first day of Auschwitz was between six and seven weeks. Peter and Otto were, however, holding out relatively well. Otto, true to his nature, attempted to remain positive. He shied away from anyone who complained all the time, preferring the company of those who could join him in a discussion about Beethoven and Schubert — not hunger and illness.

Edith and her two daughters stayed together, trying to help one another survive.

"In the period that we were in Auschwitz . . . Mrs. Frank tried very hard to keep her children alive, to keep them with her, to protect them. Naturally, we spoke to each other. But you could do absolutely nothing, only give advice like, If they go to the latrine go with them.

Because even on the way from the barracks to the latrine,
something could happen."

LENIE DE JONG–VAN NAARDEN

"Very important [for] survival for all people in concen-
tration camps were to form little groups, support groups,
and of course as mother and children and daughters, you
were a natural support group. And I think everything
from the past was faded away against this scene of
Auschwitz. It was of no importance anymore I suppose."

BLOEME EVERS-EMDEN

They existed without privacy, engulfed in a world of
tension and terror, in constant fear of an endless list of things
that could and often did bring instant death. By necessity,
many became desensitized and hardened to the pervasive
horror that had become daily life. Anne struggled to maintain
her personality and remain human.

"Anne seemed even more beautiful there than she had at
Westerbork. Of course her long hair was gone, but now
you could see that her beauty was in her eyes, which
seemed to grow bigger as she grew thinner. Her gaiety

had vanished, but she still was alert and sweet, and with her charm she sometimes secured things that the rest of us had long since given up hoping for.

For example, we each had only a gray sack to wear. But when the weather turned cold, Anne came in one day wearing a suit of men's long underwear. She had begged it somewhere. She looked screamingly funny with those long white legs, but somehow still delightful.

Though she was the youngest, Anne was the leader in her group of five people. She also gave out the bread to everyone in the barracks and she did it so fairly there was none of the usual grumbling . . .

We scarcely saw and heard these things any longer. Something protected us, kept us from seeing. But Anne had no such protection, to the last. I can still see her standing at the door and looking down the camp street as a herd of naked gypsy girls were driven by, to the crematorium, and Anne watched them going and cried. And she cried also when we marched past the Hungarian children who had already been waiting half a day in the rain in front of the gas chambers, because it was not yet their turn. And Anne nudged me, and said: 'Look, look. Their eyes . . .'

She cried. And you cannot imagine how soon most
of us came to the end of our tears."

Mrs. de Wiek

Their bad diets and the unsanitary conditions of the camps resulted in a variety of illnesses and disease. Anne contracted scabies, a contagious skin disease. It covered her entire body with reddish pimples and the itching, especially at night, was severe.

In late October 1944, there was a "selection." Those considered fit enough were sent to work in a munitions factory, clearly better than staying in Auschwitz. Anne, too sick, was sent to the scabies barracks, which was completely isolated from the rest of the camp.

". . . Margot and her mother decided to stay with Anne.
If they could have gone with our transport they would
have survived because nearly everybody in my transport
after Auschwitz survived."

Bloeme Evers-Emden

Margot stayed with Anne in the scabies barracks and contracted the disease there.

"The Frank girls looked terrible, their hands and bodies covered with spots and sores from the scabies. They applied some salve, but there was not much that they could do. They were in a very bad way."

RONNIE GOLDSTEIN–VAN CLEEF

Desperately Edith Frank searched for scraps of food for her sick daughters. A friend found a watch and gave it to Edith, who traded it for some bread, cheese, and sausages that she somehow got to her daughters.

Just days later there was yet another "selection."

"Anne encouraged Margot, and Margot walked erect into the light. There they stood for a moment, naked and shaven-headed, and Anne looked over at us with her unclouded face, looked straight and stood straight, and they were approved and passed along. We could not see what was on the other side of the light. Mrs. Frank screamed, 'The children! Oh, God!'"

MRS. DE WIEK

Anne and Margot were "selected" to be on a transport bound for Bergen-Belsen concentration camp. Their mother, having no choice, remained behind in Auschwitz.

She grew sicker and weaker by the day, dying of grief for the two daughters she could not save.

> *"She was very weak and no longer eating, scarcely in her right mind. Whatever food she was given she collected under her blanket, saying that she was saving it for her husband because he needed it — and then the bread spoiled under the blanket.*
>
> *I don't know whether she was so weakened because she was starving, or whether she had stopped eating because she was too weak to eat. There was no longer any way of telling. I watched her die without a murmur."*
>
> Mrs. de Wiek

Edith Frank died on January 6, 1945. In ten days she would have been forty-five.

Bergen-Belsen

At the end of October 1944, the Frank sisters were on a transport headed west, back toward their birthplace, Germany.

> "When our train arrived in Belsen . . . we passed through the barbed-wire gate of the camp without really noticing it, for there was no trace of any camp. No barracks, no crematorium . . .
>
> There we stood and looked around in astonishment. But soon some curious prisoners came toward us out of the wasteland. Their heads were shaved and they looked in a very bad way.
>
> 'Where does one live here?' I asked a woman. 'In tents,' she told me. 'We all sleep on the ground.' 'And is there water here?' 'Not much.' 'Latrines?' 'We have just

made a pit for ourselves.' 'And food?' 'Irregular, little of it, and bad.'

We knew what questions to ask when we arrived in a new camp — we had plenty of camp life. . . . But there was little need to ask many questions. The indications were clear enough."

Mrs. Renate L. A. *

Established in 1941 as a prisoner-of-war camp, by 1943 Bergen-Belsen (the names of the two towns it was situated between) had become an "exchange camp." Jewish prisoners with connections abroad, the right papers, or value as hostages were sent there. Eventually they were to be exchanged for German citizens and soldiers being held by the Allies (however, very few ever were). In the meantime they would be used as slave labor for the Third Reich. Families would be allowed to stay together and would remain alive.

Since March 1944, sick and exhausted prisoners — anyone judged unable to work — had been evacuated from other concentration camps and sent to Bergen-Belsen. It was now termed a "recuperation camp" in the ironic, sadistic jar-

*A pseudonym

gon that hid its true purpose: They had been sent there to die, not recuperate.

The already overcrowded, chaotic camp was unable to properly receive the thousands of people arriving daily. The authorities at Bergen-Belsen hastily constructed tents for temporary housing.

> *". . . the third night I was there we had a storm. The tents ripped and flew off, and the heavy poles came crashing down on us. The next two nights we slept in a storage shed, among the heaps of SS caps and military boots. On the third day we were driven to a block of barracks that had meanwhile been cleared. That was the beginning of our stay in Belsen."*
>
> Mrs. Renate L. A.

The extreme overcrowding and the woeful physical condition of the new arrivals led to hunger, thirst, and rampant disease: dysentery, tuberculosis, and typhus.

There was no water for days at a time, and people died crawling toward the water pump. Some desperately boiled grass, and SS guards were needed when the vat of foul-smelling, barely edible soup was taken to the huts because someone crazed by hunger might attack it. All this occurred while hundreds of Red Cross food parcels containing Ovaltine, canned meat, milk, and biscuits remained unopened and undistributed.

"...I ran across a woman who I had known at Auschwitz. She had been a block orderly there, and had had decent clothing and food. Now here she stood holding a soup kettle, scraping it out and greedily licking the dregs. When I saw that, I knew enough. It was a bad camp where not even the privileged group had enough to eat. My sister and I looked at one another, and my sister, who had just turned sixteen, said: 'No one will come out of this camp alive.'"

MRS. RENATE L. A.

"The end is the same — only the means are different. In Auschwitz it is a quick, ruthless procedure, mass murder in the gas chambers; in Belsen it is a sadistic, long drawn-out process of starvation, of violence, of terror, of the deliberate spreading of infection and disease."

HANNA LÉVY-HASS

Anne and Margot clung to each other, trying to survive despite their deteriorating condition and the horror that was enveloping them.

As late fall in northern Germany turned into winter, conditions became even more severe, even more life-threatening. The freezing winds made life that much harder to endure and everyone that much sicker.

Anne and Margot saw a woman they had met at Auschwitz:

"Anne used to tell stories after we lay down. So did Margot. Silly stories and jokes. We all took our turns telling them. Mostly they were about food. Once we talked about going to the American Hotel in Amsterdam for dinner and Anne suddenly burst into tears at the thought that we would never get back . . . we compiled a menu, masses of wonderful things to eat."

LIENTJE BRILLESLIJPER-JALDATI

"The Frank girls were almost unrecognizable since their hair had been cut off. They were much balder than we were; how that could be, I don't know. And they were cold, just like the rest of us.

It was winter and you didn't have any clothes. So all of the ingredients for illness were present. They were in bad shape. Day by day they got weaker. Nevertheless they went to the fence of the so-called free camp every day, in the hopes of getting something. They were very determined. I'm virtually certain that they met someone there whom they knew."

RACHEL VAN AMERONGEN–FRANKFOORDER

By the spring of 1944, the overwhelming majority of those living in the so-called Free Camp, a subcamp within Bergen-Belsen, were Dutch. Among them was Lies Goslar, Anne's good friend from Amsterdam.

Lies Goslar's mother had died, along with the baby, giving birth after the Franks went into hiding. In June 1943, Lies, her father, and little sister, Gabi, were rounded up by the Nazis. Because their names were on a list to immigrate to Palestine they were sent from Westerbork to the Free Camp at Bergen-Belsen in February 1944, six months before Anne and the others were discovered in hiding.

In early February 1945, Lies heard that Dutch women from Auschwitz were in the adjacent camp.

"One day a friend of mine tells me, 'You know, between all these women there is your friend Anne Frank.' And I don't know I felt very crazy because I was thinking the whole time Anne is safe and she's in Switzerland. I was sure of this, but this was what [she] said to me and so I had no choice but to go . . . near this barbed wire — this was not allowed. And the German in the watchtower was watching us and you know he would have shot if he would have caught us, but — so we couldn't see . . . there was a barbed wire with straw and we couldn't see the other side. So, I just went near at dark and I would start to call hello, hello? something like this and who answered me but Mrs. van Pels. . . . She said 'You want Anna . . . I will call her for you. Margot I can't call for you, she is very sick already, but Anna I will call for you.'"

HANNELI ELISABETH "LIES" PICK-GOSLAR

Auguste van Pels told Lies that Margot was too sick to come but she would get Anne. Separated by the barbed wire the two friends cried; then Anne spoke:

"She said, 'We don't have anything at all to eat here, almost nothing, and we are cold; we don't have any

clothes and I've gotten very thin and they shaved my hair.' That was terrible for her. She had always been very proud of her hair. It may have grown back a bit in the meantime, but it certainly wasn't the long hair she'd had before, which she playfully curled around her fingers. . . .

We agreed to meet the next evening at eight o'clock. . . . I succeeded in throwing [a] package [of food] over.

But I heard her screaming, and I called out, 'What happened?'

And Anne answered, 'Oh, the woman standing next to me caught it, and she won't give it back to me.'

Then she began to scream.

I calmed her down a bit and said, 'I'll try again but I don't know if I'll be able to.' We arranged to meet again, two or three days later, and I was actually able to throw over another package. She caught it: That was the main thing.

After these three or four meetings at the barbed-wire fence in Bergen-Belsen, I didn't see her again, because the people in Anne's camp were transferred to another section of Bergen-Belsen. That happened around the end

of February. That was the last time I saw Anne alive and
spoke to her."

Hanneli Elisabeth "Lies" Pick-Goslar

Anne was horrified by the lice and had thrown all of her clothes away, even though it was the middle of the winter. She just walked around with a blanket wrapped around her. Both girls had typhus and looked emaciated.

"They were terribly cold. They had the least desirable place in the barracks, below, near the door, which was constantly opened and closed. You heard them constantly screaming, 'Close the door, close the door,' and their voices became weaker every day.

You could really see both of them dying. . . . They were . . . the youngest among us."

Rachel van Amerongen–Frankfoorder

"It had to have been in March, as the snow was already melting as we went to look for them, but they weren't in the bunk any longer. In the quarantine (sick bunk) is where we found them. We begged them not to stay there, as people in there deteriorated so quickly and couldn't

185

bring themselves to resist, that they'd be soon at the end. Anne simply said, 'Here we both can lie on the plank bed; we'll be together and at peace.' Margot only whispered; she had a high fever.

The following day we went to them again. Margot had fallen from the bed, just barely conscious. Anne also was feverish, yet she was friendly and sweet. 'Margot's going to sleep well, and when she sleeps, I won't have to stay up.'"

LIENTJE BRILLESLIJPER-JALDATI

"Anne was sick, too, but she stayed on her feet until Margot died; only then did she give in to her illness."

JANNY BRANDES-BRILLESLIJPER

Anne, after watching her older sister slowly die, on or near her nineteenth birthday, lost her will to live.

Days later, sometime in late February or early March 1945, Annelies Marie Frank, fifteen, perished, her body thrown in a mass grave.

One month later, on April 15, 1945, Bergen-Belsen was liberated by British soldiers.

PART FOUR

SURVIVING

By the fall of 1944, Hitler's regime, knowing they were going to lose the war, began destroying the physical and documentary evidence of their monstrous crimes.

They ordered the destruction of the Auschwitz-Birkenau killing machine: dynamiting the crematoria, demolishing the electrified barbed-wire fence and guard towers, and burning incriminating documents. They packed up piles of the remaining clothing, eyeglasses, and suitcases belonging to the 1.1 million people whose lives they had taken at Auschwitz, and sent them back to Berlin for use by German civilians. Left behind in the rush were 348,820 suits for men and 836,516 dresses. They dug up the dead bodies that had been thrown into the mass graves and burned them in open pits. And they ordered an end to the gassings. There were no more at

Auschwitz after November 1944, although random killings continued.

On January 16, 1945, ten days after Edith Frank died and only a few weeks before her daughters did, Russian planes began attacking Auschwitz. Soon inmates could hear artillery and automatic-weapon fire.

Leaving the seven thousand sick and injured behind, the Germans began to flee, fearing the advancing Russian army.

Anyone who could walk was forced to march out with them. Those sixty thousand inmates were to be taken and dispersed to other concentration camps, presumably located farther away from the fast-approaching Allied forces.

In the snow and bitter cold, wearing little to protect them and already half dead from months and years of deprivation, they moved out on what was to become a death march. Thousands died from disease, illness, hunger, thirst, and exhaustion, and thousands more, unable to keep up, were shot and left by the side of the road.

One percent of all those sent to Auschwitz survived.

One of them was Otto Frank.

Two months earlier, in November 1944, weak and ill from the slave labor and beatings, Otto was losing hope.

"One day in Auschwitz I was very depressed, I had been beaten the day before and that really affected me. . . . It was a Sunday morning and I said, 'I can't get up' and then my comrades . . . said to me, 'That's not possible . . . you must get up otherwise you are lost.' And then they went to a Dutch doctor who worked with a German doctor and this Dutch doctor came to me in my barracks. He said, 'Get up and come tomorrow morning to the sick barracks and I'll speak to the German doctor so that you will be accepted.' And that is what happened and through that I was saved."

Peter van Pels dutifully visited Otto in the hospital. Otto tried to persuade Peter to stay with him and hide in the hospital. But fearing that he might be shot if found and believing he was in good enough physical condition to withstand the rigors of the evacuation march, Peter left.

Peter van Pels was right — he was in good enough shape to survive the march. However, on May 5, 1945, he died in the Mauthausen concentration camp, just days before American soldiers liberated it.

Auguste van Pels had been transferred from Bergen-Belsen to an unknown destination. It is believed she died in the spring of 1945.

Otto Frank and the other survivors still at Auschwitz summoned the strength to wave and shake the hands of their liberators. They were given food to eat, and doctors and nurses came to tend to them. However, many were too ill and their liberators had come too late. Thousands died in the days and weeks that followed.

Otto Frank was free, but like so many others he had no job, no money, no home to return to, and no future. He knew nothing of the fate of his family.

In May 1945, he wrote to his mother:

> *Dearest Mother . . . All my hope is the children. I cling to the conviction that they are alive and that we will be together again. Unfortunately Edith did not survive. She died on January 6, 1945, in the hospital of starvation. . . . What happened in all these years, we own nothing anymore. We won't find a pin when we get back. The Germans stole everything: no photograph, no letter, no documents will remain there. Financially, we had no worries during the last years. I earned good money and saved. Now all is gone. But I don't worry about this — we have gone through too much to worry about things like that. Only the children, the children are what count.*

On June 3, 1945, Otto Frank returned to Amsterdam.

Living with Miep Gies and her husband, he returned to work at his old company and spent the rest of his time searching in chaotic postwar Holland for news of his children. He contacted groups of survivors as they returned, asking if anyone knew of his two daughters. He placed ads in the "Information Requested About" section of the newspaper:

MARGOT FRANK (19) AND ANNA FRANK (16) IN JAN. ON TRANS. FROM BERGEN-BELSEN. O. FRANK, PRINSENGRACHT 263, TEL. 37059.

Those who were returning to Holland from the concentration camps were asked to put crosses next to the names of anyone whose fate they were aware of on the long lists that were posted.

Two sisters who had known the Frank girls in Auschwitz and then at the end in Bergen-Belsen did that, and Otto was notified. After having this information confirmed in person, Otto Frank now knew that his family was no more.

On the day the Franks, the van Pelses, and Fritz Pfeffer were discovered in hiding, Miep Gies returned to the secret annex that afternoon.

Everything was a mess as the Germans, looking for anything of value, had torn the rooms apart. Still scattered on the floor where they had been dumped from Otto's briefcase were Anne's diary, notebooks, and tissue-thin colored papers that she wrote on.

Knowing that the Germans would soon be coming back with a moving van to pack up all the furniture and everything else and ship it back to Germany, Miep gathered up all the papers and put the diary in her desk.

She had never read the diary, considering it private and hoping to return it to Anne after the war.

Now, hearing that Anne was not coming home:

"I took out all the papers, placing the little red-orange checkered diary on top, and carried everything into Mr. Frank's office.

Frank was sitting at his desk, his eyes murky with shock. I held out the diary and the papers to him. I said, 'Here is your daughter Anne's legacy to you.'

I could tell that he recognized the diary. He had given it to her just over three years before, on her thirteenth birthday, right before going into hiding. He touched it with the tips of his fingers. I pressed everything into his hands; then I left his office, closing the door quietly."

Otto wanted friends and relatives to read Anne's diary. After taking out some entries that he considered offensive (Anne's writing about her bodily development and her tumultuous relationship with her mother), he typed up copies to be read. Those who read it felt it should be published. Dutch publishers, believing that people were not interested in reading anything about the recently ended war, were themselves not interested.

One of the people who read the diary and believed it deserved a wider audience was Dr. Jan Romein, a well-known Dutch historian. In April 1946, he published in the newspaper an article called "A Child's Voice." The article kindled interest in the diary, which was published in 1947 in Dutch. French, English, and American editions followed. The American edition was published in 1952 after being rejected by ten publishers.

Nearly twenty-five million copies in sixty different languages of Annelies Marie Frank's diary have been sold worldwide.

I shall not remain insignificant.

— ANNE FRANK

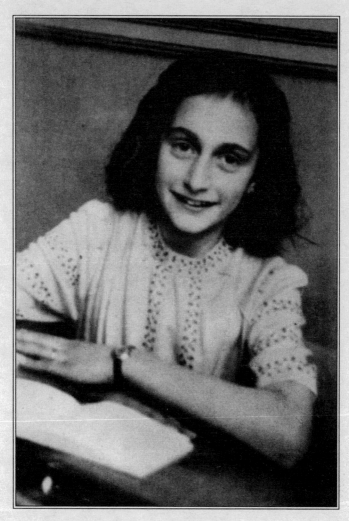

Anne Frank (1929-1945)

CHRONOLOGY

MAY 12, 1889: Otto Frank born Frankfurt, Germany

JANUARY 16, 1900: Edith Holländer born Aachen, Germany

1914–1918: World War I

MAY 12, 1925: Otto Frank and Edith Holländer marry

1925: *Mein Kampf* (*My Struggle*), autobiography of Adolf Hitler, published

FEBRUARY 16, 1926: Margot Betti Frank born Frankfurt, Germany

JUNE 12, 1929: Annelies Marie Frank born Frankfurt, Germany

OCTOBER 28, 1929: New York Stock Exchange crashes; worldwide economic crisis follows

1933:

≡ Adolf Hitler appointed German chancellor

≡ Nazis begin passing anti-Jewish laws

≡ First concentration camps established

DECEMBER 1933–FEBRUARY 1934: The Franks move to Amsterdam, Holland

MARCH 12, 1938: German army invades and annexes Austria

SEPTEMBER 29, 1938: Munich Treaty — England and France allow Germany to occupy neighboring territory

NOVEMBER 9–10, 1938: *Kristallnacht*, "Night of the Broken Glass"; anti-Jewish rioting occurs throughout Germany

1939: Westerbork refugee camp created by Dutch government

AUGUST 23, 1939: Germany and the Soviet Union sign a non-aggression pact

SEPTEMBER 1, 1939: Germany attacks Poland, forcing England and France to declare war on Germany

1939–1940: Deportation of European Jews into ghettos and concentration camps begins

1940: Auschwitz concentration camp established

≡ Germany attacks and defeats Denmark, Norway, Belgium, Luxembourg, Holland, and France

MAY 10, 1940: Germany invades Belgium, Luxembourg, France, and Holland; five days later the Dutch occupation begins

≡ Anti-Jewish laws instituted in Holland over following two years

1941: Bergen-Belsen prisoner-of-war camps established

JUNE 1941: Germany invades the Soviet Union

DECEMBER 7, 1941: Japan attacks the U.S. military base at Pearl Harbor, Hawaii, bringing America into the war

1942: Westerbork transformed by Germans into a labor camp

JANUARY 20, 1942: Wannsee (Berlin suburb) Conference — high-ranking Nazi officials devise plans for the extermination of all Jews in Europe

MAY 1942: The first mass gassings at Auschwitz occur

JUNE 12, 1942: Anne Frank receives a diary for her thirteenth birthday

JULY 5, 1942: The Franks receive a notice ordering Margot to report for deportation to Westerbork

JULY 6, 1942: The Frank family goes into hiding in the annex behind Otto Frank's office

JULY 13, 1942: The van Pels family joins the Frank family in hiding

NOVEMBER 16, 1942: Friedrich "Fritz" Pfeffer joins the two families in hiding

1943: Bergen-Belsen becomes an "exchange camp"

FEBRUARY 2, 1943: The German army surrenders to the Russians at Stalingrad

SEPTEMBER 8, 1943: Italy surrenders to the Allies

1944: Bergen-Belsen becomes a "recuperation camp"

JUNE 6, 1944: D-day — the long-awaited Allied invasion of Europe at Normandy, France, begins

JULY 20, 1944: German army officers fail in assassination attempt on Hitler's life

AUGUST 4, 1944: Those hiding in the annex are betrayed, discovered, and arrested

AUGUST 8, 1944: All eight are taken to Westerbork

SEPTEMBER 3, 1944: All eight are taken to Auschwitz-Birkenau concentration camp in Poland

OCTOBER 1944: Hermann van Pels dies

LATE OCTOBER 1944: Anne and Margot are taken to Bergen-Belsen concentration camp

DECEMBER 20, 1944: Fritz Pfeffer dies in Neuengamme concentration camp

JANUARY 6, 1945: Edith Frank dies in Auschwitz-Birkenau

JANUARY 27, 1945: Auschwitz is liberated by the Soviet Union's Red Army; survivors include Otto Frank

LATE FEBRUARY–EARLY MARCH 1945: Anne and Margot Frank die of typhus in Bergen-Belsen concentration camp

SPRING 1945: Auguste van Pels dies

APRIL 15, 1945: Bergen-Belsen is liberated by British soldiers

MAY 5, 1945: Peter van Pels dies in Mauthausen concentration camp
≡ Holland is liberated

MAY 8, 1945: Germany surrenders unconditionally to the Allies

JUNE 3, 1945: Otto Frank returns to Amsterdam

SUMMER 1945: Otto Frank learns that Anne and Margot have died in Bergen-Belsen; is given his daughter Anne's diary by Miep Gies

AUGUST 6 AND 9, 1945: The United States drops atomic bombs on the Japanese cities of Hiroshima and Nagasaki

AUGUST 14, 1945: Japan surrenders

1946: "A Child's Voice" is published

1947: First [Dutch] edition of Anne Frank's diary is published

1952: *The Diary of a Young Girl* is published in the United States

1955: The play *The Diary of Anne Frank* opens on Broadway; wins a Pulitzer Prize and Tony Award

1959: The film *The Diary of Anne Frank* is released in the United States; wins three Academy Awards

1980: Otto Frank dies

A BIBLIOGRAPHICAL ESSAY

Roses from the Earth: The Biography of Anne Frank, by Carol Ann Lee, and Melissa Müller's *Anne Frank: The Biography* are two thoroughly researched and well-written recent biographies.

Ernst Schnabel's *The Footsteps of Anne Frank* (published in the United States as *Anne Frank: A Portrait in Courage*) was one of the first books (1958), if not *the* first book, written about her. Schnabel interviewed forty-two people who knew Anne; it is these interviews that many subsequent books, including mine, are based on.

Schnabel uses pseudonyms for some of the interviewees who, presumably, did not want their real names used. Anne, fearful and protective in hiding, used pseudonyms for all the people mentioned in her diary. We can see from Schnabel's book that even thirteen years after the war had ended the fear remained.

I read all three numerous times and referred to them frequently while writing *Shadow Life*.

Amos Elon's *The Pity of It All: A History of the Jews in Germany, 1743–1933* helped me appreciate the fullness of everyday life that was the good fortune of many Jewish families. A fullness that explains their reluctance to leave their homes and their homeland in the years following 1933 and the coming to power of Adolf Hitler.

Richard J. Evans's *The Coming of the Third Reich* and Ian Kershaw's two-volume biography of Adolf Hitler, both perceptive and scholarly works, provided a political context for those same years.

To add color and texture to my portrait of Anne and her family a number of books were helpful. Ruud van der Rol and Rian Verhoeven's *Anne Frank: Beyond the Diary — A Photographic Remembrance* is meticulously annotated, adding to its visual qualities. Susan Goldman Rubin's *Searching for Anne Frank: Letters from Amsterdam to Iowa* is the story of Anne and Margot's pen-pal relationship with two sisters from Danville, Iowa. It is an important recent contribution to the literature on Anne Frank and allows us to read Anne and Margot's actual letters.

Two of Anne's best friends, Hanneli "Lies" Goslar (*Memories of Anne Frank: Reflections of a Childhood Friend*) and Jacqueline van Maarsen (*My Friend Anne Frank*), have published personal accounts that are anecdotal, honest, and illuminating.

Marion A. Kaplan's *Between Dignity and Despair: Jewish Life in Nazi Germany* and Deborah Dwork's *Children With a Star: Jewish Youth in Nazi Europe* educated me about the effects the rise of fascism and the increase in anti-Semitism had on everyday life. Andy Marino's *Herschel: The Boy Who Started World War II* answered questions I have had for years.

For specific background on the Jewish community in the Netherlands, the occupation, and the subsequent fate of that community, Dr. J. Presser's exhaustive and definitive *Ashes in the Wind: The Destruction of Dutch Jewry* was invaluable. It allowed me to convey, via Margot's diary, some insight into the activities of the Dutch underground during the war.

≡PART TWO: HIDING≡

Anne's diary was, of course, my main source for information on the family's two years in hiding. It is available in a number of editions: The one I used was *The Diary of Anne Frank: The Revised Critical Edition*. This edition allowed me to read what is essentially three versions of the diary: the one Anne originally wrote from the time she was first given her diary as a birthday present; the additions and revisions she made as she prepared it for potential publication; and the diary as it was eventually edited, translated, and published. The A, B, C serial layout takes some time getting used to but it is worth the effort.

The Revised Critical Edition contains a number of essays that were helpful in other areas as well: the early years of the Frank family; their time in Frankfurt and Amsterdam; the establishment of Otto's business; the decision and preparations to go into hiding; the betrayal and the subsequent fate of all.

Miep Gies is a transcendent person. Her book *Anne Frank Remembered* provides a unique look at the Frank family and the events that eventually overwhelmed them.

For background on Margot's interest in Zionism and her dreams of immigrating to what was to become Israel, Walter Laqueur's *A History of Zionism* is complete and compelling.

≡PART THREE: DYING≡

To reconstruct the months following the arrest of the Frank family, Schnabel's book and Willy Lindwer's *The Last Seven Months of Anne Frank* were my constant reliable guides.

Over the years I have read numerous books on Nazi Germany and the Holocaust. Conceptual research for writing Part Three of this book was based on Daniel Jonah

Goldhagen's *Hitler's Willing Executioners: Ordinary Germans and the Holocaust* and Christopher R. Browning's *The Origins of the Final Solution: The Evolution of Nazi Jewish Policy, September 1939–March 1942* as well as the Evans and Kershaw books already mentioned.

Presser's book, along with Schnabel's and Lindwer's, were my main sources for information on Westerbork. To try to understand the conception, construction, and operation of Auschwitz, I referred to Yisrael Gutman and Michael Berenbaum's *Anatomy of the Auschwitz Death Camp*, Deborah Dwork and Robert Jan van Pelt's *Auschwitz: 1270 to the Present*, and Danuta Czech's *Auschwitz Chronicle: 1939–1945*, which is a harrowing day-by-day account of how death came to the inmates trapped there.

I read many first-person accounts, which shaped Part Three. Five were particularly poetic and moving: Olga Lengyel's *Five Chimneys,* Gisella Perl's *I Was a Doctor in Auschwitz,* Sara Nomberg-Przytyk's *True Tales from a Grotesque Land,* Elie Wiesel's *The Night Trilogy,* and Rudolf Vrba's *I Cannot Forgive.* Vrba managed to escape from Auschwitz and bring the first eyewitness documentation of the operations there to the outside world.

A true understanding of the Holocaust eluded me, however. As Elie Wiesel so eloquently puts it:

"We shall never understand. Even if we manage somehow to learn every aspect of that insane project, we will never understand it. . . . I think I must have read all the books— memoirs, documents, scholarly essays and testimonies written on the subject. I understand it less and less."

≡ VIDEOS ≡

The above are all books, but two videos were essential to the writing of *Shadow Life*. Jon Blair's Academy Award–winning documentary *Anne Frank Remembered* played a key role in motivating me to write a book on Anne Frank for young readers, and its influence is throughout my book. The film *Anne Frank* is artfully directed, carefully cast, and beautifully acted. It is based on Müller's book and presents a dramatic and driving narrative without sacrificing historical accuracy. Both films are superlative, each in its own way.

≡ "WHO OWNS ANNE FRANK?" ≡

Cynthia Ozick's 1997 *New Yorker* article "Who Owns Anne Frank?" was, as I said in the Introduction, the inspiration for *Shadow Life*. The history of the diary and its publication, the agonizing story of the production and staging of the 1955 play, and the way the diary has been presented and perceived over the past half century is a complicated and complex story in itself. Reading either of the two excellent books on this, Ralph Melnick's *The Stolen Legacy of Anne Frank* or Lawrence Graver's *An Obsession with Anne Frank,* will provide fertile ground for further thought.

Watching the 1959 movie, which is now available on DVD, is instructive and disturbing because of its romanticized point of view. (Seeing the original movie poster is, alone, an unsettling experience.)

A complete bibliography follows. Readers wishing to contact me with questions can write me c/o Scholastic Inc., 557 Broadway, New York, NY 10012.

BIBLIOGRAPHY

BOOKS

ANNE FRANK STICHTING. *Anne Frank in the World, 1929–1945*. Amsterdam: Uitgeverij Bert Bakker, 1985.

BARNOUW, DAVID, AND GERROLD VAN DER STROOM, EDS. *The Diary of Anne Frank: The Critical Edition*. New York: Doubleday, 1986. *The Diary of Anne Frank: The Revised Critical Edition*. New York: Doubleday, 2001.

BLACK, EDWIN. *IBM and the Holocaust: The Strategic Alliance Between Nazi Germany and America's Most Powerful Corporation*. New York: Crown, 2001.

BLOOM, HAROLD, ED. *A Scholarly Look at the Diary of Anne Frank*. Philadelphia: Chelsea House, 1999.

BREITMAN, RICHARD. *Official Secrets: What the Nazis Planned, What the British and Americans Knew*. New York: Hill and Wang, 1998.

BRENDON, PIERS. *The Dark Valley: A Panorama of the 1930s*. New York: Alfred A. Knopf, 2000.

BROWNING, CHRISTOPHER R. *The Origins of the Final Solution: The Evolution of Nazi Jewish Policy, September 1939–March 1942*. Lincoln: University of Nebraska Press, 2004.

CARROLL, JAMES. *Constantine's Sword: The Church and the Jews*. Boston: Houghton-Mifflin, 2001.

CZECH, DANUTA. *Auschwitz Chronicle: 1939–1945*. New York: Henry Holt, 1989.

DAWIDOWICZ, LUCY S. *The War Against the Jews: 1933–1945*. New York: Holt, Rinehart and Winston, 1975.

DeCosta, Denise. *Anne Frank and Etty Hillesum: Inscribing Spirituality and Sexuality.* New Brunswick, N.J.: Rutgers University Press, 1988.

Dickens, Charles. *A Tale of Two Cities.* New York: The Modern Library, 1996.

Dwork, Deborah. *Children with a Star: Jewish Youth in Nazi Europe.* New Haven, Conn.: Yale University Press, 1991.

Dwork, Deborah, and Robert Jan van Pelt. *Auschwitz: 1270 to the Present.* New York: W.W. Norton and Company, 1996.

Elon, Amos. *Founder: A Portrait of the First Rothschild and His Time.* New York: Viking, 1996. *The Pity of It All: A History of the Jews in Germany, 1743–1933.* New York: Metropolitan Books, 2002.

Enzer, Hyman A., and Sandra Solotaroff-Enzer, eds. *Anne Frank: Reflections on Her Life and Legacy.* Urbana: University of Illinois Press, 2000.

Evans, Richard J. *The Coming of the Third Reich.* New York: The Penguin Press, 2004.

Frank, Anne. *The Diary of a Young Girl.* New York: Bantam Books, 1993.

Frank, Otto. *The Diary of a Young Girl: The Definitive Edition.* New York: Doubleday, 1991.

Friedrich, Otto. *The Kingdom of Auschwitz.* New York: Harper Perennial, 1986.

Gies, Miep, with Alison Leslie Gold. *Anne Frank Remembered: The Story of the Woman Who Helped Hide the Frank Family.* New York: Touchstone, 1987.

Goethe, Johann Wolfgang von. *The Sorrows of Young Werther* and *Novella.* New York: Vintage Classics, 1990.

Gold, Alison Leslie. *Memories of Anne Frank: Reflections of a Childhood Friend.* New York: Scholastic Inc., 1997.

GOLDHAGEN, DANIEL JONAH. *Hitler's Willing Executioners: Ordinary Germans and the Holocaust.* New York: Alfred A. Knopf, 1996. *A Moral Reckoning: The Role of the Catholic Church in the Holocaust and Its Unfulfilled Duty of Repair.* New York: Alfred A. Knopf, 2002.

GRAVER, LAWRENCE. *An Obsession with Anne Frank: Meyer Levin and the Diary.* Berkeley: University of California Press, 1995.

GRUN, BERNHARD. *The Timetables of History: A Horizontal Linkage of People and Events.* New York: Touchstone, 1963.

GUTMAN, YISRAEL, AND MICHAEL BERENBAUM. *Anatomy of the Auschwitz Death Camp.* Bloomington: Indiana University Press, 1998.

HEINE, HEINRICH. *Songs of Love and Grief.* Evanston, Ill.: Northwestern University Press, 1995.

HELLMAN, PETER, TEXT. *The Auschwitz Album: A Book Based Upon an Album Discovered by a Concentration Camp Survivor, Lili Meier.* New York: Random House, 1981.

HILBERG, RAUL. *The Destruction of the European Jews: Revised and Definitive Edition.* New York: Holmes and Meier, 1985.

HILLESUM, ETTY. *An Interrupted Life & Letters from Westerbork.* New York: Henry Holt and Co., 1996.

JOHNSON, ERIC A. *Nazi Terror: The Gestapo, Jews, and Ordinary Germans.* New York: Basic Books, 1999.

JONG, LOUIS DE. *The Netherlands and Nazi Germany.* Cambridge, Mass.: Harvard University Press, 1990.

KAPLAN, MARION A. *Between Dignity and Despair: Jewish Life in Nazi Germany.* New York: Oxford University Press, 1998.

KERSHAW, IAN. *Hitler 1889–1936 Hubris.* New York: W.W. Norton, 1998. *Hitler 1936–1945 Nemesis.* New York: W.W. Norton, 2000.

KLEMPERER, VICTOR. *I Will Bear Witness: A Diary of the Nazi Years 1933–1941*. New York: Random House, 1998. *I Will Bear Witness: A Diary of the Nazi Years 1942–1945*. New York: Random House, 1999.

KOLB, EBERHARD. *Bergen-Belsen: From 1943 to 1945*. Göttingen, Germany: Vandernhoek & Ruprecht, 1998.

KOPF, HEDDA ROSNER. *Understanding Anne Frank's Diary of a Young Girl*. Westport, Conn.: Greenwood Press, 1997.

LAQUEUR, WALTER. *A History of Zionism: From the French Revolution to the Establishment of the State of Israel*. New York: Schocken Books, 2003.

LEE, CAROL ANN. *The Hidden Life of Otto Frank*. New York: William Morrow, 2002. *Roses from the Earth: The Biography of Anne Frank*. New York: Viking, 1999.

LEITNER, ISABELLA, AND IRVING A. LEITNER. *Isabella: From Auschwitz to Freedom*. New York: Anchor Books, 1994.

LENGYEL, OLGA. *Five Chimneys: A Woman Survivor's True Story of Auschwitz*. Chicago: Academy Chicago Publishers, 1995.

LEVI, PRIMO. *Survival in Auschwitz*. New York: Touchstone, 1996.

LÉVY-HASS, HANNA. *Inside Belsen*. Sussex, England: The Harvester Press, 1982.

LINDWER, WILLY. *The Last Seven Months of Anne Frank*. New York: Anchor Books, 1991.

MAARSEN, JACQUELINE VAN. *My Friend Anne Frank*. New York: Vantage Press, 1996.

MARINO, ANDY. *Herschel: The Boy Who Started World War II*. Boston: Faber and Faber, 1995.

MELNICK, RALPH. *The Stolen Legacy of Anne Frank: Meyer Levin, Lillian Hellman and the Staging of the Diary.* New Haven, Conn.: Yale University Press, 1997.

MERTI, BETTY. *The World of Anne Frank: Readings, Activities and Resources.* Portland, Maine: J. Weston Walch, 1984.

METZGER, LOIS. *Yours, Anne: The Life of Anne Frank.* New York: Scholastic Inc., 2004.

MOORE, BOB. *Victims and Survivors: The Nazi Persecution of the Jews in the Netherlands, 1940–1945.* London: Arnold, 1997.

MÜLLER, MELISSA. *Anne Frank: The Biography.* New York: Metropolitan Books, 1998.

NOMBERG-PRZYTYK, SARA. *True Tales from a Grotesque Land.* Chapel Hill: The University of North Carolina Press, 1985.

PERL, GISELLA. *I Was a Doctor in Auschwitz.* North Stratford, N.H.: Ayer Company, 1997.

PRESSER, DR. J. *Ashes in the Wind: The Destruction of Dutch Jewry.* Detroit, Mich.: Wayne State University Press, 1988.

PRESSER, MIRJAM. *Anne Frank: A Hidden Life.* New York: Puffin Books, 2001.

READ, ANTHONY, AND DAVID FISHER. *Kristallnacht: The Nazi Night of Terror.* New York: Random House, 1989.

REILLY, JO, AND DAVID CESARANI, TONY KUSHNER, AND COLIN RICHMOND, EDS. *Belsen in History and Memory.* London: Frank Cass, 1997.

ROL, RUUD VAN DER, AND RIAN VERHOEVEN. *Anne Frank: Beyond the Diary — A Photographic Remembrance.* New York: Viking, 1993.

RUBIN, SUSAN GOLDMAN. *Searching for Anne Frank: Letters from Amsterdam to Iowa.* New York: Harry N. Abrams, 2003.

SAMMONS, JEFFREY L. *Heinrich Heine: A Modern Biography*. Princeton, N.J.: Princeton University Press, 1979.

SCHNABEL, ERNST. *The Footsteps of Anne Frank*. London: Pan Books, 1958.

SHIRER, WILLIAM L. *The Rise and Fall of the Third Reich: A History of Nazi Germany*. New York: Simon and Schuster, 1960.

SPIEGELMAN, ART. *Maus I: A Survivor's Tale — My Father Bleeds History*. New York: Pantheon, 1986.

SPIELBERG, STEVEN, AND SURVIVORS OF THE SHOAH VISUAL HISTORY FOUNDATION. *The Last Days*. New York: St. Martin's, 1999.

STEENMEIJER, ANNA G. *A Tribute to Anne Frank*. Garden City, N.Y.: Doubleday, 1971.

STROOM, GERROLD VAN DER, AND SUSAN MASSOTTY. *Anne Frank's Tales from the Secret Annex*. New York: Bantam Books, 2003.

VRBA, RUDOLF, WITH ALAN BESTIC. *I Cannot Forgive*. Vancouver, B.C.: Regent College Publishing, 1964.

WETTERAU, BRUCE. *The New York Public Library Book of Chronologies*. New York: Prentice Hall Press, 1990.

WIESEL, ELIE. *The Night Trilogy*. New York: Hill and Wang, 1985.

WYMAN, DAVID S. *The Abandonment of the Jews: America and the Holocaust, 1941–1945*. New York: Pantheon, 1984.

ARTICLES

BURUMA, IAN. "The Afterlife of Anne Frank." *The New York Review of Books*, February 19, 1998.

MELNICK, RALPH, Reply by Ian Buruma. "Anne Frank's Afterlife, Cont'd." A letter. *The New York Review of Books*, May 28, 1998.

Ozick, Cynthia, Reply by Ian Buruma. "Anne Frank's Afterlife." A letter. *The New York Review of Books*, April 9, 1998.

Ozick, Cynthia. "Who Owns Anne Frank?" *The New Yorker*, October 6, 1997.

VIDEOGRAPHY

Amen. A film by Costa-Gavras. Katharina/Renn Productions, 2002.

The American Experience: America and the Holocaust: Deceit and Indifference. WGBH Educational Foundation, 1994.

Anne Frank. Buena Vista Home Entertainment, 2001.

Anne Frank Remembered. Sony Pictures/The Jon Blair Film Company, 1995.

Anne Frank: The Life of a Young Girl. A&E Biography, 1999.

The Attic: The Hiding of Anne Frank. Cabin Fever Entertainment, 1992.

The Diary of Anne Frank. Twentieth Century Fox, 1959.

The Grey Zone. A Film by Tim Blake Nelson. Lions Gate Home Entertainment, 2002.

The Last Seven Months of Anne Frank. The Willy Lindwer Collection. 1988 Ergo Media Inc., 1995.

Leni Riefenstahl's Triumph of the Will. Synapse Films, 2001.

Steven Spielberg and the Shoah Foundation Present: The Last Days: A Film by James Moll. USA Home Entertainment. October Films, 1999.

INDEX